Criminal Justice
Recent Scholarship

Edited by
Marilyn McShane and Frank P. Williams III

A Series from LFB Scholarly

Youth Violence, Resilience, and Rehabilitation

Joan Serra Hoffman

LFB Scholarly Publishing LLC
New York 2004

Library of Congress Cataloging-in-Publication Data

Hoffman, Joan Serra, 1960-
   Youth violence, resilience, and rehabilitation / Joan Serra Hoffman.
      p. cm. -- (Criminal justice)
   Includes bibliographical references (p.   ) and index.
   ISBN 1-931202-59-1 (alk. paper)
   1. Juvenile delinquents--Rehabilitation--United States. 2. Violence in
adolescence--United States. 3. Violence in adolescence--United States-
-Prevention. 4. Youth and violence--United States. I. Title. II. Series:
Criminal justice (LFB Scholarly Publishing LLC)
   HV9104.H73 2004
   364.36'0973--dc22

2004006935

ISBN 1-931202-59-1

Printed on acid-free 250-year-life paper.

Manufactured in the United States of America.

Table of Contents

Acknowledgements

I owe a debt of gratitude to a large number of people and institutions who helped me in different ways on this book. In the years when I worked as a youth violence prevention worker and community organizer, I was lucky enough to be taken under the wing of a particularly gifted violence prevention worker, Anthony D. Borbon, who helped teach me how to speak with young people and how to work respectfully in communities. Not many people know that some of the best classes in violence prevention are those given by experienced to beginning youth workers. His courage and compassion were a considerable source of strength to me. I am indebted to him for his kindness to a novice, trying to come to terms with her professional abilities.

I am grateful as well to have been a student of singular teachers who took uncommon professional risks in their respective fields, and who provided guidance to the dissertation project on which this book is based. I particularly want to mention Deborah Prothrow-Stith, who "walks her talk" as an academic, practitioner and activist; Constance Williams, for her reassurance about the validity of children's voices; James Callahan, for his engaged irreverence, incisive questions, and biting wit; Gunnar Dybwad, for his humanism and compassion; and David G. Gil, who shepherded me through my schooling and writing of this book. Professor Gil maintains a pure vision of what a non-violent society might be. Colleagues and friends, Dieter Koch-Weser, Mauricia Alvarez, Cheryl Vince-Whitman, and James Mercy, generously served as readers and advisors for this project; I am most grateful for their interest and advice.

Over the years I worked on this study, I was fortunate to receive an award from Brandeis University to complete my research, and a Next Generation Fellowship from the Rockefeller Foundation, which helped support its completion. I wish to thank Marilyn McShane and Frank P. Williams, the series editors; and Leo Balk, my editor at LFB Scholarly, as well as Katie Baer; their careful editorial guidance and interest transformed the dissertation into a book.

Finally, I would like to thank the many young people whose stories are told in this book, and who stuck with the project through the many years it took to conceive and complete it. Together with my family, they have taught me innumerable lessons about life and death, pain, persistence and hope. Their journeys and contributions to the process of preventing violence can teach us all important lessons.

CHAPTER 1

Introduction

When I woke up from being shot, I couldn't talk, I couldn't move, I couldn't eat, and I couldn't breathe without the help of a machine. In fact, for the first six months, I couldn't communicate with anyone at all. All I could do was lie there and think. You hear gang members say all the time, "I'm not afraid to die." But let me tell you, when you are lying there gasping for air, bleeding, going into shock, rushing toward death, all that hard core is gone and all that is left is fear.

As for me, I had to learn to forgive. I had to let go of my anger toward the person who shot me, or it would have soured my life. Once I got over that boulder, I felt there was so much more that I could accomplish in rehabilitation, spiritually, mentally, and socially in my life.

—José, age 20, shot at age 17

This study emerged from a relationship with a group of young people with whom I worked as a youth worker/community organizer for city public health and hospitals departments over a six-year period, from 1990-1996. The young people whose collective experience forms the basis of the questions asked in this work were referred to programs in Boston and Los Angeles by pediatric, adolescent health, and rehabilitation practitioners, the juvenile justice system, and by other youth, as they voluntarily sought to "learn to control their anger" and achieve a "positive life." Referred because of health and criminal justice problems due to assaultive behavior, these young people had experienced many types of violence. They had encountered physical, sexual and domestic abuse, both at home and in institutions ostensibly designed to protect them. They had suffered economic, environmental, and institutional violence in the form of resource-deprived and run-down neighborhoods and schools. They had been discriminated against, and, in a few cases, had been victimized by the police. Many of the young people had been described by youth-serving practitioners as "intractable."

Over a six-year period, I learned much about their lives, families, and challenges, working directly with the young people as they began to question past involvement with violence. I observed as some of them developed into change agents, working in their respective communities in Boston and Los Angeles as organizers, advocates, and counselors, in a society increasingly skeptical about rehabilitation and in an era of human service funding retrenchment. In the years since, I kept in close touch with the study participants, continuing to work with many of them in a different professional capacity—as peers—on joint violence prevention initiatives, continuing to collaborate on this longitudinal study.

This participatory study explores the individual and collective pathways out of serious and chronic violence taken by 20 of these young men and women, mostly begun while they were still children: the period of assaultive violence involvement began for one precocious young man at age 9 and ended for another at age 24. The young people were between the ages of 20 and 32 at the time of the study's completion. The study documents their journeys, in their own words, from responses elicited by collectively generated research questions; through writings (journal entries, autobiographical statements, and other interviews) collected over a nine-year period (1990-1999) by the research participants, myself included; and observation and project notes taken by me over this period. It investigated: 1) the factors, events, personalities, processes and catalysts that contributed to or retarded the termination of assaultive conduct; 2) the factors, events, personalities, processes and catalysts which inhibited their full and non-violent development; and 3) the implications of a traumatic event for revisiting past behavior. The study contributes to a common theory of change and rehabilitation for young people who have been seriously violence involved and impacted by trauma, identifying primary and secondary antecedents to violence cessation of assaultive conduct to inform violence intervention and prevention efforts in health and community settings. Their individual words are thus interspersed among the findings, and their collective voices guide this project, minimizing the likelihood of abstract generalizations and bringing a human, flesh-and-blood reality to this work.

This study has attempted to incorporate the subjugated knowledge contained in the collective experience of these young men and women with the academic discourse on violence, especially its termination. The motivation to undertake this study was to offer, from below, an alternative to the analytic bias in much social science theory, to the racially and ethnically laden topic of assaultive youth violence. Criticized by both the political left and the right in recent years, modern U.S. social science has tended to document disadvantage among the least powerful, focusing on the reactive and pathological elements of racial and ethnic minorities and the economically disenfranchised, and on the deficits of the troubled young, at the expense of their strengths, successes, solidarity, and proactive, healthy characteristics (Pettigrew 1980). Concentrating far more on static description than dynamic process, such analyses have largely focused on the individual rather than the social—the event or behavior, rather than the context or process—and have generally favored an individualized discourse of deviance over a more socialized discourse of inequality.

Constance Williams' study of black teenage mothers, stressing the importance of comprehensive micro-level research, served as a model for my work. Conducting in-depth interviews with 30 young mothers, she explored the meaning, the perspectives, and the experiences of pregnancy and mothering for these girls, and presented a much more complex picture than the conventional findings gleaned from large-scale surveys or epidemiological studies. Like teenage mothers, youth involved in assaultive violence are a diverse group, with strengths as well as weaknesses. They too "are a population about whom policy makers express great concern but have little information" (Williams 1991, 39).

Very little is known about the termination of assaultive behavior and why some young individuals can extricate themselves from the vicious cycle of violence, changing their mindset and life circumstances, while others are not able to do so. In documenting the individual journeys of a select group of young people, I hope to show how this process of change manifests itself and unfolds over time, examining the life circumstances that occurred before such a transformation could take place. As the young people describe their journeys through a life of both perpetration and victimization of violence, I hope, to quote Geertz (1973), that "their small facts speak to large issues," shedding light on the obfuscation within the existing body of research and perhaps clarifying some of the theoretical precepts.

The voices and stories of change agents have yet to enter the official discourse of public health. In these narratives we may find the clues so urgently needed to advance the study and measurement of violence and its prevention, and support the efforts of its front-line practitioners. Current attempts to delineate and measure the pathways of such behavioral and attitudinal transformation have been hampered by insufficiently developed or "thin" causation and cessation theories and evaluation methodologies.

The public health department's conceptualization of violence, and the safe space provided by the clinic and hospital, allowed the young people in this study to try on new ways of thinking and acting. The emphasis of social environment strategies, such as job training and community organizing, seem to have also proved useful to these youngsters, who regained some measure of control over their lives, which also affected their safety, health and gave them a sense of purpose. The study findings, inductively derived from the stories, may be useful in informing future public health and hospital prevention and intervention programs and broader youth development efforts that seek to change the behavior and promote the health and well-being of their clients. The findings may also contribute to the discernment of program evaluation criteria. Lastly, they suggest youth-driven policy recommendations on how existing violence prevention, health, social welfare, youth development, victim assistance and criminal justice policies can foster change and violence desistance, challenging the dominant discourse on incorrigible youth.

The appropriation and treatment of anger and violence within the discipline of health, i.e., a clinical or medical setting, is not without its critics (Arendt 1970). The discipline of public health, like the hospital and the clinic (in Foucault's [1975] expanded term), can be cut off and isolated from the external world and from the experiential world of the youth client, becoming an institution of social control that locates the source of trouble and treatment in individual capacities, rather than social arrangements (Zola 1972; Conrad and Schneider 1980; Mosby et al. 1977, 603–680). Anger, often an expression of collective or compounded frustration, can be reduced by such narrow medicalization into a personal, psychological, or genetic "problem" requiring medication, additional treatment, and isolation. The discourse and practice of public health, however, can be liberatory, offering a space with a reach far beyond the clinical setting, allowing new ways of addressing and responding to human needs and miseries to emerge. It can also provide a forum where technical treatment offered in a respectful, non-judgmental, and socially grounded manner during a time of fear and crisis can leave a profound impression, allowing pain to be transformed into a critical practice of freedom (Scheper-Hughes 1992).

CHAPTER 2

Youth Violence

YOUTH VIOLENCE IN THE UNITED STATES

Youth interpersonal violence, by any standard or measure, is a significant national problem that has plagued the United States for decades, and has captured the interest of policy makers and social observers at various junctures in U.S. history. Recent discussions on contemporary youth violence usually focus on the post 1980 decades, and violence trends are often analyzed through two distinct periods: 1983-1994 and 1995-2000. During the first period, the nation experienced a towering number of adolescent deaths, violence-induced injuries and arrests for youth homicide. Rates of homicide among youths 15-19 years of age reached record-high levels in the latter half of the 1980s. Between 1985 and 1991, annual homicide rates among males 15-19 years old increased 154 percent (from 13 to 33 per 100,000), surpassing the rates of youths in the 25-29 and 30-34 year age groups (CDC 1994). During the 1985-1993 period, homicide arrests of young people aged 10-17 rose 154 percent, from 5.7 to 14.5 per 100,000.

In the second period, the escalating trend was reversed, with arrests for violent crimes involving youth decreasing dramatically, along with sharp decreases in youth homicide in urban areas. Homicide rates for young males began to decline in 1994 and dropped 34 percent between 1993 and 1997 (from 34 to 22.6 per 100,000). In 1997, the rate of homicide among males 15-19 years of age was 22.6 per 100,000—a decline of 12.4 percent in one year (NCIPC unpublished). While arrest rates for weapons offenses among youths 10 to 17 years of age doubled between 1987 and 1993, they dropped 24 percent by 1997 (Snyder 1997).

Although these trends are encouraging, rates remain unacceptably high. Rates of homicide among youths 15-19 years of age continue to be among the highest ever recorded in the U.S. for this age group. An important indicator of violence—confidential reports by youths themselves—reveals that the proportion of young people who acknowledge having committed serious, potentially lethal acts of physical violence has remained level since the peak of the epidemic. Yet in any given year in the late 1990s, at least ten times as many youths reported that they had engaged in some form of violent behavior that could have seriously injured or killed another person (USPHS 2002). Other dimensions of youth interpersonal violence have remained constant, despite fluctuations in numbers. Homicide continues to be the second leading cause of death for persons 15-24 years of age, and the third leading cause of death for children ages 5-14. Homicide remains the leading cause of death for African American youth. In this age group, homicide is the second leading cause of death for Latino youth. In each year since 1988, more than 80 percent of homicide victims 15-19 years of age were killed with a firearm (NCIPC unpublished). The risk of violent victimization continues to be greater for a 12-year old than for anyone age 24 or older. Homicide victims aged 10-17 are still most likely to be killed by either a friend or acquaintance as opposed to a family member. Most of these homicide victims are shot to death, and the majority of juvenile homicide victims in this age range are male. Juvenile victims generally know who their attacker is, and know that person well (Snyder and Sickmund 1995).

For every homicide, according to the National Crime Survey, there are more than 100 non-lethal assaults (NCHS 1992). Increased use of firearms in acts of aggression has not only led to an increase in lethality, and hence a greater number of completed homicides, but has also led to a greater number of survivors who are severely and permanently injured. [1]

Spinal cord injury has increased steadily as a result of violence-induced firearm injury. Once considered a wartime injury, by 1973 gunshot wounds were second only to motor vehicle accidents as the leading cause of traumatic quadriplegia and paraplegia (Smith et al. 2003). In several urban areas, spinal cord injuries have doubled or tripled; the current wave of gunshot spinal cord injuries constitutes a new generation of injury cases (Zeeb 1991), and a new patient group has emerged: youth with violence-induced spinal cord injury. The Spinal Cord Injury Model Systems Database reports that during the 1973-76 period, violence accounted for 13.3 percent of all cases entered into the database; in 1991-94, 30.4 percent (NSCISC 1994). Like all victims of violence, most of those sustaining spinal cord injury due to violence are young, and belong to minority groups. Of all violence-related spinal cord injury victims during the 1973-1992 period, 69.8 percent were non-white (Garland 1993, 21). A current study of patients with spinal cord injury caused by gunshot wounds between 1993 and 1999 notes the continued predominance of young minority patients (Smith et al. 2003).

During the last twenty years, urban trauma has been described as analogous to a chronic recurrent disease with a significant mortality rate, due to the probability of recurrence and the related high risk of experiencing the co-morbidities of substance abuse and unemployment (Sims et al. 1989, 940-947). The young injured victims are generally discharged into a resource-poor community beset with violence, so that a return to a violence-prone lifestyle or further victimization is a significant risk, ultimately resulting in another injury to themselves or others, or in death. One of the characteristics of youth acquaintance violence is a high recidivism rate among the able-bodied as well as among the disabled.[2]

The fiscal burden of violence on the health care system in the United States has been crippling. By the 1990s, the growing number of intentional injury trauma patients and the escalating costs of services for this mostly uninsured population had become a financial obstacle for trauma center expansion and maintenance. Despite a spate of surgical literature studies supporting the efficacy of trauma systems in reducing mortality from trauma and improving outcomes, trauma centers across the United States were closing—61 since 1981 (Dailey 1992, 539-547; Trunkey 1993). Overburdened public hospitals with progresssively diminishing resources and de facto rationing were described by Shoemaker et al. as reaching "a new peak of disarray, generally referred to as emergency department gridlock." This turmoil prolongs existing delays and, in turn, exacerbates the incidence of shock and shock-related organ failures. During periods of social unrest, such as the aftermath of the Los Angeles riots in 1992, these conditions escalate abruptly, and "have a devastating psychological effect on physicians and their support staff." Even more emotionally debilitating is the effect on the underserved inhabitants, leading to over-irritation, disturbed feelings, anger, demoralization, and, eventually, torrents of violent physical reaction (Shoemaker et al. 1993).

During the last twenty years, youth interpersonal violence has traditionally been considered the exclusive domain of the criminal justice system, and responses have largely focused on control strategies, law enforcement, and the alternatives offered by judicial and penal institutions. Arrests, a heavy investment in incarceration, and more severe prosecution of juveniles and children have been the popular bipartisan policy responses. Many of the nation's youth are involved in the juvenile justice system. The U.S. Department of Justice estimates that there are 2.5 million juvenile arrests each year (Snyder 2000). On an average day, approximately 109,000 youth under 18 are incarcerated (Sickmund and Wan 1999), and nearly 15 percent of these youth are housed in adult facilities that may lack services for youth (Austin et al 2000). Minority youth are over-represented in the juvenile justice system, with African American and Latino youth accounting for over 60 percent of young offenders in juvenile facilities (Snyder and Sickmund

1999). National arrests among girls for violent crime have actually risen, as have the rates for many small towns, suburbs and rural communities (Prothrow-Stith and Spivack 2004).

It is not clear that a policy of deterrence through post facto punishment and incarceration has had its intended effect. The treatment of juveniles as adults, encouraged under the Violent Crime Control and Law Enforcement Act of 1994, intended to reduce youth crime through a harsher, swifter, and more punitive response, seems not to have had the proposed effect. According to a study of youth transferred to adult criminal court in Florida, such adjudication quickly resulted in a higher rate of new crimes among those tried as adults, as compared to their counterparts whose cases are handled in juvenile court (Washington Crime News Services 1996a).

In the last several years, significant attention has been paid to the decline in youth violent crime in the United States, largely due to declines in urban youth violence rates in urban areas. Boston's reduction in youth homicide in the mid- to late 1990s, was dubbed the "Boston Miracle." Boston experienced a dramatic reduction in juvenile murder rates. Whereas there had been 73 homicides among individuals younger than 24 years of age in 1990, there were only 15 in 1999 and 2000 (Boston Police Department 2004). Los Angeles would also experience a decline, on a less dramatic scale. In the last couple of years, the rates of youth homicide have increased once more. In Boston, homicides rose 38 percent in 2000, and exploded to 68 in 2001, prompting the question if the so-called "Boston Miracle" was over. In Los Angeles, homicides have also risen after years of decline.

Of the Boston homicide victims in 1999-2001, a sharp increase has been noted among those ages 25 to 32, from 4 in 1999 to 22 in 2001, an increase attributed to the increase of felons returning to the community from prison, many of whom were previously involved in gang conflicts as juveniles. According to the Boston Police, many of these deaths are believed to be retributions or attempts to retake drug markets lost by the individuals when they were incarcerated (Boston Police Department 2004). If the homicides of the early 1990s were characterized by the Boston Police as part of a period of hot-headed street killing by youth, those after 1999 are seen as more calculated.

Whereas the problem individuals of the 1990s were often young, immature, hot-blooded and had never been to prison, those in 2001 are prison-hardened criminals. In many cases they are the same individuals who are now returning to the community after a stint in jail where they have acquired an "education in how to effectively employ violent means..." What will be needed is a focus on "impact players"–individuals seen as having a negative effect in neighborhoods regarding gang activity, drug trafficking, and firearm violence (Winship 2002, 16).

The persistent problem of interpersonal violence among the young raises an increasing number of questions and doubts about existing and past public policy responses to the problem, as well as the socio-economic costs to the individual, the community, and the nation of pursuing such policies.

At a community level, relying on incarceration and other retributive criminal justice responses without correcting the pattern of discriminatory enforcement has resulted in rates of selective and concentrated imprisonment among the young and young adult offending population. Nearly 40 percent of all California's black men in their 20s were imprisoned, on probation, or on parole in 1995, a rate nearly 8 times greater than their white counterparts. California maintains 20 percent more of its young black men in the criminal justice system than the nation does overall, though the national average rate for this group rose from 25 to 33 percent in 1995 (Juvenile Justice Digest 1996b). In Massachusetts, Latinos or Hispanics are the fastest-growing segment of the prison population, and by 1995 made up about 20 percent of this population, as compared to 9 percent in 1995 (U.S. Census Bureau 1995). Among youth, Hispanics or Latinos represent 8.8 percent of the youth population ages 10-19 in Massachusetts, but 35 percent of the youth in custody of the Department of Youth Services (DYS). Latino youth ages 10-19 in DYS custody increased by 24 percent from 1995-2000 (Citizens for Juvenile Justice 2000). Such discriminate use of force and selective incapacitation is in itself a contributing factor to repeated violent behavior.

The increasing reliance on law enforcement as the principal response to the rise in youth assaultive violence has created problems for the judicial system itself, as well as the larger goals of justice it seeks to promote. The Massachusetts juvenile justice system, once touted as a national model, is under strain. In 1985, the largest category of offenses for juveniles was property crime (such as larceny or vandalism); by 1993, violent crime had become the largest category. Nearly 43 percent of the juveniles remanded to Department of Youth Services custody had committed crimes against another person, with armed assault exceeding any other crime. Another 40 percent had committed property crimes. The budget cuts during the state's fiscal crisis of the early 1990s and the rising level of serious and violent juvenile crime has resulted in an overloaded system similar to the medical gridlock experienced in trauma and emergency room settings (Juvenile Justice Digest 1995).

A 1996 American Bar Association report highlighted similar systemic problems with juvenile justice representation across the United States. The report revealed that, on average, juvenile defenders carry a caseload of more than 500 cases a year, resulting in inadequate representation as guaranteed under the 1967 U.S. Supreme Court ruling. This overload problem has far more serious implications due to recent Congressional, state legislature, and executive agency decisions that juvenile courts respond with more punitive sanctions, longer periods of confinement for young offenders, and increased handling of juveniles in adult courts (Juvenile Justice Digest 1996c).

On a national level, relying on a criminal justice response to the problem of youth violence has economic implications for the general development of children and adolescents. During times of budget deficits, increased public expenditures in one area come at a significant cost to others. The most significant shift in spending, at various levels of government, has been from education to crime control. While the commitment to funding juvenile corrections became increasingly federalized, particularly the budgets for institutional care between 1980 and 1990, the contribution to education was halved. Together with the decline of county expenditures (as a percentage of the total budget), criminal justice expenditures, in 1995, for the first time in U.S. history, received more public funds from state, county, and municipal governments than education (Chambliss 1995, 9). A study of state government expenditures found that from 1987 to 1995, spending on prisons increased by 30 percent while spending on higher education decreased by 18 percent. Over a 2-year period from 1994 through 1995, state spending on prison construction increased by $926 million while funds for higher education fell by $954 million (Ambrosio and Schiraldi 1997; Suro 1997). For the first time in California's history, the 1996-1997 state budget appropriated more money for corrections (9.4 percent) than for higher education (8.7 percent). "As states continue to lay off teachers to pay for corrections officers, it is becoming more apparent that their citizens are poorly educated and unemployable—precisely the kind of person who fill our prisons," the study concludes (Ambrosio and Schiraldi 1997). In Massachusetts, the outcome of deliberations on the state budget for 2004 is expected to result in greater spending on prisons and jails than on public higher education for the first time (Massachusetts Taxpayers Foundation 2003).

The current after-the-fact, retributive justice policy response to the problem of youth violence and delinquency has implications for the health, development, and well being of the young both inside and outside the corrections system. Such resource allocation compounds the public health problem of death, injury and disability. The cost of the policy response to youth violence—and the opportunities foregone as a result— looms larger if health is envisaged as being more than the absence of injury and disease, but rather as a state of complete physical, mental, and social well-being with multiple determinants, according to the systems view of the "new public health." The attainment of adequate education, health care, personal security, housing, and recreational opportunity, necessary for health in the "new public health" framework, is compromised by the use of already limited resources on incarceration and prison facilities.

U.S. YOUTH VIOLENCE IN COMPARATIVE PERSPECTIVE

The high rates of violence in the United States in the late twentieth century have been described as a paradox. Unlike Western European nations or other high-income countries, violence in this country tends to be of a private nature, involving citizens fighting one another (Tilly et al. 1975; Tilly 1989). Some scholars suggest that the frame of reference for U.S. homicide comparisons should be the other Americas, and not Western Europe or Canada (Hagan 1994; Levine and Rosich 1996). Early observers of violence in the U.S. noted:

> Most of the countries we regard as acutely violent, we also regard as suffering from chronic upheaval and political instability. But the United States has long shown a political stability that compares favorably with, say, England or Scandinavia, and yet has a level of civil violence that resembles some Latin American republics or the volatile new states of Asia and Africa (Hofstader and Wallace 1970; Graham 1989, 342).

According to the World Health Organization's World Report on Violence and Health, issued in 2002, the rates of interpersonal violence in the United States vastly exceed those of any other western industrialized nation. In terms of youth violence, apart from the United States, where the rate is 11 per 100,000, most of the countries with youth homicide rates above 10 per 100,000 are either developing countries or those experiencing rapid social and economic changes (Krug et al. 2002).

Higher levels of structural violence and increasing state violence also characterize U.S. patterns of violence relative to other Western European nations (Galtung 1969). Some scholars have attributed the overrepresentation of African Americans (and other unreliably counted minority groups of low socio-economic status) in the U.S. prison system to the mobilization of law.[3] The politics of policing as a response to perceived ethnic or racial threat, directed at shifting groups of poor during the different socio-historical conjunctures in U.S. history, is a problem "seen to be particularly American, resulting from the heterogeneity and inequality of the society, in combination with its constitutionally provided creed of opportunity in the context of evident inequality." (Jackson 1995, 341)

In terms of incarceration, the United States currently imprisons a higher percentage of its population than any other nation, whether industrialized or developing, democratic or authoritarian (Chambliss 1995, 236). More than 5.6 million Americans (or one in 37 adults living in the United States) are in prison or have served time there, according to a new report by the U.S. Department of Justice (2003). The report presents lifetime chances of going to State or Federal prison by age, sex, race, and Hispanic origin. Assuming that recent incarceration rates remain unchanged, the report estimates that 6.6 percent of U.S. residents born in 2001 will go to prison at some time during their lifetime. At current levels of incarceration newborn black males in this country have a greater than a 1 in 4 chance of going to prison during their lifetimes, while Hispanic males have a 1 in 6 chance, and white males have a 1 in 23 chance of serving time.

While most nations have abolished the death penalty in law or practice, the U.S. continues to join a handful of nations with the highest numbers of executions. The U.S. has executed over 800 people since 1976, and as of December 2002, over 3,700 men and women were on death rows across the country (Amnesty International 2004a,b). The use of the death penalty against child offenders—people under 18 at the time of the crime—persists in the US, while prohibited by international human rights law. Between 1990 and September 2003, Amnesty International documented 34 executions of child offenders in eight countries—the Democratic Republic of Congo, Iran, Nigeria, Pakistan, Saudi Arabia, the US, China and Yemen. The U.S. carried out 19 executions—more than all other countries combined.

While youth gangs are found in all regions of the world, the United States contains the great majority of gang-involved cities and members, although other nations have developed their own variants of gang-like structures. Gang formation is especially pronounced in countries and communities undergoing economic transition, rapid urbanization, or where social order has eroded (Klein 1995). The start or further development of street gangs in a community generally suggests that the community has not succeeded in socializing some segments of its youth.

> Since street gangs are often composed mainly of minority youngsters, the failure often implies the specter of institutional racism. In addition, the continuation of these gangs, now comprising a gang problem, reflects on the inability of community institutions to control or roll back the problem. Social agencies, schools, and the justice system appear impotent

and thus face a public relations problem on top of their gang problem (Klein 1995).

YOUTH VIOLENCE PREVENTION IN TWO COMMUNITIES: RESEARCH PROJECT HISTORY

In 1990, I became a public health/community development worker with the city of Boston on a violence prevention project linked to the inpatient pediatric and adolescent medicine department at the city hospital. The project had expanded to cover all areas of the city as a result of a sharp increase in Boston's homicide rates and street gangs, and the mayor had declared youth violence prevention as one of his main priorities. My job at the time was to extend the research into new communities and demographic groups—specifically, the various "Latino" (Puerto Rican, Dominican, other Spanish-speaking Caribbean, and Central and South American) immigrant/migrant and ethnic groups—and incorporate these perspectives into the emerging public health approach to youth violence prevention.

During the 1980s, the Latino youth population in Boston increased substantially. The number of young men between the ages of 16 and 24 increased by 72.5 percent from 1980–1990, and the number of young women grew by 50 percent (Gaston Institute 1992). Increased Latino youth enrollment and use of youth-serving agencies, hospitals and emergency rooms provided an incentive to programs to hire workers who were bilingual and familiar with some of the experiences and life issues faced by these various subgroups.

At the city hospital and city health centers, a slow but steady increase of young Latino males (and a few young women as well) were being treated for injuries as a result of peer violence, with a steadily increasing number dying from their injuries. In the six-year period between 1985 and 1991, the overall number of adolescents treated for gunshot wounds increased 245 percent, while stabbings increased 98 percent (Boston City Hospital 1991). By 1992, the rate of gunshot and stab wounds for youth ages 15-19 had reached 43 per 10,000 (Violence Prevention Project Papers 1994). For Latino and African American youth ages 15-24, homicide was the leading cause of death; the rates in Massachusetts in 1990 were 113 and 39 per 100,000, respectively. For white youth ages 15-24, homicide ranked as the second leading cause of death taking a toll of 7.2 deaths per 100,000.

In an effort to become better informed about this community of young people, given the paucity of published research in this area, I began to recruit youth who had been victims and/or perpetrators of acquaintance violence: young males and females between the ages of 13 and 19, most of whom were Latino (predominantly Puerto Rican, but also Dominican, Honduran, Mexican, Salvadoran, and South American), African American, West Indian, or European American. They lived in Dorchester, Roxbury, Mattapan, the South End, and Mission Hill, the neighborhoods in Boston with the highest homicide, assault and other violent crime rates. These predominantly poor neighborhoods accounted for more than 90 percent of the city's African American population and 72 percent of the city's Latino population; 59 percent of its residents reported being members of other minority groups. Nearly 75 percent of the reported gunshot and stab wounds among Boston residents were to residents of these neighborhoods (Office of Health and Vital Statistics 1993).

In the process of recruitment, I learned that the program's approach to compartmentalizing youth violence was useful only to a point, for it overlooked many demographic, racial, and cultural complexities. Many young people counted as "African Americans" in youth programs were descendants of or were born as Cape Verdeans, West Africans, Caribbeans, and Central Americans. Among the native African American youth population, differences in regional origin, timing of family migration and class and family composition at times overrode the "racial" similarities on which categorical funding, program philosophy and disease counts were based. Among the "Latino" youth, similar distinctions, even within specific "poorer" neighborhoods, suggested "the differences among these subgroups—in education, employment, family structure and even age distribution—were often greater than overall differences between Latinos and non-Latinos (Duany and Pittman 1990).

As the youth brought their friends into the program—members of increasingly multi-ethnic and multi-racial street corner groups and street gangs—what also surfaced was the existence of a cross-group reality that encompassed specific groups of urban African American, Latino and other youth, including whites, or Anglo Americans. That challenged the ways in which the problem of (and solutions to) youth violence was conceptualized and addressed, often mobilizing one affected constituent group at a time. Even though my interest had been to understand the manifestation of youth violence in the Latino community, preventing such violence required that I work with the peers closest to these youth, many of whom were of a different group, ethnicity, and/or race, who included native or non-native born members, and both males and females.

If the races, ethnicities, and sometimes the nationalities of these young people were varied, many of their immediate life circumstances were similar. Ninety percent of the young people lived in families with only one parent. Eighty-five percent had dropped out of school—some as early as seventh grade, one in fifth grade. Most had parents who had not finished high school; a few had parents who had never held a full-time or part-time job. All the youth had been shot at and/or stabbed, all had witnessed acts of violence, and most were involved in street groups. Some had migrated to the "inner city," some had been born in it, but all now lived there, in areas of high poverty and homicide, areas where the social service infrastructure in place in the 1970s has been increasingly gutted. Many grew up during those years, in neighborhoods where a process described by Wacquant and Wilson as "hyperghettoization" was taking place. In this process "social ills that have long been associated with segregated poverty—violent crime, drugs, housing deterioration, family disruption, commercial blight and educational failure—have reached qualitatively different proportions and have been articulated into a new configuration that endows each with a more deadly impact than before" (Wacquant and Wilson 1989), leading to the deterioration of the stabilizing forces of the inner city.

In addition to my work in Boston, I assisted other cities in developing public health and hospital-based youth violence prevention programs. In 1992, I visited a prevention and intervention program in the pediatrics department of a rehabilitation hospital in Los Angeles. Formerly treating polio and tuberculosis patients, the hospital now handled a growing and steady stream of injured youth and young adults requiring rehabilitation due to violence-related injuries. The many children and youth in wheelchairs who passed me as I was given a tour of the facility were the most visibly affected—the tip of the injury pyramid resulting from violence and requiring trauma center services and rehabilitation. In 1992, violent injuries killed 1,023 and hospitalized 5,661 Californians under 21 years of age. The rate of hospitalized assaults for males, which excluded patients who died in the hospital, reached 98.4 per 100,000 that year (California Department of Health Services 1996). The median age of victims of gunshot wounds being transported to area trauma centers at the time was 20. Of the victims requiring trauma center treatment, 48 percent were Latino, 37 percent were African American, 10 percent were white, 5 percent were Asian, and most were uninsured. (Violence Prevention Coalition 1993). In the previous year, firearms had taken the lives of 372 Los Angeles County youth under 20 years of age. For every firearm-related death, states the literature, between 10 and 40 people are shot and ultimately survive.[4] These luckier ones, I thought, might be some of the young people I saw during my hospital tour.

Like the Boston program, the youth program I visited uses hospital, trauma, health, and rehabilitation centers, as well as the juvenile justice system, as a point of intervention and recruitment for young, predominantly urban victims of violence. The frameworks informing both programs are drawn from public health. Recognizing that youth assaultive violence and the number of youth injured due to firearm use and stabbing by their peers was both a pervasive national problem and a problem for the urban poor (with some local variation). I expanded my research to include both West and East Coast cities.

As was the case in Boston, interpersonal violence is the leading cause of death for minority youth in Los Angeles, although the extent of homicide differs. In 1992, homicide rates in Boston were one-third higher than the nation's, a relatively low rate as compared to Baltimore, St. Louis, and Philadelphia, whose homicide rates are three to six times the national rate. Despite this, in 1993 more teenagers were murdered with guns in Boston alone than in the entire country of Canada (Office of Health and Vital Statistics 1993). In 1992 there were 2,589 reported homicides in Los Angeles County; of these, 801 were deemed gang related (Violence Prevention Coalition 1993). During the previous year, 1,311 people had been arrested for homicide in Los Angeles County; 388 were under the age of 18. Among Los Angeles youth under the age of 21, the rate of hospitalization due to nonfatal gun assaults for 1991 and 1992 was 63.7 per 100,000.

My visit to Los Angeles was part of a public health response to the events that had transpired in 1992. As part of my "education" about Los Angeles, a city gang worker took me on a painstakingly slow tour of the areas where the riots broke out, driving around the neighborhoods and tracing the path of the riot as it had unfurled. The burnt-down buildings, rubble and debris left in the wake of the riot seemed just one more insult. In my eyes, this area was a chronically underdeveloped "third world" pocket in the midst of the affluent city of Los Angeles. The area's buildings and infrastructure had been devastated by another form of violence, far more protracted and discrete than the riots themselves. I did not see any youth recreational areas, transportation, jobs, libraries, museums, cultural centers, or boys and girls clubs. I saw little safe and sturdy housing. There were no health centers, other visible community facilities, nor signs of food stores that sold fresh produce. Alcohol stores, however, were plentiful, as were the prime-aged males on the street, drinking, dealing, or just passing the time. The institutional neglect, segregation, marginalization, and poverty that had worn down the neighborhood through a process of attrition, was the most shocking.

I wanted to leave. The gang worker, concerned—and also, perhaps, slightly pleased—at my discomfort, suggested that all this must be news to me. What saddened me was that, in fact, it was not news. Facets of what I saw reminded me of the extremes of wealth and underdevelopment in Brazil, where I was born and lived during parts of my adolescence. The parts of the city I saw were "third world" pockets in an advanced western capitalist nation. Yet the prevalent construction of the problem of violence (as well as the proposals for its eventual reduction) generally did not encompass a dimension of economic democracy. Segregation, and ethnic and racial distrust, created such narrow, parochial, and at times reactively, chauvinistic world views that only the "insiders" or the "native sons and daughters" could presume to attempt to unravel the problem.

These larger forces, I suspect, are closely, although indirectly, linked to the state of other urban communities and to the act of collective protest and rioting that broke out in the spring of 1992 in Los Angeles (and which spread spontaneously to other urban centers). So, too, are they linked to the high toll of homicides and injuries among youth. The Webster Commission, investigating the 1992 "spring unrest" (or riot, rebellion, or civil disturbance, depending on the viewpoint taken) following the first Rodney King beating verdicts, in fact referred to the 1965 Watts riots to help explain the recent events.

The Commission noted that already dwindling federal investments in the area had declined again since 1981. These cuts, from $23 billion to $8 billion for job training, from $6 billion to zero for general revenue sharing, and from $21 billion to $14 billion for local economic development, were accompanied by housing cuts; overall federal housing programs were cut by 8 percent. "As a result, the great gulf between rich and poor... continued to widen" (Klein 1995, 196).

During the lifetime of the young people whose risk for homicide informs this work, federal disinvestments and widening income inequality constitute the overriding meta-tale of the poorer areas of the two cities.

DEFINITION OF TERMS

The point of departure and the conceptualizations of youth violence used in this study are drawn from the discipline of public health. This report focuses on one facet of interpersonal violence: assaultive behavior. Within the spectrum of behaviors contained under the rubric of assaultive behavior, this report focuses on one of the sub-categories: acquaintance violence. An overview of these terms is provided below.

Assaultive Violence

The definition of assaultive violence includes both nonfatal and fatal interpersonal violence where physical or other force is used by one person with the intent to cause harm, injury, or death to another. Homicide—death due to injuries inflicted by another person with an intent to harm, injure, or kill by any means—is only one, though the most extreme, manifestation of assaultive violence. It is further classified as either criminal or non-criminal in nature; criminal homicide excludes both death caused by negligence and "justifiable homicide" (an act committed in self-defense or in the line of duty by a police officer). Four legal classifications are generally used to identify nonfatal injury in surveillance, research, and media reports: aggravated assault, simple assault, rape, and robbery (Rosenberg and Mercy 1991).

Aggravated assault, one of the classifications, is defined as: 1) an attack with a weapon, regardless of whether an injury is the result; 2) an attack without a weapon, resulting in either serious injury (such as broken bones, teeth, internal injuries, or loss of consciousness) or an undetermined injury requiring two or more days of hospitalization; or 3) an attempted assault with a weapon.

Simple assault is defined as an attack or an attempted attack without a weapon, which results in minor injury (such as bruises, black eyes, cuts, scratches or swelling) or in an undetermined injury requiring less than two days of hospitalization.

Rape is defined as carnal knowledge through the use of force or threat of force, and includes attempted rape.

Robbery is a completed or attempted theft of property or theft directly from a person through the use of force or the threat of force, with or without a weapon.

Both fatal and nonfatal assaultive violence can be further divided into different types, based on such characteristics as victim-offender relationship, setting, and circumstance. The most common categorization pivots around the relationship between the victim and the offender. The three most general categories of violence using this differentiation criterion are stranger, family, and acquaintance violence. This approach has been chosen because both the etiology and prevention strategies for assaultive violence generally vary by the victim-offender relationship. The research literature in public health generally presents assaultive violence and homicide as similar categories of behavior, and depicts homicide as the "completed" assault. Most strategies that would reduce assault are generally deemed to reduce homicides.

Acquaintance Homicide/Violence

Both the perpetrator and the victim of acquaintance homicide and assaultive behavior have a similar statistical "portrait." They tend to be younger than the victims and perpetrators of family homicide and are much more likely to be male, black, and poor. Offenders are usually younger than their victims, and the homicides involve handguns as the weapon of choice. Unlike the other two categories of homicide—where the victim/perpetrator roles are fixed, with one being the more constant "offender," and the other the more constant "victim" (as in domestic homicides)—in acquaintance violence, the power and use of force is more evenly distributed, and the roles more readily interchangeable (Rosenberg and Mercy 1991). The person who is victimized today may well have perpetrated in the past or come to perpetrate in the future

(Sampson and Lauritsen 1994). Homicides involving friends or acquaintances are most likely to occur within a private residence, although one-third occurs on the street. A greater percentage takes place in bars, relative to other types of killings (Ridel and Zahn 1982).

Gang/Street Group Violence

Not traditionally included in the discourse of violence as a public health issue, gang violence, or the violence committed by street groups, was an integral part of this study since many of the young people interviewed belonged to a street group or gang (as had many young people treated for injuries), and their gang involvement contributed to their greater risk of victimization and perpetration. Morales, a gang intervention researcher, has estimated that in Los Angeles, gang members are 60 times more likely to die as a result of homicide than the general population (Morales 1992). Therefore, those who associate with gang members, live nearby, or play on streets where there is gang activity, are at substantially higher risk for injury and death.

Estimates of gang-related homicide and nonfatal assaultive injury vary substantially across states and cities, due to different levels and extent of gang activity, the ability of local police to count and correctly identify them, and also because of the manner in which gang homicides and other acts are defined and counted. In cities like Los Angeles, the police deem an incident gang-related if a gang member is involved, either as victim or offender. Thus, a liquor store robbery carried out by a gang member, even if conducted for individual gain, would be classified as a gang crime. Some cities, such as Chicago and Boston, define a gang related crime more narrowly: it must involve a gang motive: an assault of retaliation, recruitment, funding the gang, and so forth.[5] Despite variation in classification among cities, and reflecting the increases counted by the federal government, the "past 10 years have seen more than a doubling of the reported gang homicide figures since what was thought to be a one-time-only peak in 1980" (Klein 1995, 17)

The issue of gang definition is a contentious one. Among gang scholars, as outlined by Ronald Huff, different definitions can lead to different conclusions about the seriousness of the problem of gangs and the gang-violence relationship (Ridel and Zahn 1982). Whereas some scholars state that gangs should not be defined, so as not to lose conceptual variation, others, such as Morash (1983), who studied gangs in Boston, debate whether criminal involvement should be included in the definition of a gang due to concern with the tautological problem (Horwitz 1983). If gangs are defined as delinquent groups, then it is impossible to investigate the members' history of delinquency independent of their gang affiliation, nor the implications for intervention and prevention (Morash 1983). Further, as stated by Miller

(1981), when "youth groups in a particular community clearly appear to present a problem, they are perceived as gangs; when they do not, that community has 'groups,' not gangs."

Researchers like Klein and Maxson have adopted the term "street gangs" to address the aging of the gang population over time. As gang members remain in their gangs longer than they used to, members now range in age from 10 to 30, and age has become less of a defining characteristic. The street setting and style have gained in importance. Gang members (mainly boys and young men, but the number of girls and young women is growing) are described as engaging in "cafeteria-style" crime, aimless and quite different from the rational calculated organization and use of violence inherent in the portrayals of "the violent criminal street gangs" offered by the Los Angeles Police Department (Klein 1995). For the purposes of this study, I have used the terms "street groups" and "street gangs" interchangeably.

Victims of gang or street group activity, as in the case of most person-to-person crime, tend to look much like the perpetrators. They generally live in the same neighborhood, are of the same ethnicity or race, fall within the same social status and age bracket, and are the same gender. The similarity in victim-perpetrator characteristics has remained largely unchanged for decades, according to research conducted on Boston and Los Angeles gang victims (Klein 1995). A retrospective study of Los Angeles adolescents and children injured or killed in drive-by shootings in 1991, found that 71 percent were documented members of "violent street gangs" according to the Los Angeles Police Department. Of those who died, 86 percent were members of street groups Hutson et al. 1994).

The reliance on guns as a characteristic of street group violence has increased, accounting for 61 percent of gang killings in Philadelphia and East Los Angeles between 1968 and 1969, and rising to 90 percent of Los Angeles homicides in the last few years (Klein 1995, 73-74).

CHAPTER 3

Youth Violence Prevention: A Public Health Approach

The way in which violence and its prevention has been addressed theoretically and programmatically over the last three decades has had a profound impact on the lives of the adolescents who grew up during this period, and on the lives of the young people who collaborated in this study. The literature reviewed as part of the historical and theoretical background for this study covers selected discourses on the contemporary study of youth violence, the development of programs to reduce their incidence, and addresses some of the themes that surfaced from the study participants' stories and perceptions. It is meant as a cursory and selective review, with further exploration of particular research and programmatic approaches embedded in the themes explored in subsequent chapters. As such, the review discusses the emergence of the study of violence as a public health issue, the theories of causation, and the current knowledge on termination. The public health literature implications for violence prevention program design and the theoretical frameworks informing the two programs from whence the study participants were recruited in the early 1990s are also touched upon.

THE EMERGENCE OF YOUTH VIOLENCE AS A PUBLIC HEALTH ISSUE

In the late 1970s, federal public health officials announced their mission to reduce the rate of interpersonal violence among the most affected population subgroup (i.e., young black males). The Centers for Disease Control and Prevention (CDC) began to document differences in the risk of homicide victimization in the United States, disseminating the results to a larger audience and attracting increased media coverage.

In 1985, the findings of the Task Force on Black and Minority Health of the Secretary of the U.S. Department of Health and Human

Services would mark the beginning of a sustained and increasingly well-funded effort to address assaultive injury among youth as a public health problem. The task force concluded that homicide was the leading cause of death for black men ages 15–34, and the calculated lifetime risk for death from homicide was 1 in 28 for black men as compared to 1 in 164 for white men. These stark facts mobilized public health, medical, and African American communities in an effort to address this critical health problem (U.S. Department of Health and Human Services 1985). In the late 1980s violence surveillance, research, and the development of preventive interventions began to be integrated within the mandate of local and regional health departments.

Public health reframed interpersonal violence as a preventable matter, providing a "big tent" framework for research and intervention that encompasses the insights and strategies of varied disciplines. The public health definition of violence as the "threatened or actual use of physical force against a person or group that either results or is likely to result in injury or death," (Mercy et al. 1993) included illegal behaviors as well as non-criminal behaviors. It offered an opportunity to reconcile frequently contradictory conclusions about youth violence, drawing from offender-based research, social and developmental science approaches on the one hand, and conventional public health approaches on the other. The public health method stresses community-based strategies, with a focus on practice and collective action, going beyond the medical model, which largely focused on the diagnosis and treatment of specific illnesses in individual patients. It identifies three levels of prevention research and practice:

1) Primary prevention activities to promote health and protect against exposure to risk factors that lead to health problems, focusing on reducing or removing risk factors by changing the environment and the community, as well as, family and individual life styles and behaviors.

2) Secondary prevention strategies to stop or slow the progression of the health problem, including screening and detection for early diagnosis, treatment and follow-up, and targeting those more susceptible to health problems due to family history, age, lifestyle, or environmental factors

3) Tertiary prevention efforts to manage and rehabilitate persons with diagnosed health conditions to reduce complications, improve their quality of life and extend their years of productivity.

The method employed by public health would follow the precepts of scientific method, a process by which scientists, collectively and over time, endeavor to construct an accurate (i.e. reliable, consistent and nonarbitrary) representation of the world. This method involves four steps: 1) the observation and description of a phenomenon or group of phenomena, 2) the formulation of an hypothesis to explain the phenomena, such as a causal mechanism or a mathematical relation, 3) the use of the hypothesis to predict the existence of other phenomena, or to predict quantitatively the results of new observations, 4) the performance of experimental tests of the predictions by several independent experimenters and properly performed experiments. Experimental science requires experimental verification of hypothetical predictions, and is built upon testable theories (Wilson 1952).

The public health method would similarly identify problems and develop solutions for entire population groups, by 1) uncovering basic knowledge about the problem, by gathering data to determine the nature of the problem, the trends in its incidence and prevalence; 2) investigating why violence occurs, and conducting research on the causes and correlates of violence through epidemiological analyses that identify risk and protective factors associated with the problem, and research on factors that may be modifiable through intervention; 3) the design, development and evaluation of the effectiveness and generalizability of interventions; and 4) the dissemination of successful models as part of a coordinated effort to educate and reach the public (U.S. Surgeon General 2002).

A significant contribution of public health was to revisit and attempt to integrate old debates on violence that had been insufficiently or separately explored by social scientists. Given the complex and multifaceted nature of assaultive violence, traditionally separate disciplinary approaches (i.e., biological, cultural, structural, interactionist, and psychosocial) advanced interpretative theories on the causation of violence, often with distinct policy and program implications. As outlined in *Violence in America: A Public Health Approach*, none of these approaches fully explain the occurrence and manifestation of violence, nor do they address the need to develop "causal explanations that combine biological, psychological, and sociological factors in ways that more clearly explain the occurrence of assaultive violence involving different perpetrators, victims, and circumstances" (Rosenberg and Fenley 1991). Kinnear (1995) identifies four main groups of causal theories of violent behavior in children and adolescents—biological, psychological/psychosocial, environmental/ situational, and societal—and similarly concludes that most scholars "believe that violent behavior is often caused by a complex interplay among many factors."

Public health would also prompt the re-examination of unanswered questions. Why were there differences among groups in their level of involvement in violence? What etiologies of violence emerged from the social, behavioral, and criminological literature? How did the choice of explanation and theory influence the types of programs and policies implemented?

The early research on interpersonal violence would be shaped by the dominant political and social scientific understandings of crime and violence. The term "violence," like the earlier study of "aggression," would be used to describe varied behaviors, often with little understanding of cause, process, time, place, or context. Writing about the contemporary study of interpersonal violence, Hawkins similarly observes that it "is included among a variety of forms of anti-social conduct whose distinct 'causes' are not differentiated." This has hampered early efforts to understand the quality and causes of the impulses and origins of such violence among children and youth, and how best to intervene and evaluate prevention efforts. Years before, in *The Anatomy of Human Destructiveness*, Fromm outlined how the equivocal use of the word "aggression" had led to much confusion. The term had been applied to "the behavior of a man defending his life against attack, a robber killing his victim . . . the sexual approach of the male to the female." In such a construct, aggression is seen as a "noxious" act, and the quality of the impulses of entirely different phenomena is irrelevant, leading to what Fromm describes as a "theoretically hopeless position," with no hope for understanding aggression's actual cause.

When exploring ethnic, racial, and social class differences in rates of violence, explanations also tended to largely focus their analysis on the values, attitudes, and beliefs that were presumed to differentiate low-violence from high-violence groups. According to Hawkins, the idea that specific ethnic, racial, and social class groups and specific sub-populations have varying rates of violence due to cultural values became an "umbrella concept," integrating many seemingly competing theories of crime and violence:

> For example, when put to the task of explaining group differences in rates of interpersonal violence, various theories that emphasize social learning, social control/containment, or psychological or psychiatric dysfunction are all strengthened to the extent that they affirm the existence of cultural or sub cultural differences. The disproportionate resort to violence is deemed to be quite understandable for dysfunctional persons who reside not only within dysfunctional families and other primary groups, but also within dysfunctional or aberrant cultural contexts (Hawkins 1993).

As a consequence, much of the literature and theory on youth assaultive violence (which, in turn, informed the first generation of program development) focused on exploring inter group differences, and the enumeration and analysis of dysfunctions. Socio-economic inequality might be seen as a contributing factor, if not a possible cause, of violence. However, programmatic and policy responses generally focused on individual, situational deficits, seen as less diffuse and more proximal, and developed interventions to address such shortfalls (Sampson and Lauritsen 1994; Tolan and Guerra 1994). Responses favored social learning, psycho-social, educational, "cultural-difference," and other such interventions, which seek to change the norms, values, beliefs, or habits of thought of certain high-risk groups. Such approaches tended to be short-term and deficit- and/or culture-specific in design. A 1996 review of 15 science-based interventions that employed a spectrum of strategies and had a rigorous evaluation design concluded that "individually oriented strategies are more common than those directed toward peer, families, schools, and communities" (Powell et al. 1996, 6). The bulk of empirically demonstrated "effective" practices were found at the individual level.

A 1996 review of public health violence prevention initiatives and their intervention/prevention principles focused on optimizing the developmental outcomes of children through the prevention or reduction of problem behaviors. These interventions employ a health promotion model[6] designed to reduce aggression and promote positive development in school-age youths, and are built on a common research base that emphasizes "the role of emotional reactivity; skills deficits; peer relationships; normative beliefs about aggression; the role of the mass media on violent behavior; the role of neoassociationistic cognitions; social cognitive problem-solving models; cognitive rehearsal; coercion; mindlessness, premature cognitive commitments; mindfulness; and goal-directed behavior" (Farrell 1996, 14).

The early proliferation of individual-level interventions is also largely due to the relative ease in studying and intervening at that level. Writing in the mid 1990s, Tolan and Guerra (1994) concluded that as a result, such efforts "get an inordinate amount of attention and their overall value may be inflated."

> With individual-level approaches, comparisons are easier to construct, random assignment is easier to impose, and follow-up is less complicated. Often, interventions at this level can be implemented without the need to obtain community or parental support, and they generally require minimal family, school, or neighborhood commitment.[7]

In Tolan and Guerra's 1994 review of adolescent violence prevention programs, they found that demonstrated "promising" initiatives could be found in interventions that address various levels or spheres of influence. Such initiatives ranged from individual group member interventions; proximal interpersonal interventions with family and peers; proximal setting efforts directed toward social groups and organizations, such as schools and neighborhoods; and societal macro-system interventions directed at characteristics of the general society, such as economic opportunity, firearm availability, or media exposure.

According to the authors, in order to develop adolescent violence prevention programs, a theoretical link must be drawn across factors that consider the occurrence of violence as dependent on multiple-level influences (p. 12). If individual-level characteristics, close interpersonal relationships, proximal social contexts, or societal-level influences are "considered separately, these factors provide competing univariate theories that explain little of the variance in adolescent antisocial behavior and are likely to explain less about violence. Even if considered collectively, this listing of risk factors does not indicate how best to target interventions."

Sampson and Lauritsen would argue for a broader approach that "leads away from a simple 'kinds of people' analysis to a focus on how social characteristics of collectivities foster violence" (1994, 89). The authors' exhaustive risk factor review concluded that suggestive links to the causes of violence can be gleaned from the ways in which individual-level and situational-level characteristics interact with "community-level factors such as (but not limited to) the ecological concentration of the urban underclass, residential mobility and population turnover, family disruption, housing and population density, criminal opportunity structures (e.g., levels of nonhousehold leisure activities, gun density), and dimensions of social organization (e.g., informal social ties, density of acquaintanceship, supervision of street-corner street groups, organizational density and strength)" (p. 90).

Between 1993 and 2002, several other comprehensive scholarly and reviews on the occurrence and patterns of youth violence, its causes and consequences, and intervention strategies, were published by federal agencies, the National Academy of Sciences, professional organizations, and university-based researchers reviewing research (Reiss and Roth 1993; Eron et al. 1994). Informed by a broad range of disciplines, this research contributed to a new level of assurance that youth violence can be both understood and prevented.

Among these publications is the Surgeon General's Report on Youth Violence (U.S. Surgeon General 2002), which provides a review of what is know about youth violence from a public health perspective, summarizing the state of the science on youth violence and synthesizing the differences in perspective of three Federal health agencies, the CDC, the National Institutes of Health, and the Substance Abuse and Mental Health Services Administration.

This report takes a conservative approach to the standard of evidence required, and draws from a contemporary knowledge base that includes study findings that have shown consistent results, no contrary results, and that have been replicated in several studies. It also reviews meta-analyses and epidemiological research, primarily general population studies that use probability samples, and cross-sectional or longitudinal designs. Giving most weight to true experimental studies, the report also included carefully designed and executed quasi-experimental studies, where true experiments were too complicated or cost-prohibitive to carry out, or when they posed unacceptable ethical questions.

This synthesis identifies and quantifies those individual, family, school, peer group, and community characteristics that place children and adolescents at risk for violent behavior, in the course of a child's or adolescents' development. The report describes how risk factors, in particular situations or groupings , can increase the likelihood of violence will occur, It also begins to identify those factors that seem to protect from the effects of risk, a nascent field of study. Informed by a developmental perspective, the report concludes that both risk and protective factors are found to vary in their predictive power depending on when they occur: As a child grows form infancy to early adulthood, some risk factors increase while others decrease in importance. Substance use, for example, is a much stronger risk factor at age 9 than it is at age 14.

The report delineates the strongest risk factors during childhood: involvement in serious but not necessarily violent criminal behavior, substance use, being male, physical aggression, low family socioeconomic status or poverty and antisocial parents. Peer influences largely supplant family influence as a child grows into adolescence. During this period, the strongest risk factors are weak ties to conventional peers, ties to antisocial or delinquent peers, belonging to a gang, and involvement in other criminal acts.

Cumulative research also underscores the linkages between youth violence and other forms of violence experienced by children and youth, such as witnessing violence in the home, or being abused physically or sexually (Fagan and Browne 1994). Parental neglect, rejection and indifference have also been found to place children at a greater risk of anti-social and aggressive behavior (Widom 1989b). A young person at risk for violence exposed to additional risk factors such as alcohol and other substance abuse, and firearm access, may experience more than one form of violence . The further impact of cultural and societal risk factors such as isolation, poverty and cultural norms that are accepting of violence can similarly result in a young person already at risk experiencing more than one form of violence.

The young who are involved in serious violence often have a lifestyle that often includes alcohol and other substance use, guns, sex, among other risky behaviors. The young who are involved in serious violence often exhibit other problem behaviors, and commit many other types of crimes, presenting challenges to intervention efforts. Successful interventions need to address not only the violent behavior of these young people, but also their lifestyles, which can be full of risk (U.S. Surgeon General 2002)

Meta-analytic studies of offender rehabilitation in the early 90s offered a standardized overview of a large proportion of hundreds of empirical studies, reviewing program effect in both clinical (beneficial outcomes in terms of personal change) as well as criminological outcome measures (Lipsey 1992). This literature suggests that interventions should target the proximal causes of the undesired outcomes associated with delinquency. Indiscriminate targeting of intervention programs is counterproductive, as are less structured and less focused approaches such as counseling. Further, the most effective rehabilitation programs, which are behavioral, skills-oriented, and multi-modal, incorporate cognitive approaches that address the "attitudes, values and beliefs that support antisocial behavior" (Gendreau and Andrews 1990). These interventions have high treatment integrity, often target the family, and have the most impact when conducted in the community or when linked structurally to community-based interventions. Another important predictor of success is the selection of medium- to high-risk offenders; rehabilitation is most successfully delivered to those offenders whose patterns of offending suggest a high probability of recidivism.

Despite these important advances, there remain important gaps in the understanding of youth violence at all levels. As stated in the Surgeon General's report, while two general onset trajectories for youth violence have been identified—an early one, in which violence begins before puberty, and a late one, in which violence begins in adolescence—very little is known about the latter. Most youth violence begins in adolescence and ends with the transition into adulthood, yet late-onset violence prevention is not widely recognized or well understood.

A comprehensive, multi-year survey of American youth offers a broad view of the onset and termination of violent behavior over time. The mid-1990s study found that serious violent offending most often begins at ages 15-16, with violent behavior peaking at 18 and declining sharply thereafter. A person over the age of 20 with no past serious violent behavior offenses is not likely to become a violent offender (National Youth Survey, as cited in Elliott 1994a; see also Elliott 1994b, 1). Although a considerable minority (more than one-fourth) of youth commits at least one act of violence before turning 18, for most young people, this behavior ceases over time. More than 80 percent of adolescent violent offenders terminate their violence by age 21, and the "criminal careers" of most violent youthful offenders generally last only one year. Despite the prevalence of delinquent behavior, 6 percent of adolescents are responsible for two-thirds of all violent crimes committed by juveniles, and approximately 40 percent of the arrests for all serious crime are of children and youth ages 10-20. After age 29, arrests for violent acts taper off dramatically. (U.S. Department of Justice 1993, 5-6; FBI 1993).

Substantial numbers of serious violent offenders emerge in adolescence without warning signs in childhood. A comprehensive community prevention strategy must address both onset patterns and ferret out their causes and risk factors. The differences in patterns of serious violence by age of onset and the relatively constant rates of individual offending have important implications for prevention and intervention programs. Early childhood programs that target at-risk children and families are critical for preventing the onset of a chronic violent career, but programs must also be developed to combat late-onset violence.

Violence Prevention Framework of the Boston and Los Angeles Programs

Although a large amount of work has been carried out to understand the problem of youth violence, no standard typology of intervention strategies exists, and no one theoretical stance appears to be dominant in terms of efficacy for prevention programs (Fields and McNamara 2003, 67). The framework of the Boston and Los Angeles programs, moreover, cannot be neatly collapsed into typologies of peer group interventions empirically evaluated to date.

In an effort to begin to address the question "What actually works to reduce violence?" Tolan and Guerra (1994) differentiated three program approaches among peer programs for youth ages 12–21: 1) shifting peer group norms to increase peer pressure for prosocial as opposed to antisocial activity; 2) preventing association with antisocial peers and/or redirecting peer group behavior toward prosocial activities; and 3) focusing on involving youth in conflict resolution with peers, such as peer mediation and conflict resolution programs.

Both the Boston and Los Angeles initiatives (begun respectively in 1990 and 1992) were established to serve the hard-to-reach adolescents who had dropped out of mainstream youth activities, such as schools and youth and community centers, and become involved in violence and crime as a way of life. In Boston, the efforts of a community-based violence prevention program (including a youth program of adolescents voluntarily referred from juvenile justice programs and health clinics, adolescent street workers, and other youth) were extended and linked to the inpatient pediatric department of the local city hospital, which housed the level one trauma center. In 1995, the program was expanded to include young patients from the neighboring spinal cord injury unit, following a hospital merger. In Los Angeles, an outpatient peer education program was established in 1992, recruiting young people from the community as well as youth from the spinal cord injury center at the rehabilitation hospital.

The injured youth, according to both programs' conceptualization, could benefit from more information about violence, risk factors for violent injury, and coping with the trauma of their injuries. Both programs' goals are to decrease adolescent morbidity and mortality and improve quality of life, and are premised on the belief that the hospitalization experience, when the young person is separated from the context in which the violence occurred, provides a "teachable moment" for the young person to revisit past conduct and learn from past mistakes. The experience of trauma is also seen as an opportunity to provide support to a young person whose emotional walls, which are generally difficult for authority figures to overcome, may be momentarily lowered, allowing for health professionals to stimulate further behavioral change.

Tolan and Guerra's conclusions about adolescent violence interventions are consistent with the meta-analytic studies of offender rehabilitation. Offering a standardized overview of a large proportion of hundreds of empirical studies, the meta-analyses review program effect in both clinical (beneficial outcomes in terms of personal change) and criminological outcome measures (Lipsey 1992). This literature suggests that interventions should target the proximal causes of the undesired outcomes associated with delinquency. Indiscriminate targeting of intervention programs is counterproductive, as are less structured and less focused approaches such as counseling. Further, the most effective rehabilitation programs, which are behavioral, skills-oriented, and multimodal, incorporate cognitive approaches that address the "attitudes, values and beliefs that support antisocial behavior." (Gendreau and Andrews 1990). These interventions have high treatment integrity, often target the family, and have the most impact when conducted in the community or when linked structurally to community-based interventions. Another important predictor of success is the selection of medium- to high-risk offenders; rehabilitation is most successfully delivered to those offenders whose patterns of offending suggest a high probability of recidivism.

An evaluation of the impact of the Boston program's multi-disciplinary violence-prevention trauma team outlines some theoretical premises common to both the Boston and Los Angeles youth initiatives. Based on Prothrow-Stith's (1987) curriculum, the programs and initiatives are informed by the "health beliefs model, self-efficacy, the theory of reasoned action and their synergy with cognitive mediation theory as expressed in developmental psychology" (De Vos et al. 1996).

According to the health beliefs model, risk behaviors can be altered, if the individuals believe in their susceptibility to, and the severity of the consequences of, the condition. They will also alter behavior if they believe in the benefits of the preventive measure and in their ability to conform to and abide by it. Through education about the barriers to healthier or risk-averse behavior and nonviolent means of reacting to situations, self-efficacy is promoted as young people become empowered to deal effectively with their situations.

Theories of reasoned action and cognitive mediation also inform the intervention programs, where the violent incident is portrayed as one of a series of events involving a range of choices and behaviors. By examining the link between the intended behaviors and their actual, ultimate behaviors, young people can learn how their habits of thought facilitate violent behavioral outcomes. They learn methods for assessing situations before they result in violence, and become aware of the range of potential responses to a volatile situation, consider alternatives to violence, and practice nonviolent conflict resolution skills. The approach emphasizes discussion with the adolescents, using their recent incident(s) and lifelike scenarios as a jumping-off point for discussion.

The program components explore the relationship between the social construction of reality through narrative and social behavior. They use the trauma associated with being shot or stabbed and consequently hospitalized as an experience that lends itself to narrative interpretation, one that often leaves the victim committing publicly to revenge at discharge. Many adolescents interpret the event of injury as one that confers hero status on them; others are left angry, seeking revenge; and yet others construct in their retelling a world too frightening and dangerous to allow for their safe return. The choice the adolescent makes in retelling the incident sets him or her on a trajectory that may lead to further violence. By redirecting the youth's narrative construction of events, theory suggests we can alter the event's meaning to deflect feelings of aggression and cast violence as part of the problem rather than any kind of solution (De Vos et al. 1996, 102). Other responses and perspectives have surfaced from the specific, grassroots work with adolescents and their communities over time. Many of these efforts are congruent or can be collapsed under articulated theoretical frameworks, even though they were not conceived as applications of such theories.

Peer group intervention, a model that informs some facets of both the Boston and Los Angeles programs, emphasizes the modification of antisocial behavior by changing the nature of the peer group interaction. It seeks to shift peer group norms, promoting youth involvement with prosocial peers, some of whom were formerly violence-involved, and redirecting the activities of antisocial peer groups and street gangs. Such peer interventions have been found to achieve "superior results in health-related outcomes through combined positive peer influence and specific skills training" (Wiist et al. 1996, 56) A meta-analysis of juvenile offender treatment programs similarly found that interventions involving change agents as part of the program setting were more likely to lead to positive outcomes (Davidson et al. 1990). Interventions of this type transcend a purely individual-level approach and, in some ways, resemble "positive peer culture" (PPC) interventions of the 1970s. The Boston and Los Angeles programs, like earlier PPC models, use an adult-guided, youth-run, small-group treatment approach.

A focus on employment and job creation underpins both the Los Angeles and Boston programs. Through a seven-week summer jobs program, a certain number of street clean-up jobs have been set aside for young people to design and carry out community health education service projects. During the school year, after-school part-time employment, volunteer involvement through the creation of a speakers bureau, peer counseling employment contracts with juvenile justice and health care institutions, and paid apprenticeships at public health departments and community agencies provide income and skills development opportunities.

Both programs borrow from different approaches, disciplines and philosophies, which they implement with varying and shifting levels of intensity and integrity, while also being shaped by the particular experiences of the young participants. Although small, working with a maximum of 25 adolescents per year, both programs are multi-faceted and constantly changing, and are therefore difficult to describe and evaluate in terms of ascribing correct weight to their various components and theories and sifting through the effects of their interactions with others.

Recent developments

The study and practice of violence prevention continues to grow substantially and is increasingly informed by other disciplines, deeper perspectives, and a more comprehensive, global approach. Among these emerging developments has been the increasing incorporation and acknowledgement of youth development theory and practice. Research on the features of positive youth development has begun to identify personal and social assets that can foster increase the healthy development and well-being of adolescents and facilitate a successful transition from childhood, through adolescence and adulthood. Such asset-based approaches are increasingly recognized as complementing more traditional risk-reduction efforts in communities (NRC and IOM 2002). Based on research involving over 100,000 children, over several years, from grades 6 through 12, the Search Institute has identified 40 developmental assets (internal and external) that when present in sufficient strength and combination, lead to positive outcomes (Scales and Leffert 1999). The internal assets identify those characteristics and behaviors that reflect positive internal growth and development, such as positive values and identities, social competencies, and commitment to learning. These internal developmental assets assist the young in making healthful and positive choices and to be better equipped for situations in life that will test their inner strength and confidence. External assets are the positive experiences young people receive from the world around them, and pivot around support and empowerment, setting boundaries and expectations, and about positive and constructive use of young people's time. The asset based approach identifies important roles that families, schools, congregations, neighborhoods, and youth organizations can play in promoting healthy development.

Although very few high-quality comprehensive experimental designs evaluations of community programs for youth have assessed their impact of youth, some high quality experimental and quasi-experimental evaluations show positive effects on a variety of health outcomes, such as decreases in the incidence of delinquency, early pregnancy, and drug use, while enhancing both the psychological and social assets of youth (NCR and IOM 2002).

Another response of public health efforts to address persistent health disparities—often the highly concentrated health problems concentrated in a small share of all neighborhoods, such as youth violence—has been to move "upstream" to address the more fundamental determinants of health. The field has begun to develop a public health framework for thinking about how poverty, social class, socio-economic segregation and other "social" factors work together to affect health, delineating methods for examining the effectiveness of interventions targeting the socio-cultural environment in order to improve health, and providing evidence of the effectiveness of selected intervention strategies in the area of early childhood education, family housing and culturally competent health care. The more traditional definition of "effectiveness" has been expanded to consider unintended positive and negative effects, economic efficiency, applicability and barriers to implementation. These broader reviews have the potential to serve as a guide to action and stimulate primary research that is conducive to more comprehensive and immediate social policy (American Journal of Preventive Medicine 2003).

Based on the adolescent violence reduction experiences of cities like Boston—with initiatives that spanned two decades of work—there is a growing understanding that the complex issue of youth violence requires multi-faceted solutions, and comprehensive approaches that ultimately engage all sectors of a community. Collective and political efforts at various levels are needed, building a broad-based coalition of support and participation at the same time that solutions are explored. The lessons of Boston underscore the need for flexibility, an inclusive and engaged process—one that defies a single approach. Preventing violence in this municipal context required changing community values, re-orienting services, and promoting a social movement, and it took time, according to Deborah Prothrow-Stith and Howard Spivak (1994), among the first pioneers of the violence prevention field.

The problem of violence has been increasingly recognized as a hemispheric problem, and the contributions of other countries in the Americas have the potential to greatly enrich work in the United States. The Plan of Action issued at the April 2001 Quebec Summit of the Americas of the Organization of American States identified violence prevention as a prerequisite in regional efforts to strengthen democracy, create prosperity, and realize human potential (OAS 2001). The research and practice contributions from other countries underscore that violence further aggravates existing inequities and presents obstacles for governance, economic and political development. It reduces foreign and domestic investments and impedes long-term growth, and people who feel unsafe can lose faith in the justice and political system. As states and municipalities across the our hemisphere face budgetary constraints, the financial demands of curbing violence must also be assessed in terms of lost opportunities to invest in efforts to prevent violence that strengthen social cohesion and build social capital.

At the United Nations (UN) meeting on UN Collaboration for the Prevention of Interpersonal Violence held in Geneva on 15-16 November 2001, the UN recognized the global and widespread impact of interpersonal violence on health, development, human rights, human security, and peace and acknowledged that the multiple and complex causes of interpersonal violence require a multi-disciplinary, multi-cultural response.

The World Report on Violence and Health, published by the World Health Organization (WHO) in 2002 (Krug et al.), is a watershed publication, marking a turning point in violence prevention efforts. The WHO definition of violence offers a broader definition of violence that encompasses other dimensions and outcomes: deprivation, maldevelopment and psychological harm. The World Health Organization defines violence as "the intentional use of physical force or power, threatened or actual, against oneself, another person, or against a group or community, that either results in or has a high likelihood of resulting in injury, death, psychological harm, maldevelopment or deprivation." The inclusion of the word "power" broadens the conventional understanding of violence to include those acts that result from a power relationship, including threats and intimidation. It encompasses discrete acts of omission, such as neglect, as well as more evident acts of commission. The broader definition also implies acts of both private and public violence. The report also defines youth as ages

15-29, an increasingly accepted international definition given rapid demographic, socio-cultural and labor market changes that have extended adolescence well into the 20s.

The report offers a broader, more sophisticated framework to stimulate increasingly coordinated preventive action and research across types of violence; to address social, economic and policy factors that transcend national boundaries; and to pursue violence prevention efforts on a regional or global scale. It offers evidence of the prevention of violence from micro-level individual and community efforts to broader national policy initiatives. Employing an ecological model, the report views violence as the result of the complex interplay of individual, relationship, social, cultural and environmental factors, underscoring that the various types of violence commonly share a number of risk factors for more than one type of violence, as well as links between different types of violence. These links between violence and the interaction between individual factors and the larger social, cultural and economic contexts have important implications for practice and policy, suggesting that addressing risk factors across the various levels of the model may contribute to decreases in more than one form of violence.

The report findings challenge violence prevention professionals to look beyond the fragmentation that has characterized the field, in which research and prevention efforts for the various types of violence have often evolved separately from one another. They argue for broader partnerships among groups with a major interest in primary and secondary prevention working in specific violence prevention fields, whether working at a local, national or global level. In sum, the report charges violence prevention professionals and their constituent and allied groups to think globally even as they act locally, exchanging information, ideas, approaches and experiences (Hoffman 2003).

CHAPTER 4

Study Methods

If you want to understand what a science is, you should look in the first instance, not at its theories or findings, and certainly not what its apologists say about it: you should look at what the practitioners of it do.

—C. Geertz

This qualitative, exploratory research study employed ethnographic and oral history approaches and involved the participants as co-researchers. The sources and methods used were as follows: 1) life history; 2) interview, and 3) autobiography, which allows entry to the phenomenology of the adolescents' own experience, revealing the texture of personal happenings, which gave rise to, sustained, and eventually led to the adolescents' abandonment of assaultive conduct.

Multiple sources of evidence were used to address the behavioral, attitudinal, and historical dimensions of the antecedents and process of abandonment of assaultive conduct. These sources included interviews, journal entries and autobiographical statements, selected archival records, chronicles of participant observation, and a field log.

The research objectives of this exploratory study are as follows:

1. To gather and study theme variation among the various pathways in and out of violent behavior, enhancing current knowledge about a little-known phenomenon. The study seeks to do this through narratives that view the process of manifestation and termination of violence from the "bottom up" within historical context. Specifically, the study seeks to identify and understand the catalysts, influences, barriers, and retardants in this process.

2. To assist in the identification of intermediate outcomes, thereby aiding in the development of future evaluation parameters and research instruments, and furthering the existing knowledge on termination of assaultive behavior. This objective will help to

overcome the important methodological limitations of the field, identified at the Carnegie Conference on Violence Prevention for Young Adolescents (Cohen and Wilson-Brewer 1991).

3. To contribute to program development in public health and hospital settings and youth acquaintance violence prevention and intervention programs, through the enumeration and description of the factors, qualities, and processes that provided windows of opportunity, decreased recidivism, and facilitated such transformation among youth.

4. To contribute to public health theory and the study of violence prevention. The study of the personal narratives will increase understanding of the particular processes and variations in termination of violent behavior, leading to clarification and even revision of the current literature on the causation of acquaintance violence.

5. To create a usable text for youth- and researcher-driven policy development in the area of violence prevention and youth development.

The study explored the following questions:

1. What factors, events, personalities, processes, and catalysts contributed to or retarded the termination of assaultive behavior among youth?

2. What factors, events, personalities, processes, and catalysts inhibited the full and nonviolent development among these children and adolescents, and what policies, if any, can foster such development?

3. What are the implications of a traumatic event for revisiting past behavior, and what can health and hospital programs do, if anything, to encourage and support youth in such situations?

The participants in this proposed research project were 20 racially and ethnically diverse young men and women, between the ages of 20 and 32 at the time of the study's completion, leaders in two similar hospital/ rehabilitation and community-based violence intervention programs in Los Angeles, California and Boston, Massachusetts. The young people had been victims and/or perpetrators of youth acquaintance violence and had been shot and/or stabbed. Most had been involved in the program for more than two years at the time of recruitment, counseling other youth, educating about acquaintance violence prevention, and participating in community service.

The majority of the participants in this study were either African American or Latino males, as this is the population most often seen at both hospitals as victims of violence in both cities, and most often referred to the program by the juvenile justice system. The number of girls and young women seen at hospitals and engaged in assaultive violence is much smaller. Nevertheless, the study included seven young women who provided useful information about their experiences as victims and/or perpetrators of youth assaultive violence.

Ten of the youth in the study suffered paralysis as a result of intentional, violent injuries; they are among the growing number of youth in urban settings who have spinal cord injuries and rely on trauma and rehabilitation center services (Weingarten and Grahm 1991). The few existing program evaluation efforts often exclude these young people with disabilities, on the assumption that participation would be too burdensome. Thus learning about this virtually unknown population whose successful outcomes (and the underlying factors and processes that facilitated such outcomes) may add to our understanding of youth who are affected by violence, youth with disabilities and able-bodied youth alike. Even their failures may shed light on the experiences of this population as victims of violence.

PARTICIPANT ISSUES

The researcher, other youth workers, and program youth identified appropriate participants, using the inclusion and exclusion criteria described in the body of the text. All participants had an informed consent form explained to them and signed it before proceeding with the interviews. The transcribers for this project signed an oath of confidentiality. Participants were informed that their participation was strictly voluntary and would in no way affect the manner in which they were treated or the services offered by the hospital or other agencies/programs with which they might have been involved. They were advised that all information would be kept confidential, and that all identifiers would be removed from their working data and any reports derived from them. The participants were informed that they did not need to answer any questions they did not want to answer, and that they were free to discontinue participation at any time, without prejudice.

There were no anticipated risks to the adolescents participating in this study. The study produced important insight into the prevention of a devastating health and social problem and suggestions on how to intervene, enabling other young people like themselves to overcome violence. The individual benefits were a chance to reflect on past successes and an opportunity to voice feelings about society in general, and offer program and policy recommendations based on their experiences. Participants revealed information that could be used against them by law enforcement and social services officials. Every attempt was made to minimize any risk or possibility of legal difficulty stemming from participants revealing sensitive information. All identifiers were removed from the data when transcribed or entered into the database. Each participant's data record was assigned a code, and a master list of names was maintained in a separate, locked file, apart from the data. Access to data was restricted to the researchers involved in the project. All identifying information was deleted from tapes, transcripts, and notes once the study was completed.

Now that the study has ended, participants own the transcripts for their own program development use or personal publication. Altogether, the benefit/risk ratio in participating was considered acceptable by all parties.

Selection criteria for participants reflected their interest in the topic, the depth of their commitment, the length of time they had done work in this area, and a demonstrated effort to change their assaultive behavior. The focus on long-term involvement is essential to capture the youths' entire journey, recognizing that they must overcome obstacles and detours as they extricate themselves from their former lives, stay alive and healthy throughout their adolescence, and do their best for their families and communities. For some, it took years before they could safely lay their past behind with surety and safety, and decrease their risk of being victimized in the future. For others, this point had not yet been reached.

The sampling design for this study also sought to provide the broadest possible representation of violence involvement and termination: perpetrators and victims; gang and non-gang involved; a mix of races, ethnicities, and genders; both younger and older program members; and people with differing life circumstances, experiences, and perspectives.

The pilot study in Boston added another sampling criterion: should be in back in school, working, and established in a new phase of their lives, to reduce the likelihood of responding within the constraints of earlier roles.

ETHNOGRAPHICAL RESEARCH DESIGNS

This study used an oral history/ethnographic approach, which is most suitable to record the life experiences of the group with integrity while satisfying the theoretical concerns of the study. Such research contrasts starkly with most standard social science investigations of the problem of youth violence, in which the investigators typically seek either to ignore or reduce contextual meaning in the interests of standardization and comparability. The critical task, as Geertz stated, is "to grasp concepts [that], for another person, are 'experience near,' and to do so well enough to place them in illuminating connection with experience-distant concepts [that] theorists have fashioned to capture the general features of social life" (Geertz 1983, 58).

The ethnographic focus on subjective meaning and process provides the best theoretical tools with which to understand a young person's "inner career of action." Whereas functionalism and conflict theory focus on the norms and structures that largely predetermine most social (violent or nonviolent) interaction, this study seeks to understand small-scale interactions. It is primarily concerned with fully explaining individuals' particular decisions and actions, which are difficult to explain by predetermined rules and external forces.

A central tenet of symbolic interactionist theory informed this study: the process of self-indication by which human action is formed, cannot be accounted for by factors that precede an act. Rather, self-interaction—a process whereby an individual notes, assesses any or all features of a situation or any feature of involvement in an act—eventually imparts a "career" to the eventual human act, an act that "may be stopped, restrained, abandoned, resurrected, postponed, intensified, concealed, transformed, or redirected" (Geertz 1983, 58). This level of decision-making and social interaction is likely to answer questions why a particular individual will commit an assaultive act, while another, whose life is shaped by the same macro-sociological forces, will not.

Little attention has been given to the phenomenology of the injured or violence-affected youth's own experience, or to the experiences of youth who desisted from acts of violence, there are few study examples to draw from. However, ethnographic research has been used to delineate such meanings, values, and shifts in thinking in similar participants in studies about attitudes toward work and job training programs and gang members' perceptions of the long-term opportunities of program participation (Corsica 1993, 301-302). Similar to the field of violence prevention, very little sound experimental research is available to inform policy and program design relevant to employment training for at-risk youth. What experimental research does exist may be suggestive but is flawed nevertheless, due to the scarcity of information on trainee retention, post-program employment in secondary labor markets, and job loss, and the paucity of indicators of program success or failure. "Success," in an evaluative sense, is often assessed in terms of cost-benefit ratios calculated on a number of criteria such as job placement rates, reductions in criminal activity and welfare dependency, and employment-related measures such as post-program earnings, taxable income, and unemployment usage, all of which are macro indicators. Gang employment training interventions have yet to explain or account for success or failure at the micro level. The methodology employed asks questions and obtains answers about dollars, cents, and numbers but cannot explain what a given income means to a gang participant, and how that affects how he/she makes decisions about looking for work, remaining at a job and desisting from lucrative gang criminal activities, all of which are crucial questions for intervention programs. In order to obtain such answers, researchers have given ethnographic data extra weight in identifying program strategies likely to work with the at-risk population of concern.

The need for ethnographic data to help discern program success indicators and criteria for program evaluation is urgent in the field of adolescent violence prevention. The first systematic nationwide review of the state of the art in violence prevention, completed in 1990, concluded that the field needed to develop a more consistent, scientific set of standards for evaluation across projects, and that the outcome measures in use at the time were neither valid nor feasible. The measurement of knowledge and attitudes can neither demonstrate nor explain a reduction in violence. A decrease in morbidity and mortality among adolescents exposed to an intervention is not a realistic yardstick against which change can be detected or demonstrated because of the low incidence of the phenomenon. Intermediate, intervening, and targeted objectives theoretically connected to the outcome (i.e., a reduction in violent behavior) need to be specified. Without the ability to name these intermediate objectives (and delineating the processes that bring them about), the ability to detect individual change at the micro level and evaluate program impact is severely reduced. This is particularly true over short time periods where expected effects may not be great, available statistical measures may not be sensitive enough and target populations may be too small. (Cohen and Wilson-Brewer 1991). Exactly what to measure and which method is most appropriate for documentation remain the pivotal questions in this debate.

According to one of the field's early evaluators, answers to these questions are likely to emerge from the young program participants. Describing the evaluation of the Boston Project completed in 1990, Hausman stated that too much emphasis had been placed on getting a large amount of data on a large number of adolescents. What was sacrificed in this process "was getting some really good, qualitative information on a smaller number of kids" (Cohen and Wilson-Brewer 1991). The evaluation lacked in-depth interviews to really understand how a smaller sample incorporated violence prevention in their own lives was, in retrospect, an important missed step in the evaluation process.

One of the field's pioneer practitioners, Deborah Prothrow-Stith, recommended exploring the experiences and narratives of the change agents, such as teachers, counselors, health care providers, community-based program staff, and others. Observational data collected for the Violence Prevention Project's evaluation made it clear to Hausman "that providers had begun to critically examine how they dealt with violence," suggesting that such information could serve as a proxy measure of long-term program success (Cohen and Wilson-Brewer 1991). When the change agents are youth, and either former perpetrators or victims, the process by which they incorporated violence prevention into their own lives may offer content suggestions to programs that serve youth in similar circumstances.

The questions this work seeks to answer are essentially historical (How did this process of transformation come about?) as opposed to definitional (What is this process?), which is inherent in the emphasis on the present of pure ethnographies, largely concerned with synchronic rather than diachronic time. In such pure accounts, both anthropological and sociological, the relevant "history" is limited, atemporal, and, as stated by Van Maanen (1988), "embedded in the daily practices and symbolic life of the group studied, and hence will be taken into account naturally." In choosing this method, the study proposed is part of a trend whereby "history is seeping back into ethnography as another 'blurred genre,' and native histories—as retellings and reconstructions—are being represented."

The processes leading to and from the perpetration of assaultive violence, while influenced by social-psychological occurrences within the minds of young offenders, are nevertheless much wider. Their course is also shaped by a longer, deeper history and structure than those grounded in daily practice and group life. The marriage of micro-level symbolic interactionist and ethnographic concepts to macro conflict theory was advocated by Goffman, who recommended pursuing "unsponsored analyses of the social arrangements enjoyed by those with institutional authority—police, generals, governments... and all those well-placed persons who are in a position to give official imprint to versions of reality" (Goffman 1988, 283). This approach would serve as a crucial step in bridging the micro and macro level of analysis and could yield a coherent view of whole societies. Although beyond the scope of this study, the history and emergence of powerful crime prevention and prison industry, as well as the reversal of a pro-rehabilitation ethos, are parts of the story that must be told, however sketchily. They are contained in the life episodes of many of the study participants who had contact with, were incarcerated by, and had specific types of interactions with law enforcement and the criminal justice system. These youth grew up during a period in which a national "moral panic" over juvenile crime intensified, culminating in the Violent Crime Control and Law Enforcement Act of 1994, which legislated an over 25-fold increase in offenses eligible for the death penalty, and allowed juveniles as young as 13 to be tried as adults.

A debate about the nature and circumstances of young offenders has generated new terms—such as "new breed" of violent offender, the "super predators," and "a lost generation"—to describe what is portrayed as the senseless, amoral, and remorseless mindset behind these murderous and violent acts. The ideological and political *raisons d'être* of such terms and political positions is bolstered by the "nothing works" study of the rehabilitation of offenders. A landmark review of offender treatment studies was published in 1975 by Lipson, Martinson, and Wilkins, and popularized in Martinson's paper "What Works? Questions and Answers About Prison Reform (1974). Their "nothing works" conclusion provided the empirical justification to turn away from the rehabilitation thrust of juvenile and adult offender programs. The "nothing works" doctrine, according to Hollin (1993, 72), "has, in the intervening years, been transformed from an interpretation of existing data to a socially constructed 'fact,' seemingly accepted by academics and policy makers alike."

This transformation in the discourse of juvenile delinquency, which so dramatically influenced the childhood, adolescence, and young adulthood of the study participants, either directly or indirectly, dates back to the 1950s. Historical analysis underscores how definitions of problems (and their solutions) are also "accounts" that are socially and historically situated. What was depicted as "delinquency" in the 1950s (a phrase that conjures up truancy, fighting, and petty theft) became, by the 1980s, an image of "youth crime." As stated by Friedman (1993, 240), in his social history of crime and punishment in the United States, "these are not (we think) 'delinquents,' nor 'wayward youth;' they are just plain criminals, adult in their violence and menace, if not their years." The narrative background of a society that in many ways suspended (or rescinded) its own ethical views and treatment of children is part of the story of the process by which these young people who were judged deviant and undeserving came to resume ethical, pro-social, and nonviolent conduct.

Like all forms of writing, including those that claim empirical neutrality, social science writing is rhetorical, political, and historically situated. Categories of thoughts are not formulated in a vacuum, nor can their departure point be neutral, rational, or objective. According to Stone (1997), reasoned analysis is necessarily political, "for it involves a ranking and compilation of causes, political interests, symbols and numbers, and a specific social construction of reality." In her words, "a political metaphor always faces a potential opponent, or competing metaphor." If the metaphor driving the prevalent policy solutions to youth violence (i.e., incarceration and containment/isolation) is one of a "Lost Generation" for whom it is feared nothing can be done, the competing metaphor driving this work is that of "voices of change."

Public health is a field of knowledge and a field of action. As such, both the discipline and its practitioners can uphold, revise, or resist the conventional wisdom and interests of scientific research and the social order, and can serve to humanize the academic institution, the clinic, and the larger society. This study was propelled by very clear sympathies—my own—as well as by an explicit and critical research agenda. It seeks to be both "active and committed" in method, as was Nancy Scheper-Hughes' medical anthropology study (1992) of infant mortality and child death in Brazil, a problem she first tackled as a health and community worker and to which she later returned as a researcher.

PARTICIPATORY RESEARCH DESIGN

This is how I feel: You come in here at six o'clock in the morning, smiling, talking about get up. Are you serious? I done been shot, my life has been changed dramatically, and you are in here smiling like it's funny. But I know you are happy to be here, and be working and learning different things, but you are learning at the expense of my pain, you know. You learning this, and you don't know what I'm going through.

—Ronnie, referring to the medical residents,
when he was hospitalized

An integral part of this study's methodology is that the young people whose lives are chronicled and scrutinized be active participants or co-investigators in the shaping and analysis of this project. As stated by Van Maanen (1988, 5), any disciplinary form of study "irrevocably influences the interests and lives of the people represented in [it]—individually and collectively, for better or worse." I felt a great responsibility to do no further violence to these young people but rather, convey and make sense of their experiences, thereby forcing revisions in academic and programmatic discourse. Research is always a politically mediated endeavor, in which one group has the power to represent another. The group studied or acted on in most applied programs or field endeavors is generally less powerful than the researcher or practitioner and often has little or no voice as to how the stories and experiences of its members are told. In opting for such a participatory research method, this study follows the increasingly common model among field workers described by Clifford (1988) as "dialogic and polyphonic," whereby texts are jointly authored. The study attempts to do this at various levels—through its design, the framing of the research questions, and the collection and analysis of life stories and journal entries—in an effort to minimize interpretation and interference from the researcher.

During my work with young people, I found, as Mishler (1984) did, that narrative and its formation were of crucial importance in the conduct of future behavior. Through narrative (and the accompanying processes of reflection, joint dialogue, and historical reconstruction) individuals made meaning of experience; how each young person constructed that meaning greatly informed how he or she eventually acted on it. The trajectory of these young people out of violence was in part made possible by such retelling and refinement of their past experience.

Telling their stories and being respectfully accepted into conversation not only resulted in a positive emotional experience for the young people, but also generated emotional resources (such as confidence, warmth, enthusiasm, and hope) with which they could negotiate successfully other future interactions. Such chains of interaction and ritual, states Collins (1981), "extend throughout every person's lifetime."

I chose a dialogic approach in an effort to correct for my own presuppositions. Recognizing that any individual's history of ideas is bound and limited, I nonetheless believed that the young people are capable of naming some of the social, economic, and individual sources of their own and their collective despair, violence, and resumption of will and hope. I also believed that I might be able to shed light on some of these facets or name others. At times, differences in interpretation, or "dissident," voices surfaced when the participants read the drafts and the study took shape. By asking in advance how their interpretation differed from my own, "dissident voices" contributed to a more sophisticated, polyvocal final text—a place where different opinions are recorded and, to some extent, reconciled.

PARTICIPANTS AS RESEARCH COLLABORATORS

This study required the participants to be research collaborators, rather than merely competent respondents. I was no longer solely a reporter, although, paradoxically, it also improved the conditions whereby more sophisticated and divergent experience surfaced, and, hopefully, allowed for a more authentic synthesis, or better reporting, to emerge.[8] The intent to move farther away from the explication or development of my own *a priori* theories and opinions was done not only to diminish the asymmetry of power in interview research in general, but was also self-serving: it represented an effort to alter my position and history with some of the participants as their advisor and/or adult practitioner. As Mishler (1986, preface) states, the interview is indeed a form of discourse, shaped and organized by asking and answering questions—"a joint product of what interviewees and interviewers talk about together and how they talk to each other"—as well as a product of how past conversations and relationships took place. A further benefit of giving respondents' own views is the higher assurance of "validity" of the data, minimizing errors of fact and judgment as a built-in check on participant interpretation.

A few primarily qualitative reports on the phenomenology of juvenile delinquency, gang membership, and related topics employ various ethnographic methods, including oral history, and serve as successful examples of obtaining both accurate and valuable input from delinquent youth. Among these are Shaw's (1930/1966) *The Jack-Roller: A Delinquent Boy's Own Story*; and Strodbeck, Short, and Kolegar's (1962) *The Analysis of Self-Descriptions by Members of Delinquent Gangs*; Bennett's (1981) *Oral History and Delinquency*; Hanson, Beschner, Walter, and Bovelle's (1985) *Life with Heroin: Voices from the Inner City*; Roberts's (1987) *The Inner World of the Black Juvenile Delinquent*; Williams's (1989) *The Cocaine Kids*; and Goldstein's (1990) *Delinquents on Delinquency*.

Similarly, there exists a precedent for using youth experience and expertise to inform adolescent program development. Both Schwitzgebel and Kolb's study of induced behavior change among adolescent multiple offenders (Schwitzgebel 1964; Schwitzgebel and Kolb 1964) and Slack's description of new methods of introducing intensive office treatment to hard-to-reach youth (Slack 1960) employed delinquent adolescents as paid experts on delinquency. This study proposes to build on that foundation, using previously violence-involved youth as experts on termination. The Schwitzgebel studies are of particular significance on a variety of levels. As part of a street corner project, they not only recruited and paid the delinquent youth as experts, engaging them in a discussion with street corner workers, but viewed this process as part of the effort to recruit the youth out of gangs and into prosocial community activity. Developed as a response to the limitations of clinic- (or other institution-) specific behavior change programs, where "treatment" effects do not persist after discharge, they anchored the program in the lives and daily experience of the participants in their community. Through discussion and meeting attendance, they reinforced and further developed the intended behavior change. The results of this process were documented in a controlled study: the young participants showed improvement in attendance at the meetings, reducing arrests by one-half, as compared to the matched controlled group one year after the study. After three years, the participants had significantly fewer arrests and significantly less time incarcerated than the control group.

HANDLING OF THE "SELF"

In choosing to conduct a research project with collaborators whose lives I am familiar with and to whom I could not be a complete outsider—a neutral or anonymous researcher—I adopted the position Zola outlined on the handling of the "self." Doubting the extent of social and emotional separation and distance needed to conduct social science studies, Zola states that "too much has been written about 'going native' or 'becoming over-identified' with the people or phenomenon one is investigating," and argues that awareness rather than non-involvement is the best defense against the idealization of the other (Zola 1982).

During the study, the young participants and I had various discussions in both the Boston and Los Angeles sites about how our roles as researchers were perceived and what the results of the research meant to the participants. In *Learning to Labour*, a participant observation study of English working-class adolescents carried out by P.E. Willis (1981), the author used a similar approach, including an edited transcription of a group discussion of such roles and meaning.

The discussion yielded unsolicited, critical observations from two of the L.A. participants about my interactions, which they had observed sporadically and critically for two years with the youth in the programs. The young people asked me about my background and personal life, always courteously, but broached topics in a way that the youth to whom I had been an advisor never had. Ronnie, who is particularly forthright, told me that he had observed me with the young people from Boston, and that they hid certain events and thoughts from me. He also told me I came across as a mother. I'd always been aware that my role as a practitioner would spill over into my new role as a researcher, but I had never heard it so succinctly stated. It made me uncomfortable because it revealed the underside of the paternalism (in this case, maternalism) and the dimension of power inherent in traditional advisor/client relationships, where certain forms of behavior are rewarded and where perceived progress toward "change" can be the most sought token of exchange for acceptance, attention, and scarce resources. I decided to exclude some of the Boston youth from the study until they graduated from the program and were working and established, in order to reduce the likelihood of them responding within the constraints and dependencies of our previous roles. I also purposefully selected those youth who had the most independent voices within the program to be part of the research collaboration.

DATA COLLECTION

The pilot project for this study began in January 1995 when I recruited the Los Angeles participants, and informed them that their participation would entail periodic follow-up, editing, and, possibly, further interviews. The Boston participants were recruited at the same time. The pilot study involved a total of six face-to-face interviews, three in Los Angeles and three in Boston.

The interviews asked about the interviewees' demographic and project relationship history. Additional questions explored facets, dimensions, processes, personality-related issues, and other dynamics that were the most important in the young people's journey into and out of a life of assaultive behavior. The impact of experienced trauma and program involvement was central to the interview research goal, as were suggestions for program improvement and/or transformation.

The themes and open-ended questions in the study were arrived at incrementally, and reflected the concerns of the participants, the cumulative experience and program-driven concerns of the two groups of youth interviewed, and my personal agenda as a practitioner and advocate. On completion of face-to-face tape-recorded interviews and their transcription, the texts were returned to the research subjects to be reviewed, corrected, and used as a departure point for further joint refinement. Additional questions about the death penalty, trying juveniles as adults, and the 1994 Violent Crime Control and Law Enforcement Act, as well as broader societal policy recommendations, were also asked.

For this study, I conducted a total of 20 face-to-face exploratory interviews with adolescents and young adults. Their interviews and life histories focused on the onset and termination of assaultive behavior, and covered a period of assaultive violence involvement that for one participant began at age nine (the youngest) and for another ended at 24 (the oldest). The interviews were carried out in an informal, conversational format, with the participants aware of and prepared to speak on the specific themes that will be touched on during the interview. See Table 1 for the demographic characteristics of the study participants.

In addition to the interviews, this study is informed by a period of observation, participation, continued dialogue, and joint reflection at the two sites: continuously in Boston over a period of six to nine years, and in six-month intervals over the past six years in Los Angeles. Field notes, other case studies, and journal entries collected over the study period, with the participants' permission, supplemented the interview data. Journal entries, letters, reflective pieces, and autobiographical statements from the youth participants and other young people in the programs, with their permission, provided additional data. Media interviews (in video or in print) granted by the young people in the past were also used.

Table 1. Study participant demographic characteristics

Name	Race/Ethnicity	Age at completion of study	Years involved in project	Gender	Disability
Delbert	Asian/West Indian	20	1994-2000	M	
Manolo	Salvadorean	20	1994-2000	M	Y
Charo	Dominican	23	1991-2000	F	
Andrea	Honduran	23	1993-1999	F	
Ruby	African American	23	1994-1998	F	
Lita	Mexican American	25	1994-2000	F	Y
George	African American	32	1994-2000	M	Y
Ronnie	African American	31	1994-2000	M	Y
Sandy	Mexican American	20	1994-2000	F	Y
Andres	Honduran	24	1992-2000	M	
Flaco	Puerto Rican	25	1992-2000	M	
José*	Puerto Rican	21	1993-1996	M	Y
Carl	African American	21	1994-2000	M	Y
Mo	African American	23	1994-1999	M	Y
Cy	African American	23	1993-1999	M	
Emmanuel	Afro-Honduran	25	1991-1999	M	
Lulu	Anglo-American	21	1993-2000	F	
Albert	Mexican American	27	1995-2000	M	Y
Erika	Mexican American and African American	24	1994-2000	F	
Martin	Cape Verdean and African American	24	1994-2000	M	

*Deceased in 1996

DATA ANALYSIS

The following principles guided the analysis of the qualitative data collected:

1. Multiple sources of evidence were used wherever possible.
2. A case study file that organizes the raw data collected was created.
3. A chain of evidence, such that each conclusion is based on supporting evidence and the context within which the information was obtained was established, and maintained (Yin 1989).

The field notes, interviews, and observations were content analyzed, a process through which emerging information categories, themes, and patterns were coded. Subsequently, the analyzed notes were studied further to identify explanatory patterns and themes that are consistent with the data collected. Any inconsistencies prompted revisions of the explanatory parameters and themes, which, in turn, were used to develop the case study of the group, through cross-case explanation building from multiple-case studies.

PILOT STUDY

Six interviews were conducted in Boston, and three in Los Angeles. Two of the six were conducted with young women, one from each city. The races and ethnicities of the pilot participants were as follows: two are African American, one is European American, one is Mexican American, one Honduran, and one is Puerto Rican. Of the six, five are U.S. born, and one is an immigrant.

The interviews lasted about two hours each and were done in one sitting at a conference room in the Los Angeles hospital, in May and October 1995. The Boston interviews were carried out during fall 1995 and spring 1996 at the Department of Health and Hospitals. All interviews but one, due to medical problems, took place at the scheduled first appointment. One difficulty was securing a quiet space in the two settings, as neither program had uninterrupted access to a quiet room with a door for privacy. The other difficulty was setting up appointments with some of the youth who did not have a telephone in their homes and whose mail service was inconsistent. At each site, one of the youth collaborators agreed to be the organizer and outreach person for the other participants, setting up appointments and accompanying me to the interview site.

I began the pilot study with an informed consent letter (Appendix A), which included a paragraph about the confidentiality of each person's responses, the precautions I would take to achieve this goal, and how no identifying information about individual participants would be included in the text. I was operating under the assumption that confidentiality was a right of the respondents, and the conventional wisdom that a guarantee of anonymity would result in more truthful responses. Also, since I was interviewing both minors and a group that was already "stigmatized," I thought that the youth would want to retain control of the conditions under which their experiences, feelings, and opinions would be made public, or "enter into the discourse with others in their social worlds" (Mishler 1986, 124). However, two of the young people told me that they wanted their names used. They are experienced organizers and wanted to be credited for what they say and think and the experiences they have lived through—they feel responsible for what they say. Becoming part of an anonymous mass or using a pseudonym would take away their right to a voice and bar them from entering "discourse" on their terms as individuals. So, for this pilot study, I opted for the suggestion of Gunnar Dybwad, used by Paget in her 1983 study of creativity, which was not to assume that everyone would choose anonymity, and to give those interviewed the option of being identified. Of the other four interviewees, three—one of whom was a minor—thought that confidentiality was appropriate and did not want to be identified. Though the fourth interviewee wished for his identity to be made public, I chose not to identify him as he was also a minor. In the course of securing approval from the Human Subjects Review Committee, the anonymity of the study participants was required in order for the study to proceed. All but one of the 20 young people, José Ojeda, who has since died, have remained anonymous.

PILOT INTERVIEW THEMES

To take George's interview as an example (verbatim excerpts are included), his trajectory into the perpetration of violent behavior, and his victimization at age 22 from a gunshot injury to his spinal cord, could be coded and interpreted as resulting from anger, multiple losses, and the breakdown, or suspension, or abandonment of morals. Consciously setting these aside at age nine, as a result of the watershed and traumatic event of having a gun pulled on him at age 9 by a police officer, and a cumulative history of rejection as a child, George describes the sequence of events that initiated his history of "disruption" and set him on a path of assaultive violence:

> The police, I think I was about nine, the police, they came and jumped out and threw guns. We were just nine-year-old boys playing out in the yard, and so I ran and hollered for my mother 'cause she could hear me from the windows. That changed the way I visualized people, from that experience with the police pulling a gun on me when I was nine years old. After that, at school, I began to become dysfunctional [laugh]. I began to act up in class, speaking the last shot. I didn't understand why a grown man would want to come down the alley and pull a gun on a nine-year-old kid, you know, we was nine years old. So, then, grades then begin to go down. When this guy pulled up on us, it was like, why us? So, when this happened it changed my whole conception of things. Like I said, I began to react more violently, I began to be disruptive in school, I began to beat up people, and I began to push aside a lot of the morals [laugh] that

my mother was passing down to me, and I took up on my own
views and do what I wanted to do.

His rehabilitation, states George, was achieved by learning to control
his anger, coming to terms with loss, and the recuperating, resuming, and
refining of his sense of morality. When George speaks of his role
models, he speaks to a different dimension, one of historical memory and
context, revealing the need for a different periodization and set of
parameters within which to understand the temporal sequence that led to
his past violent outbursts, his "criminal" history or homicide/injury "risk
profile," and his subsequent "rehabilitation." This surfaces when he
speaks of Martin Luther King and of Malcolm X; he refers to their
abilities to overcome, and to change within, despite the constraints of a
system—a system with barriers George views as reduced, but still very
much here. George was born in 1968, and the realities and conflicts of
the late 1960s influenced George's choice of role models and shaped his
construct of change. The structural violence challenged by Martin Luther
King, whom George admires because of the steadfastness in his
nonviolent position (despite great violence done to him) and by Malcolm
X, who was able to evolve in his thinking, stems from a legacy of
violence and exclusion that dates back to his grandfather. George's
grandfather, who was born around the turn of the century, also had to
contend with extreme violence and was brutally victimized. The etiology
of this reality dated back to slavery.

My grandfather, my grandfather is almost 90 years old, he grew
up in the period when slavery had just stopped, you know, he
was able to make it, and he was able to struggle through. He
couldn't read or write, but he was able to operate different
tractors, to lay plumbing through the cities of Arkansas and
Texas and Fort Worth and things like that, and he was able to,
basically, he was a laborer, you know, contributing a lot to that
city, you know, even though he had seen people hung on tree—
he had seen people brutalized, castrated, stuff like that—he
himself was able still to continue in love.

My grandfather, he, he was castrated, his genitals were cut off
by five people, Caucasians in the southern states. Even though
that happened to him, he still [laugh] was able to continue in
love, you know, to have love toward the brothers. After he
healed, he was still able to work with his bossman, you know
what I mean, and work with Caucasian people and still respect
them as men and not be, how should I say, not be violent toward
them, you know, 'cause I'm quite sure that he could have gotten

mad and gotten a gun and shoot and gone on a tirade and shoot people, but he never did do that, so I admire that.

The negative and positive experiences George had in various programs influenced his development. He encountered racial discrimination in a rehabilitation hospital, which treated a large number of minority youth injured by handguns; subsequently, George had violent outbursts, throwing things at the nurses who gave preferential treatment to Caucasians and Latinos. By contrast, he experienced total acceptance, with no strings attached, as a result of a housing referral, and this proved to be a watershed event in George's conversion. Taken in by a Chicano pastor—a former gang member who had overcome life obstacles similar to George's in the context of inner city Los Angeles in the 70s and 80s— George spent three years in a community, resulting in a sustained shift in his thinking and actions.

In George's transformation, the reduction in race bias was critical and points to the need, stated eloquently by medical researcher Felton Earls, to "clean up" the community as well as the larger society when attempting to advance knowledge and "control" youth violence. The rehabilitation department, where George received counseling to overcome his problems with violence, only served to exacerbate the problem due to perceived (and therefore, as far as George saw it, real) discrimination. Linking variation in social context with individual patterns of development, Earls advocates the implementation of specific policies to figuratively "clean up" the epidemiologists' laboratory: the community. A national gun control policy, rebuilding the infrastructure of inner cities, and reducing race bias in human services and the criminal justice system are seen as "environmental conditions equivalent to the role of sanitation in combating tuberculosis" (Earls 1991).

George believes that programs that deal with "only blacks, only Latinos, only whites—most of the programs in Los Angeles—are going to fail," because the problem of violence is "multi-dimensional." He says that he liked the way Malcolm X conceptualized violence:

> ...it's no longer a simple problem nor a black problem, it's a human problem, you know, violence and stuff like that. So, I like the way he was able to identify violence as being a human problem, not a black problem, not a brown problem, not a white problem, just a human problem, you know. He was also able to say it is not only about civil rights; it is about human rights.

The program and policy implications of this observation are substantial at the provider, policy, and societal levels. If the problem of violence is multi-dimensional and essentially one of human rights, it will require a systematic, multi-leveled effort to address it and the participation of many, within both individual programs and the larger society. This goes against the current trend of delegating to or challenging minority communities to assume responsibility for taking care of their own—a mantle of responsibility eagerly sought as necessary and based predominantly on cultural difference explanations.

George stated that a good youth violence prevention program needs "an intellectual" with "book knowledge," as well as a person who has been where the youth "are at" and understands their feelings and situations. For him, the latter pivotal person was a Chicano, whose sense of integrity, when challenged by the realities of hyperghettoization, led to a process and model of change George could relate to and learn from, a sense of integrity that was not dissonant with the models of change Martin Luther King and Malcolm X provided, and, more significantly, resonated with the goals and example set by his grandfather.

STUDY LIMITATIONS

This study was shaped by the traditions and disciplines from which it was drawn, with all their limitations as well as their strengths, and by the pre-text assumptions and fragmentations of reality that underlie such disciplines. As an ethnographic portrait of the pathways in and out of assaultive behavior of a chosen group, the image presented will be to some extent particularistic, in flux, and therefore limited. Further, the use of history, despite its advantages, brings with it a particular set of problems, since it is more difficult to discern the relative autonomy of the group and individual (and the isolation of the phenomenon being studied, i.e., assaultive violence) from both the specific and the larger macro structural processes in which it is manifested.

In giving qualitative data extra weight in identifying program strategies, ethnographers have often faced the charge that their findings lack objectivity, reliability, and generalizability (Babbie 1992, 305-6). While offering more valid findings than survey and experimental measurements through their thick, deep descriptions and investigation, such studies do involve subjective dimensions that affect formal reliability. Since respondents are not randomly selected from a specified population, as is the case in this study, questions about the generalizability of the findings to a population beyond those studied can also be raised.

Nevertheless, qualitative findings in gang ethnographies have contributed to quantitative research, generating useful hypotheses and uncovering previously unknown research amenable to empirical testing and typology formulation. For example, careful and methodical qualitative studies on gang members' attitudes toward employment have uncovered overlapping themes, despite the subjective biases of the different researchers.

Although theoretical orientations may differ, there is remarkable consistency among ethnographic accounts of gang members' attitudes toward work and job training programs and gang members' perceptions of the long-term opportunities such programs afford participants (Corsica 1993).

Other limitations might be those associated with the micro processes of adolescent development, the natural "life span" of delinquency, and maturation. Another concern might be regression to the mean, since changes occurring by virtue of the subjects starting out in extreme positions may be attributed erroneously to program effect, or disproportionate weight may be given to situational or other explanations. This could be compounded by the fact that as a youth cohort ages, the risk for being a victim or perpetrator of homicide decreases, and this risk should likewise diminish for the older participants, regardless of experience. A further limitation might be the distorted picture offered by these survivors of the problem (and resolution) of youth homicide. These informants survived to tell the story, and chose to retell their story publicly and become activists.

Despite these possible limitations, I have nonetheless chosen to tell the stories of these young survivors and now peaceful activists. I believe that their stories individually and collectively yield many lessons to be learned and unveil many myths. We believe that this information may be useful and adaptable to a larger subset of urban youth whose lives are affected by violence.

CHAPTER 5

Trauma, Resiliency and Rehabilitation

What do you know? It's your rivals from around the way. They beat you up bad, you can hardly speak. You are in the hospital with bad memories. The doctors are confused and don't know what to do. Now, is this life good for you?

—Claire, age 14, stabbed at age 13

The phenomenon of recurrent violence and the meaning of traumatic injury among adolescent young men and women in the inner city have been particularly difficult to explain. Demographic factors, such as income, age, and ethnicity, as well as a host of other community, situational, and individual factors, have been cited as being associated with violent injury—with witnessing, as well as with committing, a violent act against someone else. However, none of these factors provide an explanation for the dynamics of recurrent violence itself, nor do they shed light on termination. Similarly, the available literature on the effects of exposure to violence on the mental health of adolescents, while empirically demonstrating a relationship between exposure to violence and symptoms of psychological distress, does not offer an understanding of the effect of a traumatic event on revisiting past behavior. Traumatic events overwhelm the ordinary human adaptations to life, they "generally involve threats to life or bodily integrity, or a close personal encounter with violence or death. They confront human beings with the extremities of helplessness and terror, and evoke the responses of catastrophe" (Herman 1997, 33). The common denominator of psychological trauma is a feeling of intense fear, helplessness, loss of control, and threat of annihilation.

Empirical studies conducted to date on the effects of exposure to violence on the mental health of adolescents have focused on specific sub-populations of adolescents living in high-violence neighborhoods. A study of inner city black adolescents found that symptoms of depression and hopelessness were associated with self-reported use of violence: a correlation was found between violent behavior, lack of purpose, and the expectation not to be alive at age 25 (DuRant et al. 1996). Another study of public high school students found that certain types of violence exposure were highly associated with specific categories of trauma symptoms. Having been a recent witness or victim of home violence, having been sexually d or assaulted, or having been a past victim of threats, slaps/hits/punches, beatings, or muggings were strongly associated with anxiety, dissociation, stress, and depression. Important predictors of anger included having been a recent victim or witness of home violence, or having been a past witness to threats, slaps/hits/punches, beatings, or muggings (Singer et al. 1995).

These more recent studies both reinforce and expand on earlier studies that concluded that exposure to various types of violence as either a victim or witness was associated with psychological trauma. Earlier descriptive clinical studies among youth on the effects of exposure to war and the impact of such acute trauma as witnessing a sniper attack suggest that exposure to violence is associated with anxiety, post-traumatic stress disorder symptoms, depression, and aggression (Pynoos and Eth 1985; Bell and Jenkins 1991). Other studies on the mental health and behavioral effects of children's and adolescent exposure to familial abuse found similar results, including difficulty controlling anger, aggressive behavior, chronic anxiety, substance abuse, and post-traumatic stress disorder. Stress, depression, anxiety, school failure, reduced interest in play, and suicidal ideation have also been linked to repeated exposure to violence. The negative effects of stress and anger on children's health have been amply documented.

Such efforts to detail the incidence and effects of exposure to violence underscore the need for health care, school, and community institutions to screen adolescents for violence exposure and to address violence-related symptoms. They also suggest that more nuanced, longitudinal studies among varied groups of adolescents and children are required to attain a clearer understanding of the scope and particularities of different types of violence exposure. However, these efforts do not provide insight into the process and at times paradoxical consequences of violent injury for victims, perpetrators, or witnesses. The process of termination of violence and its relationship to exposure to trauma is similarly not understood. Such critical limitations have portentous repercussions for the development of interventions and perhaps for prevention efforts as well.

The literature on children and adolescents who are exposed to the trauma of violence suggests that not all children or adolescents directly exposed to violence develop stress-related disorders. In an article on adolescent and pediatric assault victim's needs, clinicians note that for most individuals, "responses wax and wane between mild positive and negative reactions" (AAP 1996). Clinicians also observe the reaction of some children who "use a negative experience to motivate them toward positive behaviors, such as greater avoidance of high-risk behaviors, spiritual and/or civic development, or a greater investment in their education, describing it as the 'Batman Syndrome.' The authors point out that there is little research describing what allows some children to turn a negative experience into a positive motivation, and no epidemiological studies that document how frequently this transformation occurs.

Providers of hospital-based pediatric and emergency care, community health and community survivor groups, youth workers, and family members have anecdotally described similar experiences among "hard core" youth. Some of the young people describe their dramatic transformation process as a "wake-up call—a response to a near-death experience, often in tandem with hospitalization and its aftermath. While some study participants describe getting shot or stabbed, or witnessing violent injury to others, as an "awakening," akin to being "slammed against a wall," others saw it as another episode of little consequence in their lives—hardly forcing a re-examination of past behaviors. Several young people describe how near-death experience, hospitalization, or exposure to violence reinforced a delinquent identity and propelled them further into active violence perpetration and crime, illustrating the amply documented trajectory of juvenile delinquency found in many criminology studies.

The stories of the young people in this study suggest a complex and paradoxical relationship between exposure to violence and its effect on perpetration, victimization, and witnessing. The detailed narratives about the events leading to (and from) injury and trauma allow a better understanding of these experiences and relationships from the young person's perspective. Important themes and concepts emerge in their collective experience of trauma, allowing a glimpse into what enabled them to turn a negative experience into a positive motivation.

I Knew It Was Coming: Getting Shot as a Rite of Passage

Like serving time in a juvenile or adult correctional facility, getting shot and even sustaining paralysis was seen as a rite of passage—"earning stripes" for the neighborhood or street group/gang—by some of the youth participants. Like the experience of expulsion or dropping out of school, involvement with juvenile (and in some cases adult) corrections and detention, beatings and stabbings have long been rites of induction or steps in the development of a delinquent identity, often referred to in autobiographies of gang and delinquent groups of the 1960s and 1970s and in the literature of delinquency. During the period in which the study participants entered into adolescence and young adulthood, the experience and "the nature of the violent act has changed from the fist, stick and knife to the gun... the handgun had replaced the fist or knife as the weapon of choice" (Canada 1995).

In the mid 1980s, the number of juvenile homicides involving a firearm started to spiral upwards while the number of non-firearms homicides held steady. By 1994, nearly 80 percent of the youth homicides among young people ages 15 to 19 were committed with a firearm, with four times as many children killed with a gun in 1994 as in 1984. While firearm homicide rates would decrease from 1994 to 1998, the proportion of youth homicides committed with a firearm would remain consistently high through out the decade, with 80 percent of youth homicides in the 15-to-19-year old age group committed with guns (NCIPC 2000).

For the young people interviewed in this study, for their siblings and friends, getting shot, familiarity with emergency rooms, and admission to trauma and rehabilitation centers were inevitable aspects of living their street lives. Death, too, was an increasingly contemplated aspect of their lifestyle and existence. During the decade of the 1990s, the codes of conduct on the streets in Boston and Los Angeles underwent a major and lethal shift with the increasing availability and use of weapons in altercations between youth. The further proliferation of semiautomatic guns, capable of firing up to 17 bullets without reloading, would contribute to an increase in lethality and allow for a new level of injury severity. In 1992, firearms were used in 70 percent of homicides involving adolescents (American Academy of Pediatrics 1992) and in 90 percent of gang-related homicides in Los Angeles (Hutson et al. 1994).

Like most child and adolescent victims of drive-by shootings in Los Angeles, most of the young participants in this study were shot in the inner city, during the summer, on public streets, and at night (Hutson et al. 1994). Although all children and adolescents in these neighborhoods were at an increased risk of getting shot due to drug trafficking and the number of street gangs and groups, these youth understood their heightened risk vis-à-vis other youth. This increased risk of homicide was calculated in one study as being 60 times greater for gang members than for the general population (Morales 1992).

In Boston, Mo fully expected to be shot; it was just a question of when. Although recognizing that death might be an outcome, he never fathomed the possibility of paralysis:

I know it was coming someday, you know. I just didn't know it was gonna come like that. I didn't know that I was gonna pay for it the way I did, you know, by being paralyzed... It was a wake-up call. And like I said, I knew it was coming someday. I just didn't know when, you know, 'cause of all the stuff that I did. I was involved in drive-by shootings, shootin' at other people, and stuff like that. I knew it was gonna come sooner or later. I knew it was gonna come. It was expected, but it wasn't expected for it to come the way it came. So I mean, you know, it put me in the position that I'm in. I always figured that, hey, the only way I'm gonna get out this gang and this drug-selling is I'm gonna wind up in jail for a while, or I'm gonna end up dead, you know. Every time I thought about myself getting shot, you know, it was death, you know. I never thought of being shot and living afterwards.

When he was shot at age 22 in Los Angeles, George had expected the bullet for some time. What surprised him about this shooting was the age of those pulling the trigger:

Before I got shot, well, about 19 months before I got shot, I had a dream that I got shot. So I actually dreamed about me getting shot. And in the dream I had seen myself laying on the ground shot. So I always knew that if I continued to do what I was doing that eventually I would be shot. So the day that I got shot, I felt like I was gonna get shot that day. And I just felt it. I was on the porch, and after I walked off the porch across the street, it was two guys standing there. They were teenagers probably, about 13 or 14 years old; they did not look like they were in a gang...

Albert was shot on three separate occasions, at ages 14, 15, and 17, in Los Angeles. In the first two incidents, he was the intended target. The third time, he was shot accidentally by one of his friends. Albert describes the times he was shot; the first was a drive-by shooting:

We were just walking to the store and somebody just started letting off on us. A car pulled up, and they just started blasting on us. The second time I got shot, I was involved in a shoot-out with somebody, and I ended up catching a bullet. The last one that confined me to a wheelchair was actually an accidental shooting; it was an accidental shooting where I was just messing with guns and the gun went off and hit me in my stomach. I was shot at age 17. The bullet lodged, it struck me through the front of my stomach, and it lodged in my spine, which confined me to a wheelchair for the rest of my life.

Albert describes being "scared, real scared; I thought I was dying" when he was shot, yet he would later describe getting shot and sustaining a disability as "earning stripes for the neighborhood. That's the way I took it. I was the one that could take bullets. You know, I took 'em for the neighborhood and ain't nobody could hurt me."

The phenomenon of sustaining a life-changing disability as a rite of passage into street or gang groups and life, described by Albert, is relatively new. It is more prevalent in large cities like Los Angeles and Chicago, with a large number of gunshot victims and many well-established street gangs or groups. It is more accentuated in Los Angeles than in Boston because of the number of gun injuries, availability of weapons, and number of organized street groups in greater Los Angeles. Although happening on a smaller scale in Boston, the phenomenon of gun-induced injury as the growing etiology of new spinal cord injury cases is a national trend in urban areas across the country. While no national incidence studies have been conducted since the 1970s, data from the National Spinal Cord Injury Database show that violence-related injuries have increased dramatically: from 13.9 percent in 1973-77 to 21.8 percent in 1994-98, with violence becoming an increasingly more common cause of injury among African American and Latino males (Nobunaga et al. 1999). Available information about these victims, in terms of number, specific cause of injury, and degree of long-term disability, continues to be sketchy.

The young people in this study accepted the likelihood of death as normal or expected and envisaged the possibility of paralysis and other severe disability as a potential outcome of day-to-day life. Some might ascribe this acceptance to sub-cultural value systems. However, the participants also expressed a realistic assessment of and perhaps necessary accommodation to the dangers and possible costs involved of living a certain lifestyle: the widespread use of guns, the pervasiveness of trauma, the strong likelihood of hospitalization for injury, and the ancillary risks of employment in the drug trade.

As in the case of Albert, other young participants had been shot or stabbed several times, and had witnessed many other incidents, before sustaining a wound that they would describe as a "turnaround" event in their lives. The young people attributed the important and transformational nature of a particular episode to many reasons. For Ronnie, the severity of the last wound made the costs of continuing his former lifestyle prohibitive. Ronnie had been shot in the leg when he was in high school, shot once more in the back when he was 20, and hospitalized for a third time at age 24 for multiple gunshot wounds, sustaining a spinal cord injury. After the third shooting, he decided to leave his life of drug dealing and violence, not because of his injury or loss of mobility, but, rather, as he found out returning once more to the streets, because the cost/benefit ratio of doing business, and the level of violence he would have to employ, was no longer worthwhile. When asked what made him change his behavior, Ronnie replied:

> Being in the wheelchair, now, I couldn't do the things I used to. I still can go out there and sell dope, but people can run and keep the money. Like, "I ain't gonna pay you" and try to push me, then, I have to shoot them. And I'm not, dag, it's not worth me going through all that. I don't want to have to worry if they gonna bring my money back. I have to chase this dude down for this, and if he don't bring it I have to pay somebody to beat him up. Then he can come back and beat me up. Then I have to just shoot him. Like I say, that's too much to worry about, so the thing for me was to don't do it.

Ronnie's assessment of the heightened cost of doing business following his disability is similar to the cost/benefit analysis described by Adler, which drove the operations and values of the crack capitalist generation that surfaced in the mid to late '80s. Adler contends that these "ghetto capitalists" are not vastly different from mainstream entrepreneurs, and that theirs is not a "culture of poverty" (Adler 1995, 6). Ronnie similarly understood his niche in the marketplace and the increased level of risk in his operation. He realized that, given his disability, he was no longer able to be an independent dealer but would have to employ the services of a wrecking crew; he no longer commanded the authority nor instilled the fear sitting in a wheelchair that he once did as an upright man.

What Do I Have to Offer Life but Hell? Incapacitation Did Not Lead to Cessation

As in cases where youth suffered gunshot wounds, sustaining a spinal cord injury per se did not lead to the cessation of assaultive conduct or the conscious rejection of life-threatening situations or people. Shot at age 14 and sustaining a disability, Carl nevertheless went back out, dealing drugs with a vengeance. For him, getting shot and losing his mobility was not a deterrent. Like other youth, the anger Carl felt was further compounded by his injury. Shortly after his second hospitalization (because of secondary disabling conditions due to his spinal cord injury), Carl would slip back into his former life:

That put me on bed rest from January '93 to April '93, and it was just like after that everything went downhill. I started dealing with my disability. I started taking my feelings out on innocent bystanders. I got back into things... I got back into selling drugs, stuff like that, 'cause I just didn't have respect for myself or no one else. My life in general, I just didn't care anymore, 'cause I said, look how I'm living. What does this life have to offer me? So what do I have to offer life but hell?

According to veteran youth and gang workers working in cities with a high volume of gang shootings and disabilities, becoming injured and sustaining a severe and permanent past injury once provided a well-earned "retirement" from gang activities or a sanctioned farewell to identifying openly with the gang. During the lifetime of the study participants, this was no longer the norm. A chaplain at a rehabilitation center in Los Angeles that treats many gang-related shooting victims who sustain disabilities commented on the circumstances that could influence if a severe disability provided a way out:

There is a silent code in the gang that says, "You don't get out"... But when you are disabled, it's acceptable. A lot of the gang members are relieved to find themselves in a chair. Unless they are higher up. It depends how important they are in the gang. If it is just an average kid, he's relieved." For many the experience drives them deeper into the life. Getting shot can seem a promotion to a career whose very initiation was violent; the wheelchair is a badge of honor for someone who was elated when he was first beaten up because he knew he had finally been 'jumped' into the neighborhood. Being chair bound stokes despair in those for whom despair is the social glue (Rymer 1992).

After being shot and permanently disabled at age 14, Manolo discovered that his gang (and its rival gang) had accommodated their routine and code of conduct to absorb the rising number of youth with spinal cord injuries back into their ranks. Manolo described one such encounter:

I went to this big meeting with gangs of people from different gangs. One of the guys in a wheelchair from another enemy gang in the meeting told me, "What's up?" and do I want to go head up with him? I was mad, you know. Then I looked at him and said, "What do you mean?" And he took off his shirt, he

looked big and everything, but I don't care. I just looked at him,
I said, "What you gonna get out of it? If I fight you, what we
gonna get out of it?" I told him, "I fight you, we gonna get
something good out of it." I didn't fight him, 'cause he didn't
tell me what we gonna get good out of it, so he called me a
punk, and I just looked at him and said "Yeah, whatever."

I Have Never Had Anybody So Close to Me Die Before: **Witnessing Trauma to a Loved One**

Seventeen-year-old Ruby questioned her involvement with her peers and
past life after witnessing the death of somebody she especially loved:

I have never had anybody so close to me die before. I was so
scared, I didn't come out of the house. I didn't want to be on the
streets anymore because I was scared for my own life.

Ruby underwent a rapid transformation after this death, joining a
youth violence intervention support group and helping organize a peace
march through the neighborhood in which her boyfriend had been shot
and killed. She remained steadfast in her resolve, choosing to ignore the
taunts of the rival group during the funeral mass, and did not take part in
any of the retaliatory acts of violence planned by her friends. A month
after the death, Ruby began speaking to other young people about the
consequences of joining a gang, and the benefits of renouncing gang
membership as a means of "staying out of trouble and taking care of
myself."

Witnessing the death of somebody close, especially if that person
was viewed as "innocent," could similarly trigger reassessment of a
violent lifestyle. This was especially true among the young people
interviewed who were most deeply into the life and who frequently
contemplated their own death. Describing the death of his cousin, who
was shot in the head while riding in the car alongside him on an outing
one evening, Mo said that he wished that he himself had taken the bullet.
It was in this drive-by shooting that Mo was shot in the back and lost the
mobility in his legs:

Why did my cousin have to die, you know? Why couldn't it
have been me that died, you know? Why couldn't my cousin
live... I mean, my cousin, he has a daughter. So I mean, now his
daughter's growin' up without a father... I didn't have no child
at the time, you know. So it was like I'd give my life to bring

his life back so he could see his child grow. But, unfortunately, he was the one that had to pass away.

The idea that his tainted conduct could have harmed his cousin, and by extension his niece, contributed significantly to Mo's reconsideration of his life to date. It was as if his life was no longer his own but an extension of his cousin's, and therefore had to be lived cleanly. He was 20 years old when he lost his 18-year-old cousin. The other passenger in the car, a 15-year-old friend, was also shot but survived. Mo reflected on this experience:

> Losin' my cousin, you know… sometimes I feel as if I'm living a double life here, you know. For me and for my cousin.

The redirection in his life was marked by a decision as resolute as Ruby's. Mo says:

> The trauma of the incident woke me up. It woke me up to realize, you know, that at, you know, you can't go back, you can't do that, you know. This is a change, you know. You gotta sit down, put your life together, you know, and get out there and accomplish things, you know.

This redirection happened soon after getting shot. "It was probably about, you know, two, two or three months after. Because, I mean, the first couple of months, I was still in shock, you know. I couldn't believe that, you know, it happened."

Sooner or Later They Are Going to Find Out Who My Father and My Brother Are: Fear of Harm to Others

Fear of a traumatic event happening to "innocent" loved ones, felt even among those who witnessed and perpetrated the highest number of acts of violence toward others their age, often precipitated examination of past behaviors. This fear frequently provided the impetus to break away from violent conduct and toward a different life. Andres, age 16, explained it thusly:

> I saw that by doing things that I was doing, it was putting other people I love in danger. You know, so that was one of the first steps that helped me out, that I saw that, you know, I wanted something else, I didn't want to live like that for the rest of my life. It wasn't living, it was dying. Basically, it was dying and that was one of the first steps. Basically, the more dirt you do,

the more you get known, the more enemies you make. But it was basically so I had people looking for me most of like every other day. You know, just pick a day, and if they don't get me, sooner or later they are going to find out who my father and my brother are. My father, they could have killed him. I didn't care. I wanted to kill him myself and could have. But I just never brought myself to do it because, I mean, he was my father. I couldn't take a life when he gave me the life. If I would have stayed there, I would have died, I would have died... and if I wouldn't have died, my father would have died or my brother would have died. They would have gotten them and then possibly gotten me.

Carl's fear for his mother—that the violent consequences of his drug dealing could catch up with her—similarly influenced his decision to change his life at 15 and stop dealing drugs:

My mother went back to doing drugs before because she was kind of stressed out, you know what I'm saying. It was just like, damn, my mom is on this shit. I'm selling this shit. I might as well sell it to my own fucking mother. So I just stopped. Fuck it.

I've Gone Through So Much, What Else Could He Do To Me?
Cumulative Exposure to Violence

Like Andres, other participants stressed how they had become war weary, tired of the hyper-vigilance and the cumulative fear in their lives. Witnessing, perpetrating, and being victimized by violence took its toll on them over time. The fear was often accompanied by boredom and uneasiness with the total lack of structure in almost all facets of their lives—a characteristic of the lives of gang-involved youth (Klein 1995). The many idle, empty hours waiting for action, between short bouts of excitement—especially among those who were deeper in the life (i.e., had dropped out of school, did not participate in community activities, and were living with other peers)—also became old and tiring. These realizations, however, often did not occur simultaneously, and it was generally when the young people reached the late teens or early to mid-twenties that they became aware that ceasing to be destructive and becoming integrated and productive were two separate, although ultimately intertwined, processes. It took even more time for this realization to materialize into a wish, along with the necessary discipline to transform their lives. This was especially true among the young people who lacked the most structure in their lives, especially adult support.

Flaco describes being so tired of the violence and of his existence in such a life, having lost three cousins and friends over the last three years in shootings. When he chose to turn his back on an acquaintance—who was armed, and with whom he had had a series of altercations in the distant past—he fully expected to be shot in the back. "Every step I took, I thought I was gonna get shot, I took one step, then another, and the shot did not come, so I just kept on walking, each step I said, 'He's gonna shoot me,' but he never did. I thought he would." This courageous act exemplifies the "walk away" lesson that violence prevention approaches seek to inculcate. Yet in this reality, such an act was one of utter recklessness, demonstrating how facile prescriptions often fall short. Flaco has a flat affect when he relayed the details of this incident. He did not recount the incident as an accomplishment, in a hurried or excited tone; on that day, he says, he just didn't have it in him any more to fight back and he felt as if, at that moment, he had nothing to lose.

Andrea describes her life up to age 17. Raped by a group of men at age eight in her Central American homeland, she was brought to the United States illegally at age 10 to live with her mother and abusive live-in boyfriend. By age 15, she had run away from home, assaulted the live-in boyfriend, served a sentence at a juvenile corrections facility, and lived on the streets for three months before deciding to join a Los Angeles street group for protection and as a survival alternative to prostitution. At 16 she gave birth to a son, fathered by one of the boys in her gang, and continued to do drive-bys up until delivery. By age 17, she had attained the high rank of shooter and enforcer in her clique of a highly organized street gang in Los Angeles and was regularly using cocaine and heroin to help her carry out her work.

Andrea exhibited the traits of "locura," described by Vigil in his study of street socialization and violence among Chicano gang members. Locura or Loco behavior is a wildness or controlled insanity, both a mindset and an instrumental contrivance in which one thinks and acts in a daring, courageous, and especially crazy fashion in the face of adversity. Such socialization and locura behavior varies immensely among gang members and largely accounts for the difference in their level of commitment to and involvement with gang violence. Like other adolescent and pre-adolescent barrio youth who spend most of their childhood unsupervised on the streets, under the direction of older peers, Andrea learned how to deal with many new realities on the streets and, most critically, how to manage the sense of personal fear engendered by street life. In doing so, she helped perpetuate a street culture and mindset. As Vigil notes:

The more loco individuals have usually experienced a problematic life since childhood, undergoing emotional insecurity. Having internalized feelings of self-hatred, fed and intensified by feelings of personal worthlessness and generally the worthlessness of others, they constitute a kind of "psycho-social death." (Vigil 1990)

Andrea's story illustrates the ways in which personal and social backgrounds shape antisocial sentiments and actions. In her mind, the mistreatment and aggression she experienced became internalized to a point where a state of locura was maintained. Since she perceived her home, the street, and her street peers as crazy, it was relatively easy to redirect that attitude toward others. Many barrio youth have had nicknames that glorify this value, such as Psycho, Killer and Loco, which affirms the significance of this behavior.

Vigil described this psycho-social mindset through the words of a young man he interviewed for his study: "I was afraid, but I couldn't be afraid. My head goes on like a TV set that has poor reception and a lot of static, and I got real mad and was pounding his head against the cement" (Vigil 1990, 237). The young people who participated in the study commonly described such rage and extreme fear. José describes it as the equation of fear and anger with violence. He remembers his inability to distinguish "the difference between fear and anger. And I did not know you could get angry without doing violence." George, an African American ex-Blood member, describes this mindset as "calmed out exteriorly. But inside me, I was in a rage. And you repress your feelings till eventually you have only three emotions: extreme anger, extreme sadness, and a halfway sort of happiness."

According to Vigil, this loco mindset has become requisite for street survival and a behavioral standard for identification and emulation:

It helps assuage fear, for the fight-flight dilemma (and even the middle ground of fright) is resolved by the gang whose members collectively value locura as an escape or safety valve from this anxiety. There is also a practical, perhaps more important, facet to locura. A loco is sometimes a highly valued property of the gang, for this person can singly match (or stop) the challenges of rival barrios, or function to rally and incite other less loco prone members to rise to the occasion. (Vigil 1990, 238)

Most street youth experience a certain amount of trepidation and anxiety about locura behavior, with some individuals needing to experience only one incident before they reexamine and disavow their violent lifestyles, as was the case for some study participants who witnessed, were victimized by, or participated in a stabbing or shooting and experienced its aftermath (e.g., death, injury, disability, and grieving). As with Andrea and Andres, the contemplation and decision to disengage and disavow is reached after a prolonged period of exposure (in terms of the amount and severity of the victimization, witnessing, and perpetration) and a prolonged period of numbing. Andres describes engaging in his first shooting at age 11, at the prompting of older gang members, and the deadening of his feelings that would soon follow:

> I had to show that I was down for my 'hood, that I would do anything for my 'hood. I felt lousy after that, I would have nightmares about it for days to come… after that it was easy, there were no nightmares, no remorse, no repent.

These very traits of recklessness, craziness, and unpredictability that enabled Andrea to manage the personal fear engendered by street life also equipped her with the abilities to transcend it. This was also true for other youth interviewed. The traits of locura and the ability to repress fear—qualities that gave Andrea such a strong reputation on the street and placed her and others in such danger—served her well as she took another turn, away from deviant and violent behavior. Other adolescent gang members who had less problematic backgrounds and less intense street experiences feared Andrea. These young members had to cope with fear at two levels: a general fear of the streets and a specific fear of other peers. Andrea grew weary of the empty "excitement, always looking at the present, until one day something came over me and told me to think about the things I was doing wrong. At first, I did not want to think about the facts but I knew sooner or later I had to do it." Choosing to leave this group carried with it a sanction, and Andrea had to go into hiding because a contract was placed on her for desertion, eventually leaving the state to remain safe. Andrea, who had been described as "reckless" by both her family and other providers—a trait that had previously earned her praise and fear from her street youth peers—now committed her most incautious act, even by the standards of the gang members.

I Kept Thinking About My Mother: The Centrality of Mothers and Families

Of the young people interviewed, three spent most of their lives in a household with two parents, and the remainder grew up in households headed by their mothers or grandmothers or in institutional settings. The centrality of mothers and grandmothers in their lives—and their concerns about these women witnessing or experiencing the consequences of their violent acts—was a recurrent theme in the stories young people told of their journeys into and out of their involvement with violence. Delbert describes his family, especially his mother, as "his conscience," and he looks back to when he was 13:

> I guess she was my conscience, you know, I always had that feelin' that I was doin' somethin' wrong, and when I really heard my mother talkin' to my aunt I was like, yo, this sucks. I never really want to disappoint my mother in anything I did, I didn't want to disappoint her. I mean, I did some bad stuff, and I was like, damn! I can't do that, I can't disappoint my mother. And when I saw that dude get stabbed, I was like, what if I end up like this dude? I mean… damn! And then I hurt her? I was like, yo, it's time for me to get outta this.

Cy was sent away as a child and grew up in a "Home for Little Wanderers." At age 20, recalling his abandonment led him to consider leaving behind his life of brawling, drinking, and theft and explore the possibility of forming and keeping a stable family. By this time, Cy had experienced several arrests as a juvenile, for assault at age 14 and for car theft at ages 15 and 18, and had been arrested for assault and battery on a police officer at age 19. He recounts how he "was just getting arrested every other week, for disturbing the peace. Destruction of property." When he was 20, he met a woman whom he would later marry; she had a young son, who reminded Cy of himself:

> I was small, right? It reminds me of my mother, just me and my mother alone. And it's harder that, you know, just it be the kid and the mother, and I know deep down inside that they need help, you know. You know a woman could use help, you know, with a kid, because the kid is a big responsibility, so. 'cause I know that my mother needed help, and I needed somebody to be there for me when she wasn't there, so that's my commitment.

In Cy's own reckoning, this process of transformation—consciously deciding to take another path—took a year and a half to two years. It involved going back to school and graduating with a general equivalency diploma at age 21, working at various jobs for one year while completing an urban Peace Corps program, and being selected to be part of a national demonstration project in civic leadership development for twenty young men 18 and over who were involved with the criminal justice system for violent offenses. In this program, Cy cleared up his outstanding warrants, which was part of the program requirements, and made a clean start. Cleaning up his record, trying to find an employer who would hire him given his past record, and staying positive throughout the process was difficult. It was only possible, he said because of "my commitment to my wife and my stepson.... But I know if I wasn't married or have a stepson, I would probably be right back out there. It's so easy."

Andres describes the bond he has with his mother. Born a sickly child in Central America, he survived an illness that took many babies in the region:

> Because my mother told me that when I was a little kid I had died, clinically dead. And then she asked God, if you want to take him from me, take him from me now or while he still haven't grown up and I haven't got started, you know, I haven't gotten to it 'cause I don't want you to take him later on in life. You know and many times I hear my mother say that I'm like, damn, I'm meant for something else, basically, I feel that's something else, something better than what I was, what I went through. Something better than what I thought I would have.

Ronnie's decision to stop selling drugs for the last time was also prompted by having dragged in his mother and shamed her publicly through his activities:

> The last time I was out, I think I was set up. Somebody told on me. It was probably one of my friends. I'm like, if they told on me, then what if they tell again? They raided my house. They had my mother all outside in her nightclothes. They ram shacked the house, and for me to see my mother's face when I did get busted in her house, I was like, I'll never do that again. So I told myself I would sell drugs no more. So I haven't. I'm a good boy.

When he was shot at 14, Carl "didn't panic, didn't cry." When he saw that he was unable to move, and saw himself through his mother's and grandmother's eyes, the gravity of what had just happened sunk in:

> When I started seeing myself like this, I started crying and shit like that. My mother, she really couldn't say nothing. My godmother, she really couldn't say nothing but damn sorry this happened.

I Need to Live to See My Daughter: Child-Centered Orientation

Charo said that she had contemplated suicide on several occasions, but her fear of what would happen to her children kept her from giving up: "I didn't wanna die 'cause I'm gonna be no good dead, and what's gonna happen to my kids?" Charo's fear that her own children's witnessing would lead them to eventually become either perpetrators or victims of domestic violence, become depressed or influence them to perpetrate acquaintance violence due to the anger experienced from violence witnessed at home, led her to reexamine her life. Her concerns about the spillover effects of exposure are validated by current research findings that underscore the links between different forms of violence. Associations have been found between exposure to violence in the home and being a victim or perpetrator of violence in adolescence and adulthood (Maxfield and Widom 1996); and research has shown the association between suicidal behavior and several types of violence, including child maltreatment (Brown et al. 1999).

> I don't want my daughter to look at beatings as being normal. That's how come I wanted to make it different for her. I don't want my son to beat up his girlfriend. And I don't want them to be violent at school. I don't want them to have all this anger where they have to show that anger in school.

Throughout her many visits to the emergency room and time spent recovering at home from domestic assaults, Charo thought about her life:

> I had a lot of time to think, and I thought about a lot of things, and I'm like, there's not gonna be a change. This is not gonna get any better for my kids. And just seein' my kids suffer... You're not really realizing, you're ignoring what's happening to you, but you're not really realizing what's happening to your child. You think that your child is totally unaware of what's going on, but they know everything. And then you start seeing things, the way that your child reacts to like somebody going like this *[lifts her hand suddenly]* getting like all scared, and if somebody's like crying or somebody's trying to fight and they just, you know, they start getting scared because they're like, you know, somebody's gonna hurt each other. So they tend to get really nervous, and my kids, still to this day, are like that. And they're scared of loud voices or if somebody's arguing or whatever. I was like, you know what? My kids are not gonna have to go through this... I'm not gonna let my kids go through this, you know. And I started realizing what they were going

through, which was hell. How scared and how terrified my son was when his mom was getting beaten up in front of him, you know. And how he wanted to help me and he couldn't.

Flaco recognized that the protection offered by the gang was illusory and decided he was not going to suffer any more wounds due to the activities and lifestyle of his street peers. Like other young fathers or older brothers who referred to young children as precipitating a reassessment of their life choices, Flaco recognized at age 19 that he needed to stay alive and out of trouble for his baby daughter:

I got out 'cause I started thinking, you know, it's not worth it. I got my daughter. I need to live to see my daughter. I can't be out there getting myself in trouble. Getting myself shot up for nobody else. I mean, they wasn't gonna take a bullet for me, so why should I take a bullet for them?

It Took Many Things: **Multiple Factors Lead To Re-examination**

Although some of the participants could point to a watershed event that forced a re-examination of their lives on the street, their retellings point to a series of events. Mo describes getting shot and sustaining a spinal cord injury as a transformative event in his decision to terminate his street life and drug dealing:

I'm not gonna lie. My injury. I mean, getting shot. That's what made me change 'cause, I mean… if I didn't get shot, I don't think I would have changed for a while, you know. I think I probably wouldn't have changed until I was probably about 27, 28 years old. Then I probably wouldn't even had changed then. So I mean… I think, I think me… me being shot, you know, and being in the situation that I'm in now, had a big effect on that to make me change everything.

Nevertheless, he reflects that he doesn't "think it was just getting shot:"

It was just that, you know, getting shot and then, my family almost lost me, you know, and I see the pain that they went through and, you know, stuff like that. And, losing my cousin, too, you know. So I mean, sometimes I feel as if, like, I'm living a double life here, you know, for me and for my cousin.

The young people looked back on the effect violence and trauma had on their past behavior, the list of factors and processes to which they attributed their transformation grew. The dynamics that prompted re-examination were highly individualized and unlikely to be conveyed by any single event or even a listing or cluster of events.

I Went Deeper Into It: Trauma and the Development of a Violence Career

While episodes of violence suffered or witnessed could prompt many to re-examine their lives and question the worth of their activities, sometimes, violence had the opposite effect. Other outcomes cited included reinforcing self-perceptions of personal worthlessness and powerlessness, feelings of guilt, and the belief that there is little else to lose: "That feeling of pressure. That feeling that I'm not worthy."

The experience of getting shot, witnessing violence and trauma was also described by the young people as a motivation for revenge, and involved a conscious will to engage in retaliatory acts of perpetration. An adoption of a more ruthless persona was also a common consequence, as the young person chose to turn the rage and fear outward. George describes how his delinquency and physical fighting escalated when he was 12 years old, precipitated by the death of his brother. That event was a watershed, causing George to become more deeply involved in violence, and take with him the neighborhood friends who looked up to him:

> We were stealing out of stores, vandalizing houses; we were actually committing robberies. I think that's when it really, really got real, real bad. My brother, my oldest brother, got killed, and when he got killed, that's when I like, forget it. Then I started pulling guns on people and doing things like that frequently. My brother, he wasn't a gang member or nothing. He was what we would call in ghetto language a square. *[laughs]* He was a square. And he had been robbed and shot in the head... I was 12 then, so after that happened, I went off. I just said, forget it. I started robbing, stealing, and everything. He was the voice in my life. He was one of my role models. More of a power image you could say; he would tell me different things and talk to me, counsel me, and stuff like that... Then I went deeper into it. That's what happened. Once I made that transition, the other guys, you know, they followed.

The aftermath of a traumatic, violent incident can also influence whether a young person moves further along a violence path. The aftermath of the event may uphold a vision of the world in which vengeance, retribution, and "becoming hard" are reinforced, seemingly the only—or only viable—option. Flaco had such a response after witnessing the shooting of his cousin:

> My cousin got shot right there in my face. My mind went crazy. I was only about 15, 16 when this happened. And I still got, I mean, I get flashbacks and stuff like that. Somebody had paid them to go hit up the leader. And it was my cousin, and I was with him. We came from a party, whatever. A car, this dude called him over. He's like, I don't know you. Pulled out a gun, he shot him. It was like, I went blank. I pulled out my gun. I started shooting back, you know, shooting back.

Anything Would Have Helped: Hospitalization as a Window of Opportunity

The young people in this study reported many visits to emergency rooms and clinics for a variety of wounds caused by acts of interpersonal violence. The circumstances under which their injuries occurred and the ages at which the visits were made varied. Depending on the severity of the injuries suffered, some were discharged, others were admitted to a hospital for treatment, while still others were transferred for rehabilitation, depending on the severity of the injuries suffered. Most often the young people were the victims of violence, but they also accompanied relatives and friends for treatment or visited them in pediatric inpatient and rehabilitation departments.

Manolo was hospitalized for violence-related lesions inflicted by other children for the first time when he was just seven years old. Of all the study participants, his violence-related injury "career" would begin at the earliest age. Ronnie would be hospitalized for a violence-related injury for the last time when he was 24, admitted for multiple shotgun injuries as a victim of a carjacking. Of all the study participants, Ronnie would be the oldest in the group to sustain a violence-related injury. The study participants made various hospital visits to be treated for lacerations or gunshot injuries, which occurred in a variety of situations: altercations involving their grievances with other children or youth; wounds due to gang induction "beat-ins;" casualties incurred while living or working in the streets; beatings suffered when leaving a gang (usually in mid- to late adolescence). The visit to the emergency room and admission to the pediatric or adolescent inpatient clinic became the routine, ritual ending to each gradation of involvement in violence, punctuating important episodes in the youths' personal histories, as they witnessed the violence-induced injuries and deaths of older siblings, relatives, and friends, and sustained injury and great pain themselves. The young people in the study admitted to an inpatient spinal cord injury rehabilitation unit resembled other young violence-induced spinal cord injury patients, with half of the study participants having been previously admitted to the emergency room or for a gunshot injury and receiving treatment for other types of violent injury. A study of patients admitted to an inpatient spinal cord injury rehabilitation unit between 1990 and 1998 found that 30 percent had sustained a previous gunshot wound, 16 percent had another violent injury requiring treatment, and 59 percent had prior involvement in the justice system (Ragucci et al. 2001).

These experiences were fraught with fear for many of the young people, regardless of whether the visit was made for a superficial stab wound or a more serious gunshot injury. Their fear was sometimes masked as apathy or extreme acting out behavior. But the fear was deeply felt and expressed by even the most "hard core" of the young people when they, or others close to them, sustained serious injuries that required emergency care and hospitalization: "When you are lying there gasping for air, bleeding, going into shock, rushing towards death, all that hard core is gone and all that is left is fear."

Another prevalent feeling was quiet or angry desperation. Andres spoke for most of the young participants as he described his visits to the emergency room (four times from ages 11–15, due to street violence-related injuries) and his admission for stab wounds. Looking back on those visits, he describes himself as "desperate, I was looking for anything, anything would have helped. Anybody talking to me would have helped. You know it was just the situation I was in where it wasn't that I didn't have love at home. It's just that I was looking for something else and I thought I had found it in a gang though. But I was wrong."

Hospitalization following a traumatic injury encompassed a wide range of experiences for the young participants. Although almost all of the young people mentioned their hospitalization experience (in varying degrees) as a propitious time for providers to have reached them and their peers, it was not generally an opportunity seized by health staff. Ronnie described how he was treated the first and second time he was shot in the leg, echoing the experience of other youth who described "getting stitched up and then getting the boot."

> And I went back, and they patched me up and told me I'd be all right. And sent me home. That was it. I was shot in the leg. They gave me a couple of bandages, told me to change 'em and come back in a such and such amount of time. They said the bullet shouldn't move but just come back anyway. And that was

it. The police came and ask me what happened. I told them I
was going to get some cereal and some dudes shot me. You
know, you don't tell them you did this.

Ronnie's experience echoes the findings of a study of patients in an
inpatient spinal cord injury rehabilitation unit admitted for gunshot-
related spinal cord injury between 1990 and 1998. The study identified a
total of 55 opportunities for social service interventions among the
patients admitted, finding that social service intervention was initiated
only once, and concluding that more aggressive efforts at social service
intervention could be an effective means to deter future disability
(Ragucci et al. 2001).

All I Could Do Was Lie There and Think: Incapacitation and Contemplation

The incapacitation suffered as a result of injury, as well as being away
from their neighborhoods, peers, former lifestyles, and family members,
created a space for contemplation, in which the youth could revisit their
lives in relative privacy, isolation, and safety. In anecdotal reports in
other studies, hospital staff report that the hospitalization experience
sometimes lowers the emotional walls of adolescents who tend to put up
walls between themselves and adults, especially authority figures (De
Vos et al. 1996). The young people themselves describe a similar
process, in which they contemplated and re-examined their lives,
choices, and "attitudes," and personal organization of their experiences.
They had levels of varying resistance to this early stage of change;
though there were oscillations in their resolve, the process frequently
initiated or further strengthened a more "positive" feeling about
themselves and their relationships with others.

For José, the trauma and aftermath of getting shot only strengthened
his resolve to continue along a path of nonviolence. Having decided to
turn his "life and community around," he was then shot by a bullet
intended for his brother, a drug-dealing gang member. At age 17, José
was paralyzed from the neck down, at times unable to breathe without
the aid of a ventilator. As with other youth, José's serious trauma
provided much quiet time to contemplate his past life experiences and
behaviors and reinforce the new life paths he had chosen. According to
José:

> When I woke up from being shot, I couldn't talk, I couldn't
> move, I couldn't eat, and I couldn't breathe without the aid of a
> machine. In fact, for the first six months, all I could do was lie
> there and think.

José suffered the greatest immobility as the result of violence-induced trauma and was hospitalized the longest of all study participants. The aftermath of his injury offered him time to further temper the decision to distance himself from destructive gang activities and carefully assess his life and choices. Although he had begun to make a change, and chosen a positive path one year before he was shot and paralyzed, he still "had a lot to learn." Looking back, he ascribed his survival to this event, which "made me strong, taught me discipline and how to deal with myself and others."

I'm Gonna Smoke Him: Contemplation and Vengeance

The time spent in hospitalization could also be used to explore revenge fantasies and develop plans for retaliation. Sometimes these plans were carried out, and other times they were abandoned. Manolo speaks for many of the study youth when he recounts his ruminations on "getting even," recalling the detailed plan he had conceived and refined during his lengthy hospital and rehabilitation center stay at age 14:

> And I was planning that when I get out, I'm gonna go to this fool's house 'cause I know the guy that shot me, so I'm gonna go to his house and smoke him. Go to his house, knock on his door, you know, put a girl on his door and tell the girl to tell him to come here, come to the alley. And I was just gonna tell her to move out the way. Cause I'm coming, I'm gonna shoot him up. That's what I had planned in my head.

They're Coming to Finish the Job: Fear of Further Harm

Many of the young people did not feel safe from further harm while in the hospital. For Carl, not even the pediatrics intensive care unit provided a sense of safety. Looking back on his hospitalization he recollects, "It was so tough for me in the hospital 'cause I thought they was gonna come kill me. I didn't know who the hell to look out for."

Often, the young people gave inaccurate or incomplete histories because of their distrust of the medical establishment and their perception of clinicians as far removed from their own realities. Fear of retaliation, concerns about police involvement, and the belief that the interventions offered could not keep them safe after discharge were some of the common themes they expressed. Incomplete histories made it difficult, if not impossible, at times to provide the needed care to the young patient, and refer him or her to the necessary interventions.

The fear of retaliation, concerns about police involvement, and distrust of the medical establishment are among the obstacles to identifying victims of violence cited by the Task Force on Adolescent Assault Victim Needs (AAP 1996). The initial history given by the patient is often incomplete or inaccurate. As Carl explains, he was shot by a group of young men who were looking for his 19-year-old cousin, with whom they had a conflict:

> Some bullshit back in high school when he was going to high school. They found out I was his cousin and just seen me one day and shot me. Just like that. I didn't know these dudes from a hole in the wall.

The staff at the emergency room intensive care unit, and rehabilitation hospital asked him what happened:

> But it was just like I wasn't ready to talk about it. As far as I'm concerned, I didn't know the reason then. As far as I'm concerned, it was a case of mistaken identity. But deep down in my head, I knew what the fuck they shot me for. But nobody else needed to know that. It was none of their business.

Turning to the police or criminal justice system as a means of allaying their fears or preventing further intentional injury was not an option for these young people. Although all the youth who were admitted for gunshots and stab wounds knew who the perpetrator was, or to what set, group, or gang the perpetrator belonged, they had such distrust and negative perceptions of the criminal justice system that they did not fathom turning there for help or redress. Many had criminal records of their own, or outstanding warrants for their arrests. They perceived the police to be ineffective, unresponsive, and uncaring; in many cases, they equated "police" with "brutality" and "the criminal justice system" with "injustice."

Nothing but Another Gang Banger: Clinician and Clinic Perceptions

A change in identity (such as feeling like a damaged or evil person) is one of the psychiatric disorders associated with extreme stress among individuals who have been exposed to the trauma of violence, regardless of past association with crime or delinquency. Among youth involved in delinquent and criminal activity, the extreme stress due to exposure to violent trauma can serve to intensify an already stigmatized identity. Clinicians' perceptions of these young victims as dangerous and unworthy of restorative care may further reinforce changes in identity and lead to the emergence of a "harder core" among some of the participants, who were already tainted by their association with gangs, delinquency status, place of residence, race, ethnicity or nationality, and insurance status.

The chaotic, under-funded trauma centers themselves, experiencing "medical gridlock," could also underscore the young peoples' negative self-perception because of the substandard care they received. Suffering from an "accelerating inability to meet demands for acute medical services, expressions of the increasing social disorganization of poor communities initiated and continued in considerable part by government policy" (Wallace 1990), these centers are often perceived as noxious environments. After being shot the second time and being told that he was going to the public hospital that handled most uninsured gunshot victims in Los Angeles, Ronnie had to be restrained. He remembers resisting and crying out as he was transported to this facility (ironically named after the slain civil rights leader and teacher of nonviolence, Martin Luther King):

> "What ya'll doing? I heard this here hospital kill people." "Cause the name of it is Martin Luther King, but we call it Killer King. I'm like, "Ya'll kill people in here." I'm like, "Don't hurt me in here." They have been known to not take care of people when they get shot. They have been known to actually leave people down there that have been shot and not give them the proper treatment, 'cause I guess they overcrowded. I really don't know. But as far as I can remember, we just called it Killer King. I mean, you can go in there for a stab wound that's not that severe, and before you know it, you look around and you dead, you know. And they just wasn't taking care of people like they was supposed to. I didn't want my mom seeing me all bloody and coming out of the hospital. And I didn't have a belt on, 'cause they took my belt. And this lady say, "That's good; he ain't nothing but another gang banger."

Studies of pediatric and adolescent victims of gunshot wounds in high-risk communities (similar to the neighborhoods in which the study participants lived) refer to the often multiple losses of loved ones to violent or nonviolent death, substance abuse, or prison (Barlow et al. 1982; Durkin et al. 1994). Like prisons, public health and medical facilities are the institutions of last recourse, where the consequences of a life misspent are attended to, sometimes for the last time. Flaco resisted going to the adolescent health clinic at the local public hospital to receive a check-up, or to see a dentist for the first time in 10 years, because of the visceral fear associated with the trauma and death of his cousins, who had died either at or on the way to that hospital. He also was ashamed and angry at the treatment received by his mentally ill mother at the public psychiatric facility attached to the hospital. The hospital itself came to augur mistreatment, injury, and death.

Similar to the effect of incarceration and psychiatric admission on the development of a "criminal/mental illness career," both the experience of getting shot and admitted to the hospital and the aftermath of this experience also solidify the stigmatized identify and damaged self-perception of the young. Carl describes the events following his discharge:

> Even went back to selling drugs after I got hurt. It's easy. It's even easier now than it was before. I went back to life in the fast lane. You in this lane that's going so fast that you can't even think what move to make next because this fast lane is carrying you within it. You know what I'm saying. What people don't know is that this is the kind of lane that has its own disposition. This is the lane that's pulling back from all of the rest of the normal lanes. So people looking at you judgmental. They're judging you because you're in that fast lane, and you don't even know it until you smash into a wall like I did. It wasn't like I smashed into that wall. That wall came and found me. Smashed into me.

They Don't Treat All Patients the Same: The Violence of Discrimination

Institutionalized racism (the systematic deprivation of equal access to opportunity) and discrimination are factors that contribute to the high rate of interpersonal violence among African Americans. Criminologist William Oliver suggests that institutional racism has led to feelings of powerlessness and self-hatred and lowered self-esteem among many African American youth, especially males. According to Oliver, it has also prevented a considerable number of African American males from achieving manhood through legitimate means and has led to an alternative notion of manhood in which overt toughness is one of the dominant traits (Oliver 1994, 57). Given the established, albeit not clearly understood, relationship between racism and other types of discrimination and the perpetration of and victimization by violence, it was important for the clinics to eliminate or minimize all forms of discrimination. Only then could the youth begin to use the incident of trauma as an opportunity to reassess their lives and to adopt an alternative, less "tough" persona.

The participants describe many instances of discrimination in the clinic that exacerbated and further hardened the posture of the young African American and Latino men and women. Whereas many had grown to expect and accept such mistreatment in other institutional settings, the post-injury period made them feel especially vulnerable and fearful, and the inability to receive equal access to services only intensified their hard-core behavior and overt toughness.

When he was hospitalized for his spinal cord injury, George was concerned that his legs, already paralyzed, would stiffen, further hampering his ability to drag them and lift his torso into a wheelchair. He observed the treatment from the staff:

> They would come and administer what they call "range and motion" to your leg. To keep your legs from getting too stiff and stuff... Because Latinos and Caucasian that come to my room, they would do these things. But me, not too much, you know. So I got mad and angry. I used to get real mad; I'd throw stuff at them. I'd just get mad like that, 'cause I felt that you're not treating me the way you're treating everybody else, so I'd just throw stuff at different people who'd come in my room. Act out. But I just wanted to be treated the same way that you treat that Latino and that Caucasian.

Delbert described the treatment received by one of the young patients he would later mentor, a young African American man who had sustained paralysis due to a gunshot injury, as compared to another white young man on the floor:

> They took the TV from them—the patients, the regular old patients—and gave it to this dude. They gave him, like, all the nurses and all the, you know, the attention, and they just neglected the regular patients who was there before just 'cause he had some kind of fame to him. He was a hockey star. He was an all-American, rich white kid who played hockey for this big school, and they totally neglected the, the regular people, the people who needed, probably, the help the most 'cause they couldn't afford the help. And that, I would have to say, is mad negative. You can't get more negative than that, denying people their rights, what they need, what they deserve.

Others told of respectful interactions with those of other races and ethnicities in a time of crisis and profound fear, describing them as transformative. These small, respectful, and humane conversations and interactions had the unexpected result of forcing a change in the world-view and self-image of these youths. Andres describes one such encounter:

And I said to him, I said, "Oh, oh, here comes another white person," you know, he's feeling guilty because, oh, "I'm white," and they are doing all these things to feel better, please kids, you know, I mean to people of color. That was my first impression. After I got to know the people, I knew it wasn't like that at all, and that they were truly about, about helping people out, and I was just the kid, you know.

I Didn't Want to be in Watts: The Clinic as a Window to the Outside World

The young people sometimes described the clinics and hospital as having provided a window to an outside world, to other ways of living and possibilities, and serving as an introduction to different cultures. These are functions that schools are meant to fulfill, but for the young people in the study, schools had not done so, for a variety of reasons. For Ronnie, a broader view of the world was made possible by his attentive and engaged English doctors:

> People from London that was there that took care of me, and that kind of made my day, you know. They would come in the room [Ronnie imitates the accent]. And I'd just crack up, and I'd be laughing. And I'd be like, "When you gonna take these tubes out of my nose?" And they like, "Today's your lucky day," and they took them out. And they'd always be coming in talking to me. I'd be like asking them about London, you know, 'cause I didn't want to be in Watts or whatever. So when they used to tell me I used to like just picture myself over there. It rains all the time. There're like castles and that lush green land. So I, when they'd be talking to me, I'd close my eyes and picture myself over there. And they used to just tell me. We'd be sitting talking for hours, you know, and I'm like, "That's crazy. I want to go to London." I'm like, "Are there black people over there?" And they say, like, "Yeah, there are black people." I say, "I bet they talk funny, huh?" And she'd say, "No, they talk like me." And I'd say, "Well, you talk funny to me." Oh, it was cool. They'd treat me real nice.

In the best scenario, the clinic not only exposed the young patient to alternate ways of thinking and being in the world, but also delivered the means through which a new life—or one's true life—could be lived. At age 14, Carl was referred to a hospital school as part of his rehabilitation plan:

When I came here and got exposed to what I can do, what I haven't seen, it was a whole new ballgame. Let's pull out the rug, and let's get ready for this new life.

A recent study on young victims of violence similarly found that youth can change their lifestyles to avoid becoming repeat visitors when changes are initiated by the physicians and staff in the emergency department, who view this as an opportunity to counsel (Mitka 2002; Zunz and Rosen 2003). In Carl's case, given his spinal cord injury and paralysis, envisioning another life of possibilities was seen as especially critical and part of the treatment plan not generally extended to other less permanently injured victims of violence. Carl was taught to take care of himself and reintroduced to sports. He resumed his schooling in an institution where he was expected to graduate, he met new people, and he did some traveling:

I was exposed to caring for myself in the position I'm in now. Caring for myself on an everyday living basis. As far as coming here, it gave me back inclusion, where playing sports is what I always looked for in a high school. Not necessarily academics, but it's definitely keeping me where I'm supposed to be. Graduated. Just the whole support here is like one big family. Even though it's corrupt, but that's with any family. You got bullshit in your family that you don't agree with all the time, but you have to live with that. You know what I'm saying. Just some of the people that I've met. And I'm telling you, going out of state, one of those trips and stuff like that, playing ball, track and field, going to camps—all this shit helped me a lot. It got me exposed to the outside world. This is what it is. This is what's out there. I can be there and see this shit now. Where I felt like I was sheltered by Boston. I felt like I never thought I would go to Oklahoma three times, Baltimore twice. Yeah. Illinois twice, Wisconsin, Colorado. I never thought none of that.

He Treated Me Like a Father: The Importance of Clinician Interactions

The quality and warmth of the human interaction between the staff and the patient was a key factor in how the youth interpreted the event of trauma and its aftermath. Ronnie described his English doctors as treating him really nicely, with interest and respect. Mo remembers the janitor, Herman, an older African American gentleman and family man, who showed him tenderness and gave him advice after hours, and who was brought in to calm Mo down after his frequent rages against the psychologists and social workers. Manolo describes his neurosurgeon, "Doctor M," as "his father." Dr. M performed many of Manolo's surgeries, the first when he was just 14, but it was Dr. M's interest in Manolo as a total person that really touched the young man. Dr. M checked in on him, kept in touch over the years, and took an active interest in Manolo's development, and he was not afraid of Manolo's past. The presence of this neurosurgeon in his life—a series of short, sometimes fleeting, but high-quality interactions, over time—was greater than that of Manolo's own father, a man Manolo could barely remember: "He [Dr. M] says I'm his son, and he is like my father, Dr. M, he's a father to me."

Other youth described their relationship with providers as engendering a sense of loyalty, trust, and caring, as if the providers were an alternate family, the "family" that many of the young people sought when joining a street group. The youth felt they "owed" something to the staff members who had treated them fairly and who they trusted to stick by them, just as they would have trusted a fellow street group member who had protected them—only this time, the young people would have to "do the right thing" by behaving and staying positive. Ronnie described two hospital staff members:

> There was Rudi Lopez. He was there for me. Liza, she was there when my own therapist wasn't. You know, my therapist wasn't there. It was always the OT and Liza. Just somebody who come through like a home girl. But she was head of everybody, but she would come through. And I, like, used to share with her, you know. "What's up, dog, how you doing?" She'd say, "I'm all right." So it was just the chosen few.

It Was Good While It Lasted: Limited Impact of a Hospital-Based Violence Intervention

Martin describes getting stabbed as "a little bit of a wake-up call. It allowed me to meet people and get hooked up with some violence prevention groups, but it was nothin' that really stayed... I didn't learn my lesson yet." He was counseled on the inpatient pediatric floor a couple of times by a therapist before being discharged. This therapist educated him about anger management and risk factors for homicide:

> Well, I listened and said yeah, you know. It was good while it lasted, but it still stuck with me, and it came back to haunt me later 'cause I got stabbed *[again]* that November, and then like

a week and a half after I got stabbed, I had to go back in the hospital 'cause one of my cuts got infected.

Martin received very little community follow-up other than a weekly support meeting; he was released back into the community and into the same life situation, this time with the experience of having suffered a serious stab wound. His search for protection, for "something to hold on to," upon his return to an unresolved set of issues he faced on the street led him to seek a more efficient, more lethal weapon this time around. It could be argued that Martin's hospital education about his risk for homicide victimization, while temporarily steeling his resolve to stay out of trouble on his return to the community, may also have heightened his fear of the probability of revictimization, leading him to take precautionary, "preventive" measures of a different sort:

First, when I first went around the way, I was kinda like scary. But after like a few days, I was back outside, and that's when I started gettin', I said now I need to get me somethin' to hold on to, and then I... that's when we started... that's when we got that piece to hold on to, and then the next year is when I had got into that trouble with the gun situation.

This experience of weakening resolve or "backsliding" was not unique to Martin. Among the young people who identified the experience of injury and hospitalization as causing them to reconsider their lives and lifestyles, this re-assessment alone was not sufficient to change their behavior once they returned to the larger community. This was also true among the young people who were moved to reassess their involvement in violence after witnessing the victimization of others. Wanting to effect a change and carrying it out were two different things. Speaking to some facets of this process, the evaluation of the Boston hospital-based intervention for 12–17 year olds that served Martin concluded that the "success of a hospital-based violence-prevention program may depend on the availability and linkage between community-based programs and the hospital" (De Vos et al. 1996). On a deeper level, it may also depend on the extent to which these linkages are tantamount to a perceived, as well as an actual, safety and development net.

What Do You Do in Real Life When These Guys Are Ready to Whoop You? The Reality of Community Re-Entry

The quality of the hospitalization and community re-entry experience following violent injury both had an important effect on whether the experience of trauma propelled the young people further along a delinquency career or redirected their lives. Martin said that he "enjoyed" the violence intervention he received in the hospital and in the follow-up community meetings:

> But it really didn't do nothin' when I was, like, out and at home, goin' out to the bus stop. That's when it's really, that's when it really hits home, when you gotta walk down the street, when you gotta go to the bus stop, when you gotta go to the store. That's when it's really different than bein' at those meetings. What do you do in real life when these guys are ready to whoop you?

Martin believes that the impact of a specific hospital-based intervention depends on the young person's level of violence involvement and the level of violence in his or her neighborhood:

> Talkin' to somebody about it and lettin' all your anger out… for some people it don't work 'cause, you know, they're from certain neighborhoods, and when you go outside, it's immediately danger, it's immediate danger. And so it don't work that easy for some people. I mean, it worked pretty good for me. I stuck with the violence program for a while. Then I started… I had bought a gun. I started bringing it with me to the violence prevention meeting. But you know, it only works so far for some people.

Carl pointed out that moral support from staff in clinical, community, and other institutional settings can only go so far. Youth can be taught about situations that are likely to result in violence, such as associating with violent peers, using alcohol or drugs, and possessing a firearm or other weapons. They can be helped to develop the skills they need to solve differences without violence and be taught conflict resolution, using nonviolent techniques. Carl's comment on school-based programs can be generalized to interventions in other settings:

> Moral support only goes so far when you're not on a 24-hour basis, you know, so it was like I only seen them probably like six hours out of the day. You know what I'm saying? And then I went home to a whole different atmosphere. You know what I'm saying? It wasn't necessarily peer pressure, it was just a mainstream game.

I'm Glad the Program Teens Came Along: Role of Peers

For most of the study participants, peers played a dominant role in their trajectory towards and away from violence, and in mediating their interactions in a largely hostile world. Peers and peer groups provided solace, protection, support, caring, and a sense of belonging, reasons that have been well documented in the literature on gangs and deviant youth groups. If their homes and neighborhoods are threatening and unpredictable, in the absence of other private or public interventions, then an alternate group and adaptational construct must be fashioned by the youth themselves to counter these pressures. The peer groups—as well as their reckless, crazy, and unpredictable (albeit deviant and violent) behavior –were adaptive, although bringing heightened opportunities to be victimized by, perpetrate, and witness violence.

Paradoxically, when the young people began to question their lifestyles and develop alternate perceptions of violence and trauma, returning to the streets and to their old peer group became another threatening and unpredictable dimension of their lives.

Although Manolo admired his neurosurgeon and Miguel, the violence intervention coordinator who visited him after his hospitalization and during his rehabilitation, these providers were unable to reach him in other ways:

> My doctor and Miguel. Miguel came to my bed, and, you know, talked to me about the program. I came, and I thought it was boring at first. This thing is boring, I don't want to come back here, you know what I'm saying. I'm just about fed up with this. And I don't want to hear about them, 'cause they can't talk to me about stopping the violence. For me it was already too late, too late for them to be coming and tell me that, because the damage had already happened to me. What can I do like this?

However, the program's adolescent counselors, other young people who understood his experience on the street, were able to help Manolo, keeping him from "getting stuck on stupid," replaying revenge fantasies in his head, and enabling him to move on with his life:

> I'm glad the program teens came along. I kept thinking about it. I said to myself, you know, if I shot this fool, what am I gonna get out of it? Am I gonna just, am I gonna walk again? Say I'll take this fool's feet, I'll take his life just for my legs. I said to myself, nah. That can't be possible. You know, I can't walk.

Exposure to Multiple Forms of Violence

Many of the young participants witnessed or were victimized by multiple forms of violence; they explicitly stated that the violence caused them to channel their feelings of fear, impotence, anger, and frustration into acts of perpetration on the street and in school. The violence they experienced took various forms: witnessing the physical, sexual, and physical abuse of their mothers and sisters at the hands of their partners; experiencing abuse in their own intimate relationships; being the victim or perpetrator of sexual and physical abuse as a child; and witnessing, or engaging in, physical fights with the partners of their mothers. The young people describe being brutalized as children and adolescents by adults whom they should be able to trust, and by people from whom they could not escape. The manifestation of violence in one realm (e.g., on the street, between acquaintances) experienced by the young participants as victimizers, victims, or witnesses was often a reaction to violence experienced in another realm (e.g., domestic, sexual, structural conditions).

Child Abuse and Neglect

Manolo was beaten regularly at home, starting at about age six, and soon was on the path toward delinquency, throwing rocks at people in the neighborhood, leaving school in the sixth grade, being inducted into a gang at age 11 in order to gain friends and power, and completing five stints in juvenile hall for grand theft auto. He could not fathom striking back at his mother, nor did he possess the means to control her almost daily whippings at home; therefore, like many of the other young people, Manolo displaced his anger and rage onto others his age on the streets:

> And for me, I take a whipping like—whatever. You know, I wouldn't cry or nothing. I'd just let her whip me until she want... And she'd hit me harder and harder to try to get me to cry, and I wouldn't cry. Every time she'd hit me, I'd get used to it. That's when I used to say, if my mom can hit me, then I can go hit somebody. I'm gonna go take it out on somebody else. She used to hit me hard. I was like, you can't faze me. I had fights—a lot of fights. I think I used to say to myself, if my mom's gonna hit me, I'm gonna go hit somebody else. 'cause my mom would hit me *[bam]*. I'd go outside and knock somebody out. Go at it with them and start fighting for no reason, just because my mom hit me.

As a child and young adolescent, Charo was frequently tied up and whipped with a belt by her older brother, who was often put in charge of her supervision in the absence of her mother and stepfathers. The most painful of her childhood memories, however, was her mother's lack of involvement in Charo's life as she was growing up. This neglect caused her to lash out; by the time she reached high school, her fits of anger became rage:

> It escalated to the point where I stabbed this boy, stabbed him in his arm. And it was like... I was throwing chairs around. I was really into really hurting people, really hurting them bad. I got into fights with teachers, guys, girls, I didn't care. Physical fights. Physical fights. I would throw trashcans at teachers 'cause they were so big, and I would throw trashcans, and the barrels, and I would throw chairs around. Once I got started, I was just, it was like no stopping me. I would fight anybody that would come near me. It was like, really violent type of behavior. I was angry because of the situation that I had goin' on at home, and because I felt that nobody really cared. And I really wanted some attention from my mom and I wasn't gettin' any attention from her, not being good or being bad. It didn't really matter to her what I did, it really didn't matter, the way for me to get the anger out, all the anger that I was accumulating 'cause I wouldn't talk about the problems that I had. I wouldn't talk to anybody about them. And it's like all this anger that I was accumulating, that's the only way for me to express it. That's how I felt. The anger was still there. I had to beat that person enough so I could feel better.

Cy was sent to an institution at age 10 because of parental neglect and abuse; his mother requested that he be placed in an institution because "she did not want me at home." Flaco's mother, a loving woman who was diagnosed as a schizophrenic, had frequent hallucinatory episodes, during which she was unable to take care of herself and her four children, and disowned them as her own. The children who remained at home with her were unable to sleep; they periodically went without heat or utilities and frequently had no food in the house by mid-month. They were almost always hungry at the end of each month:

> My mother wasn't well, had nowhere to go, and I was always, I had nowhere to go. You know, I woke up either at my cousin's house or a friend's house or get up in the morning and leave so

early to go to school or work. That was rough, you know. And nowhere to go, and always hungry and stuff. I couldn't handle it.

Domestic Violence

According to Andres, his sense of hopelessness and his frustration with his father's repeated violent behavior toward his mother was part of what drove him out of the house to seek protection and solace from a group of peers and adolescents on the street:

> It really hurt me to see her cry night after night because of the things my father did to her, so I stayed away from home so I would not have to see it. That is one of the main reasons I joined a gang. A big part of it was that I needed a place that I could fit in and not see my mother go through so much pain.

At age 11, Andres sought to be inducted into a gang to protect himself from another street group who repeatedly taunted and beat him. Soon after being "beaten in" by the gang—severely enough that his mother took him to the emergency room—Andres was soon after ordered to shoot another child—one of the group of kids whose taunting and bullying had brought Andres to seek gang induction in the first place:

> It happened a few weeks after that. I had got some friends, and I had gotten to know people, you know, and I had forgotten all about those kids. I didn't care about them. I had people to hang out with now, I have friends now, you know, and when they said, "You got to go take care of them," I said, "Damn." It was like… Let's just say my nuts just dropped *[laughter]*. Let's just say that it was strong, I was just like, you know, here I was, 11, about to take a life, and I knew that after that my life would never be the same.

In order to be able to pull the trigger, Andres said, he visualized his father abusing his mother. Albert similarly remembers how he felt when seeing his father, a second-generation gang member, beat his mother:

> Just real angry, I had a lot of anger inside me growing up 'cause of when I was a kid, I had a lesson, I remember the domestic violence to Mom and Dad. Dad beating Moms, and I could never have did nothing about it, and it wasn't till I grew up and just take all my anger on my enemies on the streets and stuff like that.

Domestic violence was just one of the many types of violence Albert witnessed at home:

> One of my brothers died. He was killed. I still have one younger brother. In my family, in the home there was a lot of violence. The messy violence. Drug dealing in the house. I always used to see a lot of violence in the house. My father, he'd sell a lot of drugs, and he used to have friends over, and there was always fights and shootings in the house. Grew up around, oh, just looking at all that stuff… He never showed me how to do anything. But the only thing he ever showed me was just to hustle, how to live on the streets, stuff like that.

Albert's father had specific expectations:

> If I got in a fight, I better have won. There wasn't too much of him going with me to ball games. I, he always have the best toys, the best kinds of clothes growing up, but never had someone there for me and my Little League games or anything like that. There was never that love from him.

By the time he was 15, Albert was already living on his own, following in his father's footsteps:

> I was living on the streets with my homeboys; we'd have a room in a motel, room we'd pay for by selling drugs. We'd rent hotel for months, or at times I would stay at home girl's house. She would have us all living there, too. So a typical day would be getting up in the morning, I'd buy different clothes every day, and I'd have my home girl bring our clothes to us the night before, and it will be all ironed so she would bring it to the hotel. We'd get up, we'd pay for the room, order pizza, eat, go back to the neighborhood, slang rocks all day just kickback with about 12–15 homeboys, bullshitting, having fun. Customers keep coming to us, and we're just making money, making money. Go down to the streets, go buy something to drink. Gunshots would happen on a daily basis, and we'd hear gunshots—either we'd be shooting at somebody or somebody drive by shooting at us. Go back to the neighborhood, get drunk, pick up some weapons, and just go blast off somebody too, whether they did something to us or not.

By the time Albert turned 16, he had been expelled from three school districts:

> I was involved in a shooting during Nutrition, and it led police to investigate me, and I ended up put behind bars in jail, and I got kicked out of *[the second school]* due to my gang-related activities in the school. I started a shoot-out in front of the school. And the last school district, I cracked a teacher's ribs with the stapler.

By the time he was 19, Albert had been charged with grand theft auto, possession of a concealed weapon, weapon sales, terrorist threats, attempted murder, and shooting, and entering a dwelling with an intent to kill, and had spent time in youth authority and juvenile halls. At 19, he was sent to the penitentiary for three-and-a-half years, some of it served in a supermax facility where he was kept in isolation for 22 hours a day.

Incest and Other Sexual Abuse

Lulu, Charo, Andrea, and Erika were all victims of incest as children, and one of the young men, Emmanuel, had also been sexually abused. Erika describes her repeated abuse:

> I was like eight or nine, and it happened repeatedly. And I remember one time my mom had left somewhere. My grandmother was across the street cleaning some apartments, because she cleans houses for a living and all that. And at that time, he, I guess he must have been hiding. I didn't know what the issue was. But I had a skirt, a miniskirt, not too short. The kind that people wore in the mid-'80s, and he tried to stick a screwdriver in. And I was fighting and wrestling and screaming, and it tripped me out that my godfather, which was his brother, and everybody, all his brothers were there, and nobody lifted one finger to defend me. On the contrary, they got mad because I was yelling and screaming. And after that I never felt part of the family. His sisters, sisters would come and give everybody presents but me. And so I used to nut out big time over that kind of stuff.

Suicide

Lulu and Erika had attempted suicide by taking pills; Andrea's suicide attempts were more indirect: placing herself in situations with an extreme probability that she would be shot and possibly killed, and playing Russian roulette with a loaded gun. Andrea's homicidal behavior masked her suicidal tendencies. Charo's domestic violence injuries brought her to the emergency rooms and health clinics more than 20 times, starting at age 14. Following one of these visits, Charo explicitly stated her wish to die:

> There was one time when they wanted to keep me there 'cause I used to want to kill myself at the time. I was like, you know, it's better if I just finish it. Myself. I was like, he ain't gonna kill me. I'm gonna kill myself. That's the way I felt. Like, you know... and even when I got into fights with him, I was like, you know what? I'd take knives, and I would start, like, kind of kill myself, and I'd be like, I'm just gonna kill myself 'cause you're not gonna kill me. You're not gonna be the person to kill me. I'm gonna kill myself. I was like, 17.

Community and Structural Violence

Outside the home, the participants had witnessed—and a few had experienced—brutality by the police; they had seen organized police S.W.A.T. team operations, helicopter patrols, undercover arrests in their neighborhoods, and other acts of "justifiable violence" and militarization. They had seen other forms of physical aggression and crime-related violence perpetrated by peers and neighbors. They had also witnessed the misuse of power and force by the public servants depicted by the larger society as protectors, such as the police. During the early 1990s, the police in Boston had a "stop and frisk" policy as a means to curb youth crime, routinely stopping the young people in this study and their friends, slamming them against the wall on their way to the Boys and Girls Club for their weekly violence prevention group support meetings. The participants who had been jailed or otherwise institutionalized described instances of inmate violence, including rape, and excessive use of force by the institutions' wardens.

Carl's mother was sent to jail for assault when Carl was 10 years old; he was then moved from relative to relative until his mother was released several years later. Other participants similarly describe being separated from their brothers and fathers as they too, served time in jail. Most of the young people describe living in economically and racially/ethnically segregated, resource-deprived neighborhoods with poor city services—the homicide "hot spots" of the city. These young people lived in the least developed neighborhoods, with few job opportunities and high rates of unemployment or underemployment.

Their neighborhoods each had monikers describing the community's traits; for example, Bell Gardens was "Bell Garbage,' and Mattapan was "Murderpan." They describe living in substandard housing and attending run-down, poorly equipped schools, some of which had been decertified due to the poverty of standards and teaching. Many of the participants had experienced homelessness, had used city food banks, had known hunger, and had gone without heat at various times in their young lives.

Writing on violence, injustice, and war, David Gil describes how societal violence (defined as aspects of "normal" social life, such as unemployment, income inequality, discrimination) "tends to set in motion chain reactions of counter-violence from its victims," noting that this counter-violence is usually not directed at the sources of societal violence in the institutional order of society, but rather displaced onto helpless and powerless victims. In his interpretation, "domestic violence and violent crime, as well as suicide addictions and mental ills, are direct and indirect expressions of counter-violence." Although his writing primarily focuses on adults in accounting for the socially structured violation of the developmental needs of individuals, Gil's analysis is especially pertinent to understanding of interpersonal counter-violence among children and adolescents.

These young people experienced the effects of what Gil describes as initiating (systemic) societal violence through the direct and indirect expressions of counter-violence at the hands of their families, friends, and institutions in their neighborhoods. As a consequence, the youths' behavior can also seem insensate and brutish:

> Violent, destructive and self-destructive attitudes and behaviors of individuals and groups will often seem senseless and irrational to observers of isolated episodes. However, when such episodes are viewed in the context of individual and social history, they seem no longer senseless and irrational, but reveal their inner logic as "counter violence" to violent societal practices and conditions. (Gil 1990, 289)

According to Gil, the consistent thwarting of the individuals' developmental needs blocks constructive energy and transforms it into a destructive energy. Such basic human needs are enumerated by Gil and others as: 1) biological-material; 2) social-psychological; 3) productive-creative; 4) security; 5) self-actualization; and 6) spiritual. Among the blocked needs that surfaced from the young people's accounts in this study were the stable provision of biological necessities (such as food, shelter, and heat), as well as regular access to other life-sustaining and enhancing goods and services, such as health care, particularly in a society and culture where the expectation and actual quantity and quality of consumption of such services is high.

In terms of their social-psychological needs, the positive, affirming life chances of the young people interviewed were diminished by the life circumstances of their families and communities. For most, the odds of forming stable, meaningful social relationships, and developing a sense of belonging to a community of mutual respect, acceptance, affirmation, care, and love were diminished, as were their opportunities for self-discovery and for the emergence of a positive self-identity. The subtexts of their stories reveal the precariousness and lack of stability in their lives, an existential anxiety along with the scarcity of life-sustaining goods, stable social relations, acceptance, care, and love.

Youth development scholars have identified several concrete risks in adolescence that can impair positive, or life-affirming development among youth:

> First, renegotiation of the relationship with one's parents can be so turbulent that a permanent rift and alienation between youth and their family emerges. Second, adolescents can get so caught up with a deviant peer group and its behaviors and circumstances that seriously endanger their ability to make a successful transition into mainstream adulthood. Third, adolescents can fail to make social connections with the kinds of adults and social institutions that can help them make the transition into mainstream adulthood. Fourth, educational opportunities can be so limited that some adolescents fail to acquire the intellectual and soft skills needed to move successfully into the labor market. Fifth, experiences with civic engagement and social institutions can be so minimal or so poorly designed that some adolescents fail to develop either the will or the skills necessary to participate fully as adult community members. Finally, experiences of racism, prejudice, and cultural intolerance can so alienate some adolescents that they withdraw from or rebel against, mainstream society and conventional social institutions (NRC and IOM 2002).

The early, prolonged, and chronic exposure to multiple forms of violence and trauma experienced by the study youth would exacerbate these risks, and posed particular challenges to the complex process of adolescent development. Integrating adolescence into a general life-span model of development, Erikson (1968) outlined the specific challenges for children between the ages of 10 and 18: developing a sense of mastery, identity, and intimacy. Each of the tasks involved in this development process are carried out in complex social as well as cultural and historical settings, optimal progress depending on the psychosocial, physical and cognitive assets of the individual, available social supports and the developmental appropriateness of each of the social settings encountered by young people as they go through adolescence. The tasks are: 1) changing the nature of the relationship between young people and their parents so youth can assume a more mature role in the social fabric of their communities; 2) exploring new personal, social, and sexual roles and identities; 3) transforming peer relationships into deeper friendships and intimate partnerships; and 4) participating in a series of experiences and choices that facilitate future economic independence and interdependence (NRC and IOM 2002).

The larger settings in which the youth participants lived influenced how these developmental tasks would unfold, as well as their subsequent development. Ecological transactional theory, describing various ecological contexts with varying proximities to the individual, offers a framework for understanding the impact of context when assessing a young person's responses to community violence. Bronfenbrenner (1979) described these various contexts, from the individual (including cognitions, temperament and behavior), the micro system (family relationships), exosystem (neighborhood and community factors) and the larger macro system (public policy and cultural values). According to this framework, exposure to violence in the community is likely to influence the multiple levels of the ecology. Recent research suggests that rates of maltreatment are significantly higher among youth exposed to higher levels of community violence, compared to those exposed to low levels of community violence, lending support to the hypothesis that risk factors in the exosystem may be associated with risk problems in the micro system. Moreover, both child maltreatment and exposure to violence were associated with children's psychosocial functioning (Lynch and Cicchetti). The reciprocal relationship among the varied levels of a young person's ecology underscores the importance of contextual factors that mediate or moderate the relationship between exposure to community violence and symptoms of distress. This research underscores as well the importance of considering how characteristics of the child's environment influence the adaptation to trauma, moving beyond individual symptoms and focuses on the context-specific difficulties youth experience following exposure to violence (Phelps et al. 2002).

While previous experience and learning were critical in shaping the individual capacities, values, and attitudes of the young participants, the experiences with trauma and its aftermath were also critical for their well-being and preparation for the future, setting the stage for future capacities, values, and attitudes.

It Was A Wake Up Call: Violence and Its Effect on Termination

A substantial body of research on the cycle of violence suggests that a history of violence is the strongest developmental predictor of a child's involvement in violence; early aggression commonly escalates into later violence and broadens into other antisocial behavior. These theories stress the extensive developmental continuity and consistency in the child's or adolescent's patterns of aggression. For a review of such theories see Pepler and Slaby (1994). The premise of such theories is that repeated exposure to violence gradually diminishes one's ability to discern violence as wrong, instead teaching the young person that violence is a means to solve conflicts and assert oneself. Since aggressive habits learned early in life are the foundation of later behavior, social and cultural influences in early childhood may exert a lifelong impact on children's attitudes toward violence and likelihood of their involvement with violence.

Although some theorists believe that violence is the direct, inevitable result of extreme anger or inadequate impulse control, other researchers suggest that inadequate impulse or emotional control only puts an individual at risk for violence if violent acts are that person's *preferred* response, learned through past experiences.

Studies on the consequences of trauma in children and adolescents suggest that it may permanently change a victim's view of the world. Childhood trauma studies have consistently found changes in orientation toward the future including negative expectation, a foreshortened future, and altered attitudes toward marriage, career and having children. Trauma "may disrupt developmental achievements and may cause delays in, deficits of, or failures of multisystem developmental achievements in motor, emotional, language, psychosocial and cognitive skills" (Debellis 1997). Trauma may also impact psychosexual and moral development, possibly leading to psychiatric, psychosocial, social, cognitive and medical consequences, with trauma resulting from interpersonal origins considered to be more likely to be chronic, more severe and harder to treat because of compounded difficulties in establishing a therapeutic alliance, for it involves repairing wounds of an interpersonal traumatic event. A convenience sample study (Fein et al. 2002) of violently injured urban youth, ages 12 to 24 treated in the emergency department, found acute stress symptoms seem to be common, and suggested that acute stress symptoms, assessed in the immediate aftermath of a traumatic injury, are useful indicators for later post-traumatic stress many weeks or months later.

The stories of the young people in this study suggest a more complicated relationship between a history of exposure to violence and later violence perpetration, and, by extension, the termination of violent behavior. If early exposure gradually diminished the ability of the young people to discern violence as wrong, the cumulative exposure to the effects of violence also led many to re-examine their own past involvement and perceive violence as wrong. This was the case even among the very violence-involved youth, whose early and severe aggression profiles would ordinarily make them unlikely candidates for violence cessation.

Further, although victimized as children, the young people in this study did not themselves prey on younger children; instead, they selectively channeled their anger, using violence only as a preferred response with certain individuals and situations (their peers and selected adult authority figures: teachers, health and social workers, probation officers, the police, or their mother's boyfriends). Their child-centered perspective—due to the victimization they themselves experienced during those years—kept them from expressing their rage and frustration on the young, implying a measure of control, direction and empathy. Further, for many, the act of witnessing their conduct's effects on the young prompted a re-examination of their violent lifestyles and behavior. A study of factors that prevented gun acquisition and carrying among incarcerated adolescent males reported that gun-experienced adolescents specifically identified those individuals whom they would refrain from carrying a gun.

> Quite striking was that about a quarter of gun-experienced adolescents specifically described not carrying a gun around younger family members or friends to keep these children from inadvertently being injured by the adolescent's gun. One revealed how, because of his younger siblings, he did not keep his gun in the house: "You ain't supposed to keep a gun leaded in the house. I got little brothers…" Another youth stated he would not carry a gun to his baby's mother's house. The reason being "Her little brother's…They nosy… like playin' with stuff. They may play with it, and one get shot." (Freed et al. 2001)

These findings have important implications for preventive interventions among high-risk adolescents, for the concern of unintentionally harming the innocent young can be discussed during anticipatory guidance visits to physicians as well as during acute visits related to interpersonal injury.

Some of the study participants said that their outrage toward certain forms of violence, either witnessed or experienced, could trigger their own involvement in street or youth violence. For example, their feelings of anger and impotence, brought about by domestic violence and sexual abuse, influenced their adoption of violent conduct on the streets and in schools against their peers and authority figures. But this anger could also serve as a catalyst to move them further along a path towards cessation of violence. The stories of the youth suggest that the quality of the impulse that prompted their involvement with, questioning of, and eventual cessation of, violence was varied.

What Happened to Me Made Me Strong: Trauma as an Opportunity

Many of the young people who sustained a spinal cord injury due to gunshots said that they had lost their legs but gained a life—a theme that requires a cautious attempt at explanation. Looking back on the young people he counseled, Delbert noted the precipitating circumstances that resulted in the young people being admitted to the hospital and the mindset change that ensued:

> Some of them were just accidents. Some of them just stupidity, like fighting over a gold chain or something. And some of them, it was a wake-up call. Some of them was just out there doing some hideous things. And it was like, POW! They lost their legs, they gained a conscience.

For some of the young men who became injured as a result of violence, the injury and its aftermath allowed their true selves to emerge. This was a common theme in many of the narratives of the young people interviewed. For those with spinal cord injuries, this transformation was symbolically equated with the loss of their legs, which forced them to literally and figuratively slow down. Carl says:

> I feel like I am a better man now that I am in this chair. I'm the best man I could be. 'cause back then, this wasn't me.

He specifies that it was not the chair that made the difference:

> It's just getting shot in general. That light. That stoplight that was put into my road while I was going along in the fast lane, that wall. That's what knocked some sense into me. I was going so fast, how hard I hit it, the impact.

These interpretations suggest that young people were not "shot or shocked straight," not unlike the "scared straight" programs in detention settings that attempt to scare adolescents into reconsidering their involvement in delinquency.

That Little Voice Inside You that Tells You Right from Wrong:
Resumption of the Ethical

Many of the youth refer to the incidents they witnessed and experienced
as an awakening, which led them to question their identities and the
consequences of their acts of violence. They reassessed the effects of
their behavior on family, friends, and community. The incident of
trauma, for some, had a paradoxical, unexpected effect, which reinforced
their sense of worth and purpose and their desire and respect for life.
This was also true among the most "hardened" of the youth, who had the
most violent histories. The experience of trauma and its aftermath could
open up a new world, and, according to Delbert, age 18, "make you hear
again that little voice inside you that tells you right from wrong" and
either "makes you remember or develop a conscience." Writing about
detention camps and prisons, Buber (1952) describes extraordinary
situations that not only signal a moral collapse but warrant a "suspension
of the ethical" in accordance with the will and duty to survive. The
troubling relations between the youth and children, witnessed,
perpetrated, and experienced by the young people in this study (and
described under the category of acquaintance violence), indicate a moral
collapse of a different order, and a suspension or stunting of the ethical.
Out of these troubling circumstances, questioning of old (and
increasingly false) moral perceptions and dilemmas could surface. Carl
describes this awakening of a different consciousness, which began to
manifest itself when he was around 14, following his injury and
disability:

> It was just like, damn, I'm tired of living like this, you know. I
> want to get out of this feeling. I'm tired of feeling like shit's
> fucked up when really it's not. I'm only thinking it's fucked up,
> you know what I'm saying, because this is what I see.

The young people who participated in this study said that in certain
circumstances, exposure to violence and its aftermath had the unexpected
result of forging a different consciousness, a new way of seeing and
understanding. This altered state challenged their mindset about the
violent events they had witnessed, perpetrated, and been victimized by,
and signaled an eventual end to passive acceptance of their previous
relationship with their world, their established way of life, their
relationships, and their environment. Exposure to violence and trauma at
times led to reflecting, questioning, and imagining alternatives to their
reality, offering a point of departure for reconstructing that reality, and
forcing a re-ordering of their symbolic universe.

The perspectives on violence as a health problem and the responses
offered by health institutions could offer new ways of seeing and a new

"home" for these young people, providing a sense of belonging, an introduction to a set of behavior codes, standards and ethics, and a lens through which to make sense of their own experience and involvement with violence and injury. In redefining the problem of violence as a knowable and preventable issue, a public health perspective could provide a path toward a different understanding of their current life circumstances. In some cases, trauma and its aftermath (e.g., supportive interventions, the services received, and the quality of caring interactions that followed the violent incident) opened a door for the young people, which allowed them to begin to verbalize their feelings and thoughts about their lives and their community situation. It also allowed for integration into the community and/or school or faith communities, enabling them to sustain that self-questioning and positive momentum, and reducing their risk of revictimization and/or retaliatory perpetration. For some, the supportive health setting and specialized interventions provided opportunities for enrichment, improved ability to access services, and exposure to sustained, consistent caring of instrumental peers and adults.

The implications of a traumatic event for revisiting past behavior and prompting an awakening varied among the individuals whose transformations are chronicled in this study. Even though these young people were similar in terms of their demographic and social characteristics, they differed from one other in many ways. In addition to differences in gender, race, ethnicity, and nationality, they differed in age and development, levels of poverty and social capital within their families and neighborhoods, family histories, experience with social services and school, health histories, residential histories, and individual characteristics, among others. All these dimensions influenced how the young people made sense of, ascribed meaning to, and adopted a critical consciousness of their past behavior. The varied, underlying rationales for their involvement in and perceptions of violence (and the logic that led to cessation) stem from the contexts in which these young people lived. It is clear from their stories, and the themes within them, that the situations of violence and the situations that prompted their questioning of violence were not only autonomously or culturally produced; they also have a social history and must be understood within a larger social context and within a moral order that has suspended the ethical in its relations toward these children.

CHAPTER 6

The Process of Change

What made me change? I don't know. I thought to myself that, you know what I'm saying, that I can't go back out there on the streets like this in the chair. I could, my hands still work, can, pick up a gun, you know what I'm saying? I still got the heart to do it, but for what? What am I gonna get out of it? I think about it right now, you know I'm getting old now. I'm 17 now, and I ain't gonna say I'm all that, but next year I'll be 18 years old. I gotta handle my responsibility for my own life. I can't just be out there throwing my life away. I gotta have a job, you know, I gotta stand up for myself.

—Manolo

It is something dramatic, something that just slaps you, like you were asleep. That the whole time that everything was happening, you were asleep and there's something punching you in your sleep and you finally just wake up and say, whoa.

—Andres

I believe in change, I believe people could change, I'm a prime example of that. We can save them, we can save their lives. I really do, I believe that with a passion. Nobody could tell me different cause I'd call them a liar and I'd back up and roll away cause I do believe this.

—Albert

Defining change is much more difficult than many theories have acknowledged. Studies of intentional modification of behaviors demonstrate that while change is possible, it nevertheless involves a process that is not well understood. Hundreds of psychotherapy outcome studies have shown that people do successfully change with the help of

105

professional treatment, yet the studies have shed little light on how that transformation was achieved. Many studies also have demonstrated that the majority of people change without the benefits of intervention. These studies similarly explain little about how people are able to change on their own.

The process of change is perhaps more difficult to accompany and understand among adolescents because of their varied developmental stages. Moreover, young people may find it difficult to articulate the passages involved. There is an added barrier in understanding the process of transformation among minority young people: the models and yardsticks for achievement and adolescent development have been formulated for a majority population of adolescents of different race, ethnicity, nationality, class, and life circumstances. On another level, mentioning of the word "change" in reference to the change of consciousness among stigmatized groups, and youth involved in violence and crime, evokes distrustful and at times hostile reactions. Scripts of recidivism, criminality and not stories of redemption are expected.

The affected individuals often describe the experience of change differently than the professionals observing the transformation. This difference has been observed in studies of psychotherapy, but is also generalizable to other helping professions. In addition, the helpers' perceptions of change and the strategies for effecting it are often different than those with whom they are working (Mahoney 1991). Since no studies have been conducted on the perceptions of change of violence-involved adolescents in health and hospital settings, this study offers a glimpse of how one sample of such self-selecting adolescents viewed this process.

CONTRIBUTORS TO TERMINATION

In making sense of young people's experiences of change, I examined selected sets of theories. Some of the theories were picked because of their prevalent use in the field in to describe behavioral and personal change, while others were selected because they shed light on other, less explored aspects of their trajectories of violence victimization and perpetration. The frameworks of these disparate theories provide important theoretical scaffolds against which to analyze the themes that surface in the stories of the transformation of the young people.

Practitioners in prevention fields draw upon various theories to explain behavior change, placing the behavior of the individual at the center of their frame of reference. Prochaska and DiClemente's stages of change theory (1992) offers a useful framework through which to study an individual's readiness for change. According to their theory, modification of addictive behavior involves the progression through five stages: precontemplation, contemplation, preparation, action, and the final stage of maintenance. It is a framework that can incorporate competing theories of change, such as self-efficacy theory and decisional balance theory. Prochaska and DiClemente identify a finite and common set of change processes used to progress through these stages.

The previous chapter recounted how the young people in this study exposed to violence and its consequences subsequently forged a different consciousness. In Prochaska and DiClemente's typology, these young people could be categorized as having attained the stage of contemplation, a stage in which the individuals are more open to dramatic relief experiences, observations, confrontations and interpretations, which raise emotions and can lower negative affect if the person changes:

> As individuals became more conscious of themselves and the nature of their problems, they were more likely to reevaluate their values, problems, and themselves and the nature of their problems, and themselves both affectively and cognitively. The more central their problems were to their self-identity, the more their reevaluation involved altering their sense of self. Contemplators also reevaluated the effects their addictive behaviors had on their environments, especially the people with whom they were closest. They struggle with questions such as "How do I think and feel about living in a deteriorating environment that places my family or friends at increasing risk for disease, poverty, or imprisonment?" (Prochaska and DiClemente 1992, 1109)

Ten processes of change, spanning varied theoretical approaches to treatment, are proposed in their model, and underlie the progression through the remaining stages of change (preparation, action and maintenance). These processes are: 1) consciousness raising, in which the individual's level of awareness to the problem is increased; 2) self-evaluation, which involves both a cognitive and affective re-evaluation of the self; 3) environmental re-evaluation whereby a person contemplates changes in response to consequences present in the environment; 4) self-liberation, the awareness and choosing of new alternatives by an individual; 5) social liberation resulting from environmental changes, leading to more alternatives; 6) counter conditioning, changing of responses to the environment; 7) stimulus control, modifying the environment to fit an individual's responses; 8) contingency management, involving changes in the individual that occur when there are changes in the environment; 9) dramatic relief, the process of evoking of blocked emotions, of catharsis, by observing emotional scenes in the environment; and 10) helping relationship, identified as the process that fosters change in both therapy and the natural environment. The model proposes that individuals who successfully change are likely to use these processes when initiating change, and these processes have been identified in the behavior of people in therapy as well as among those who change on their own.

Prochaska and DiClemente's theory of the stages of change has been used in research on correctional interventions with offender populations. Some criminologists have cited this model of change as offering the conceptual focus that has been lacking in the development of an assessment strategy of treatment readiness and responsivity with offenders (Serin and Kennedy 1999). The stories of transformation of the young people indicate that some of these processes are more prominent and suggest that these may be especially important to investigate in relation to termination.

In her study of the aftermath of violence, Herman speaks to another dimension of the process of transformation of import to this study: the ways in which individuals recover from violence. The study of the recovery process surfaced from many observations of combat veterans and others who experienced trauma; few address interpersonal violence traumatization issues among adolescents. Such studies have found the core experiences of psychological trauma to be disempowerment and disconnection, making recovery a process that cannot occur in isolation.

Recovery, in Herman's scheme, is seen as unfolding in three stages: 1) establishment of safety (a gradual shift from unpredictable danger to reliable safety); 2) remembrance and mourning (from disassociated trauma to acknowledged memory); and 3) reconnection with ordinary life (movement away from stigmatized isolation to restored social connection) (Herman 1997). The young people in this study were often both victims and perpetrators of violent acts, and cessation and recovery from violence were processes that were inextricably linked.

It Has to Start at You First Before Anyone Else: Change Comes From Within

All the young people who participated in this study remarked that the momentum and desire to change has to come from within. Carl describes a fellow patient also paralyzed due to gun violence who tried to reach him and advise him about getting out of his street life, "He was trying to talk to me, but I wasn't trying to hear the shit he was saying. Man, because he was paralyzed from the neck down. I wasn't disrespecting him by not hearing him. It was just that I was already shut off from the world and he just couldn't understand that."

In retrospect, Carl was so shut off from the world, that he was skeptical about whether anyone could have reached him. "I would hear him out see how he was. But we different, I don't care how you put it, there is no comparison. My being in the wheelchair is different and I look different than everyone, it is my disposition as an individual, what can I say?"

Ronnie remembers making a conscious decision to try something new, and ask for help. "Kind of let my guard down and let a couple of them in. I said, 'You can be my friend; I want you to help me,' cause at first I didn't want nobody helping me."

Cy similarly describes how he made a change. "I had to make a decision, you know. I had to work to where I got to right now. I had to decide how I want my life to be. So it was all about decision making."

Mo describes this consciousness as "realizing, you know, that you can't go back, you can't do that. This is a change. You gotta sit down, put your life together, and get out there and accomplish things."

In reflecting on their own and others' change, the study participants agreed that the ability to change is not predetermined and that in most cases, if given a chance, even the least likely candidates can make that transition. Delbert reflects on the improbable transformation among one of his violence prevention youth counselors:

> How he got good, I have no idea. But I know he developed his conscience somehow. There's no doubting that 'cause if you hear his story, and then you look at him, and you like, how the hell do you do what you do today? Then you have to, you must admire this dude. There's no choice. I don't care who you are. People would say that he was one of those that was lost. I mean, they thought I was lost when I was little, but they probably thought he was the anti-Christ.

Their stories and explanations reject the traditional view of motivation, that the ability and willingness to change is due to a personality characteristic, or are qualities that an individual young person either does or does not possess. Further, having committed violent or even heinous acts does not preclude change.

In looking back at her own transformation, Charo does not believe that she was different from the other women who can't make a change. According to her:

We all have it in us, it's just that it's difficult to see when you're going through this, and you're taking all this crap, and you're just giving yourself no worth whatsoever. But, I think we all have it in us. How I am inside, I think everybody has that place that where they can change. It's just you have to kinda like get there, and it can be far. You have to really believe yourself into thinking, knowing that are gonna do this, and that you are strong enough to get where you wanna get. Because sometimes you think you're stupid. That's another thing, you just start thinking, I'm not strong, I can't really do this. I can't. I'm not gonna function. I'm not gonna do this the way other people do. They did it because they grew up. They had no problems. You know. I can't. But you just have to believe that you could.

In recounting their own progress and those of others, the young participants recognized varying levels of change readiness, commenting on whether an individual was "ready for change" and internally motivated to make a transition, with or without a formal intervention. As one participant commented about one of the many hospital admissions experienced:

You know, they cared for me, they did seem sincere. It didn't make an impact, I acted like a smart ass and I told them a bunch of lies.

Carl remembers when he was shot and hospitalized and how at the time, he was not ready to even contemplate change, "Because I wouldn't let it happen, because I shut the door." In other cases, states Erika:

I've observed where people are not in that stage yet. That's like premature, you know, they're in a premature state where they don't want to, they don't want to go to school, yet. They don't feel right, and they might want to make a change, but emotionally they're not really ready. Mentally, they're not really ready to go to school, to go to a program, they're not ready for that. And all you can do is stop by and say "hi, how you doing? Oh well, you know, give me a call some time." Or some times, even just call. And some times it takes months, you know, before you can build people's trust and before people can feel like going somewhere. And some people might not ever go with you to these programs. And some people go to other programs, or some people might just go to a local adult school and get their life together.

Erika, and many of the young participants, underscore that the process of change often unfolds incrementally, in moving one young person to begin to consider the effect of individual actions on others, in beginning to explore new ways of thinking, in taking a step towards adopting a new behavior.

Albert recounts how he had been trying to change, even before he went in for the last time at the state penitentiary. He had attempted to leave the life of gangs and drugs behind, and had succeeded partially, taking preparatory steps by enrolling in school, although he continued dealing part time to pay his bills.

> Well, actually I was trying; I was trying to before I even went in. I went back to school. I was going to this Institute, I wanted to be in electronics. I'd finished two semesters; I had made honors both semesters with the 4.0 in my first semester and 3.56 in my second semester. So, I was doing good at school there. I was trying mostly because I had a girlfriend at the time that I was trying to settle down with and I had a lot of responsibilities being that she was living with me and I had to support her, raise her. So I started with her at the age of 17 and when I was 19 I was ready to the point where I was just relaxing. I sold the drugs to go to school. It would be like I'd be in school and then I'd get take off go make 500 bucks or something or maybe I'd just stay in school and then after school I'd go right back and go deliver something, that's how I was paying for things.

It would be in the state penitentiary, and between the ages of 20 and 21, that Albert would finally have the contemplation time needed to make a definite break, and the opportunity to

> learn common sense. I spent 22 hours a day in a cell for 18 months. There was a lot of time to think a lot of time to decide on what I really wanted to do in life, where I was headed, and I thought during that time, I sat down and thought a lot about my family. What did I want to do in my life? Did I want to end up like Masalle, who was 56 years old who had lived in that cell for 9 years. He still went to the gangs, still was shooting heroin, did I want to end up like him? I came to a conclusion that I had finally graduated at gangster school, which is state penitentiary. What do you want to become all your life? You want to be part of a prison organization, you want to be part of it? I became a part of it, and I'd seen that wasn't going to lead you nowhere. Those people twice my age still gang bang, still talking shit, but

they are all locked up in prison not having nothing in life and I just learned to realize that wasn't for me. I didn't want to do that, I was a two-time loser, two strikes, one more and I was going to catch 25 to life. And I knew that if I continued in that life, had kept on being as scareless as I had been, using impetuous thinking, that I would never get anywhere in life. What made me change? I just wanted to better myself. I made a decision that I wasn't going to be a statistic. Everybody said, "You ain't never going to make it, you are going to end up dead or you are going to be in prison and you're going to catch 25-life, you're going to do this." Everybody was always quick to point a finger at me and I'm just doing the opposite of what they want. You know I don't want to be a statistic. I just learned common sense.

Thinking about changing, wanting to change, being ready for change, beginning to change and maintaining that change were separate phases identified in the stories of the young participants, and speak to varying levels and types of responsivity, with important implications for treatment in hospital and other settings. The young people describe being "hard," "knuckleheaded" or a "smart ass," trapped in what Prochaska and DiClemente (1992) name a precontemplation stage. Like the thousands of self-changers studied by these authors, they "processed less information about their problems, devoted less time and energy to reevaluating themselves, and experienced fewer emotional reactions to the negative aspects of their problems." Ronnie remembers back to the first time he was hospitalized, and doubts that any intervention at the time would have had much long-term effect unless the individual himself wished to make a change. There might be a temporary effect induced by the scare, or attention:

Maybe had somebody there to talk to me, but it wouldn't have did no good. Cause this is how I feel, that you're gonna do what you want to do regardless. But as long as you got someone telling you that you could do something different, it would make that person feel good. But, I feel like this: you can't tell nobody what to do, I can't tell nobody what to do, I can just suggest. It will be upon that person to do, if they want to do. Now, when they get in trouble, of course they want to listen then. You can have somebody there for them, but it's still the mindset. When they get out, do they want to change? They'll have to want to change for themselves.

Models of recovery from trauma are also premised on the principle that the survivor "must be the author and arbiter of her own recovery. Others may offer advice, support, assistance, affection and care, but not cure" (Herman 1997, 133). Helpful practice helps the individual to control the behavior but does not strive to control the individual.

Although responsivity and motivation are widely recognized as key factors mediating the success of treatment programs in correctional and other interventions, the precise role of these variables is not clearly understood. Further, few professionals have the experience to intuitively assess responsivity and change readiness, for the signs are often contradictory. As George explains:

> When I did get shot and ended up in the hospital I still would behave violently and stuff like that. I was into myself, I would kick back and my mind would be on other things. I didn't really want to go back out to do violent things, to go back to that life, but my behavior, I had an acting out behavior, I still was acting out but inside me that was not what I wanted to be or to do, you see, but if you would walk up to me you'd see me acting out and cursing, you know, you'd say, he don't want to change, but I did, you know.

Albert would reflect on the young people who were contemplating making a change whom he counseled over the years at the hospital, in schools and communities. In his opinion, the ages of the young people made a difference as to how susceptible they would be to outside influences as motivators towards change:

> I think mostly it's got to be based on their part of their being willing to make the change, cause they are old enough to decide that. I mean a kid you could still sort of change them. You could still make them, somebody might to get a chance to decide that they really want to change. When they are older, when they are adults, they have to make that change. They are the ones who have to make that change nobody is going to actually change them.

With many of the young people and children learning at very early ages to fend for themselves due to lack of adult guidance and support, it becomes tricky to determine the extent to which autonomous resolve does or does not influence the transformation process by chronological age alone. As Carl states, and the lives of Andres, Albert, Andrea, George and others similarly attest, many children have to get used to fending for themselves and providing for their needs at a very young age.

Carl's mother bore him when she was 15, and when Carl was 10 she was imprisoned for attempted murder, leaving Carl to fend for himself for four years as he was shuttled between various relatives. By the time his mother was released, Carl was used to being on his own, and resisted adult guidance:

> When I turned 14 in '92, my mother got out, so we were living together and then she had another baby. I was already out of hand you know, doing my own thing, you know what I'm saying. So I was used to caring for myself and she was just trying to tame me to something I wasn't, something she wanted me to be.

You Need Some Kind of Guidance: **A Person Cannot Change Alone**

All the young participants mentioned that while the wish to change must and can only come from the individual, it is difficult to do so alone. As stated by Martin,

> I feel the person is the only person that can change. Other people can help, other people can give them advice, but nobody can change somebody. You can't change me. I can't change you. Only you can change you. But other people can be of assistance. I think a person can change, but they need help from other people, and insight.

The young people recognized that external factors influence the internal change process and the motivation to change. A young person, according to Andrea:

> needs some kind of guidance, needs some kinds of answers from somebody. You know, luckily I got mine. And you definitely need support.

Working as a gang violence prevention peer educator since the age of 16 and as a domestic violence advocate since she was 20, Charo sees herself today as a guide, a facilitator of change:

> Maybe I can make it so they don't have to take that long, as long as I took, as long as it took me to realize it. Even though you can't really help if a person doesn't want to, it's like telling like a blind person crossing the street, you can say "you wanna hold my hand so I could help you cross?" I could only help you

cross if you decide to move. If you don't wanna move, there's nothing I can do. You had to decide to move, make that first step in order for me to help you across the street, you know. That's really how it goes in this type of situation. You have to be willing. You have to do, too. I'm just here to tell you that I'm here for you, and I'm here to show you that you can do it. You can do this. You can be somebody. You can do so much with your life. You can make such a difference that you're not even probably aware of it.

Besides the effect of trauma as a catalyst on an individual's disposition to evaluate circumstances, the personal decision to change almost always required additional help in order to sustain the momentum. Delbert summarizes the opinions of most of the study participants with his statement that:

It's not possible to change alone, you might have feelings at some times, but without somebody to push you in that direction, I don't think you can, you can't change totally alone. You'd have to have something, somebody pushing you.

Erika sums up this process and the relative weight of internal and external factors pointing to the symbiotic nature of change:

It's up to you for yourself to wanna change. But once you have the mind, or the desire, to change, even though if you're doing wrong, you need people to help you because some times you fall, or you make mistakes, and you need people to kind of hold on to you, so you keep walking that road. First of all, the change starts alone, because you, yourself, have to change. The change starts with you, because nobody can change you. You have to decide to wanna change. You have to decide what kind of background, or what kind of road you want to take. But on that road, you're gonna need somebody to help you. I'd be a fool to say that I did this by myself. No, I didn't do this by myself. First of all it took people, and I wanted to change. I didn't know what school to check. I didn't know what nursing program was the best for me. I didn't know who would take me. I didn't know what, so I had to have people to help me. There's no such thing as you change by yourself.

The young people's stories underscore the need for support during the episodes of emotional intensity and as the young person restructures the memories, beliefs and self-appraisals. Charo describes how support made her process of transformation possible:

> From my point of view it's very important to have somebody that supports you and somebody that's there, and somebody who's at a level in life where they're wise, have this understanding. Also that you can say, you know, this person, over here, in this position, they're really like caring about what I do and they're really telling me that I can, I have their support. It's good to always talk to someone who is not gonna judge you, when you tell'em. If that person has not gone through your situation, they'll say "well, I can't relate to what you're going through right now. But I understand it's difficult for you to go through this, and I understand that you have pain. And, you know, if there's anything that I can do to make that pain better, you know, in taking care of you, as well, then I'm here if there's anything I can help with."

For George, this support person is an "instrumental adult" who is "attentive to what the youth are saying" but still able to lead, to "filter through some of the ideas that the youth is giving, and kind of pinpoint some things try to help the youth to pursue them." The need for this person is critical, according to Manolo, because:

> Often, those who seek to change and do really need help, don't know what to do. All they know is the street knowledge. And sometimes a person with street knowledge is looking for help and other people don't want to give it to them.

The motivation to change has been described as an interactional and interpersonal process that can be influenced in a positive way by a clinician or service provider (Miller and Rollnick 1991). For the young people in this study, the positive interaction with a helping person was the experience most often cited as contributing to the decision to change and/or maintaining of the resolve to make a change. The interactions with that helping person often made it possible for the young person to sublimate feelings of doubt, fear and guilt about the lives they were leading into a plan for sustained change towards a positive life. Motivation and sustaining the wish to change for these adolescents was a dynamic process, in which a helping relationship, either in a health and hospital setting, other institutional, or community environment played was of utmost importance.

Albert's transformation involved making up his mind not to end up a lifer like other inmates and examining the life choices that brought him to where he was. Knowing there was an alternative and a corrections officer who took an interest in guiding and teaching him was central to making the decision to change. The expected path for Albert would have been to end up like 56-year old Masalle, a lifer with a heroin habit. His corrections officer, also 56 years of age, showed him that there was "another side of the coin."

> I used to go out and work for the corrections officer, I was his clerk and his lead porter and he gave me the position—I was in charge of 4 other convicts, they were over 300 plus pounds, all straight pintos, been there for years. But I was in charge of them, I had to tell them what to do. I had to tell them where to clean, how to feed. He made me a leader there. He showed me I could, could do this. The C.O. was named Howard and he showed me on the other side of the coin, how good life could be. He would tell me how much he got paid. How his kids were. He owned houses, he had a beautiful wife. He'd leave that place and go home to his wife, he'd take vacations, he was 56 years old also. But he made it and he could go home and just relax. He didn't have to go home and worry about getting shot or worrying about feeding his kids or the next slam that he's going to get in his arm. He showed me you could make it, you know. You could make it out there. He was real caring, he was a good old man and I was stuck in the middle of that, and I chose to want to be like Howard someday.

She Touched My Heart: One Person Can Make a Difference

All the young people identified the role of at least one caring person as having a role in their decision to leave a certain lifestyle, question certain subcultures, and attempt to lead a new, safer life. For many, the nature of that caring relationship was intense, and came from unexpected places, and at times from unfamiliar people.

Whatever the backgrounds of such caring persons, their consideration of the young persons' gender, ethnicity, race, age, learning styles, social background and life experiences contributed to the engagement of the young person in the process of change and developing a helping bond, or therapeutic alliance. Failure to consider these broader factors often leads people to an inaccurate assessment of the motivation or readiness of individual youth. While the young people and their helping adults did not necessarily have to share similar characteristics, backgrounds, or histories of involvement with violence, the relationship (in treatment and otherwise) was enhanced when the helpers were cognizant of these factors. These individuals reached the young people at various stages, sometimes in dramatic but often in imperceptible ways. Often, when the young people were anxious or felt vulnerable, they were the most open to a different way of thinking about their situation and most likely to try on a new way of behaving. However, they often needed a caring relationship to provide a secure base from which they could explore new thoughts and behavior further.

For George, this individual was a Latino pastor and his congregation, who took him under his wing in 1990 after he left the hospital with nowhere to go. The pastor stayed with him for three years during all the ups and downs involved George's emotional, social and moral rehabilitation. His transformation was aided by other lay individuals and professionals:

> It's given me joy, because the people there, they would love me as I was. They was like brothers and sisters. And they would love me. And that helped me get rid of a lot of anger. The love, the loving me the way I was with no expectations, helped. Then, the counseling, and a lot of the classes we used to go to on the dynamics we went through. A lot of that stuff really helped, cause I was able to learn some things and I was able to connect back to some of my beliefs, connect back to some the rules I had forgotten along the way, I believe, and then eventually connect back to how I felt, you know. And I was able to connect all the way back to how I felt when that lady when I was a little four year old boy, made me get out of the yard and called me a bunch of names and made me leave out of her yard from playing with her son. So I had to re-experience all those feelings again, so I would feel the feelings all over again, you know. But this time I wouldn't lash out, or I wouldn't suppress them or anything like that. I would release those feeling in positive outlets and that helped me.

A caring adult made it possible for all the young people interviewed to try something new, a difficult decision given their marginalization. The young people also needed sustained caring and empathy in order to consider any educational interventions during a time of crisis. Before conflict resolution or anger management could be discussed, it was necessary for the young people to believe that they could do something, and that they had the unwavering support of another in this process. And, as many literatures document, there can be no real learning without novelty—that is, without a challenge to or elaboration of what has become familiar. Carl describes the characteristics of those who were able to reach him, paving the way for suggestions on how to encourage change in others:

> You got to be that person who understands the shit that that little kid has been through in order for you to change them. Because if you come up to a little kid giving him advice, you know what I'm saying, about what he can do better and you don't diddly squat about what he's been through, what he did wrong, how he did wrong, how he ever came to that point, and making that decision to do wrong, he won't listen to you. You see what I'm saying? If you didn't know, I wouldn't listen. But if you knew, I heard what you had to say, and it touched me. Because I felt you and I felt like you felt me.

For Carl, one instrumental adult to reach him after his gun-induced disability was his basketball coach, an Irish-American young woman. He was 15 years of age and she gave him

> the encouragement, the strive you know what I'm saying... She touched my heart as soon as I came here. Made sure I had everything I needed. Gave me the foundation. She takes part in what kind of a man I am today.

She touched Carl's heart because, unlike others.

> She extended her hand when I was reaching. I was trained to do shit on my own, so I was one of those kids who wouldn't reach, not unless I knew the hand was out there ready to grab it.

Accustomed to receiving short term or unreliable support from helping professionals, or from other adults in their lives, the young people describe the reluctance to accept a hand without testing. They expressed a need to be convinced that this person will "stick around" before trusting them. At times the young person would act out, display aggression, and even intentionally insult the adult or person being tested. Helping adults need to understand the varied reactions of the young people, and need to examine their own expectations of grateful conduct.

> Sometimes when you're helping people, people don't always welcome, don't react the way we think they should. Sometimes we think that they should react thankful and just be jumping like

little dogs and cats when you are wiggling the bone or the food. And it is not like that, because sometimes people don't show emotion. Sometimes people are very reserved, how they feel, and don't want to let people know.

How the help was offered and the attentiveness of the helper were important in assisting the termination of assaultive behavior. Martin describes the effect of this helper in his life as due to:

The man himself, his skill, and his interest in wanting to work with young people. I knew that he was wanting to work, and by what he did for me, that was one of the most fulfilling things. Just how I feel like I can't repay him 'cause that was the turning point, that was the point that made me wanna go to school. I wasn't gonna go to college, but seeing another lighter side of things was, that was the turning point.

The qualities of the man himself, a psychotherapist and gang intervention specialist, were:

Honesty. Trust. Honesty. Trust. Open. And caring. Must have been the caring, but trust, mostly, because I could tell him the story, and him coming to court with me, just meeting me, and not even saying yeah, he's the one; he's the trigger man. But just saying that I've worked with him, and I know he's capable of handling himself. Putting that trust in me, those are all good qualities.

The observations made by Martin and other youth in the study on the importance of supportive relationships for violence-involved youth is consistent with research findings on positive support with adults in other settings. In school settings, positive support from teachers is associated to greater educational success, and when teachers have positive expectations for students, they perform better (Comer 1998; Eccles et al. 1998; Ford and Harris 1996). If students care about what the teachers think and expect from them, their academic performance and social conduct improve and they care more about doing well in school (Jackson and Davis 2000).

For most of the young people in this study it was the actions of, and not the words spoken by, these individuals that earned their trust. Often, given the seriousness of the precipitating circumstances that led the youth into the hospital, clinic or other intervention facility, the helping professionals took a risk in advocating for a young person and believing in their potential for change. Martin describes how an advisor came to court to testify on his behalf:

> Mr. B started talking saying that, you know, he had done some work with me, and stuff, and sees that I'm capable of handling myself. And the judge went along with it. So I felt like I owed him something. That's what kept me hooked up with him. Like I owe him. That was like the immediate turn around for my life. He came to court. He took the time out, came to court with me, and then, basically saved my ass, basically. It was him.

It would be trust, expressed at another level by Mr. B, that would help Martin move from contemplating change to action. He attributes the influence of trust in:

> both parts because, because he put his trust in me to help, to help me, and to start guiding me. And then he put his trust in me again to relay that message to others. Well, it started because he wanted me to tell my story to a few people. I started doing that, and they started getting me some kind of training, and started doing workshops and talking to other young people about my little situation and how violence is not the route, and that there's other ways to do it, and even if you're in it, that you can get out. There's no saying you can't get out. So, that's kind of how I got hooked up.

> So it was both ways… and, and when I'd seen the reaction on the kids and how they were listening 'cause I was, I was just like them. I know their attention span can go very short when you're listening to some old person who doesn't know what they're talking about. So when a young person comes and talks, they usually tend to listen a little more 'cause they wanna hear what you're gonna say. So both parts were very helpful to me.

Erika remembers a community priest to whom she first confided her difficulties and past problems.

> He was nice. I would sing in his choir, and he would put up with me, and he gave me some clothes 'cause I really did have clothes, but not something that was decent. I trusted him because he was honest. It wasn't a thing of okay, I'm giving you this, and sleep with me or be my girlfriend, or this or that. It was more of a daughter or a father figure. A close father figure.

That's what I would say about it. And then I was still doing, you know, what I was doing. He knew what I was doing 'cause I was honest. We would sit down and talk for hours and hours about like, like my stuff. And he would talk to me and listen.

Erika also acknowledges the influence of her supervisor at work, a woman who would become her mentor,

Because she was very supportive of me. I didn't have no experience, you know. She really gave me a chance. I did a lot of work in the violence prevention coalition, with the committee and she taught me a lot of things, how to operate a computer, how to answer a phone, how to answer a fax, how to dress for executive meetings. I used to go there sometimes in tennis shoes and a crazy dress. It was like a housedress, almost. And I really learned how to dress, how to carry myself about, and she gave me a nice example. She was always classy. I used to like the way she dressed, in nice two-pieces, and the way she would talk, the way she would speak, those proper words. And she taught me how to write business letters and she would cross it out and correct it and re-word it for me. And despite her very busy schedule, she really, really was a big change in my life. She really made a big difference, and when I went to school and I asked her look, I'm gonna need to go at least an hour or two early out of here, she gave me a break and she said, okay. I asked her if I could change my schedule so that I would still work the same amount of hours, but I would work and juggle my schedule. She still helped me and she even went out and, and there was times she would buy me a hamburger. I didn't have no money or anything, and she would buy, take me out for a burger. And she'd take me to meetings and she'd put on her, her jazz, and she's young at heart, you know. She was in her sixties, but she was young at heart. And when it was my graduation, she went, and it really touched me because I even made invitations, flyers on the computer, and I mailed one to my mom and everyone. And none of my family members came, except my husband, a couple of church friends. And of all the people, she went.

From the perspective of the young people in this study, the supportive and instrumental relationships were less dependent on the professional qualifications of the community adults or program staff. What mattered most was the individual's attitude towards them, their commitment, consistency of the messages they taught, and who communicated warmth and caring while setting consistent rules and expectations (McLaughlin 2000).

Not all the individuals who reached and helped the young people make a change were professionals or adults. In Cy's case:

> What made me change is I met this girl. She used to tell me you need to get a job and go back to school. There ain't nothing on the streets. So, I took her advice and went back to school. I got my diploma. So that made me feel good. Then from there, I was just ready to um, blast off and work. After I got my diploma, I wanted to do something with myself. I did two years of community service as soon as I graduated from school. She was there with me the whole time, and stuff like that, when I was having, you know, problems. When I fell off, she lifted me right back up so I can stand on my own two feet. It took me a year and a half to stand on my own two feet.

According to all the young participants, not having such an adult often keeps the young victim and/or perpetrator from making a change:

> It's like they're not really thinking that anybody cares about them, you know. And when you're thinking that nobody really cares for you, that doesn't really help at all. Life doesn't help you to move on and to do something good 'cause you're like, nobody cares, nobody's really showing any type of interest. Nobody's letting me know that they care about me or they wanna something for me or whatever or that they're willing to give me an opportunity. Sometimes even a job can make a difference, you know, like "I'm gonna give you this opportunity and this job because I believe in you." You know? And that can make a difference. And also not getting the job can also make a difference. And you're like "See, I knew I wouldn't get this. I know nobody's gonna give me a chance. Why keep trying?" And so you go back to what's easy. Killing, or whatever. Selling drugs. What's easy.

Having such a helping adult or guide early in your life can help a young person avoid many negative outcomes, if that adult has insight, sincerity and distinguishes bad behavior from intrinsic human worth.

If children or high school students have someone that shows interest, or shows any type of relief for you, it's like 'okay, you're having this hard time, and you're being stubborn or whatever,' and no matter what the behavior is, they're treating you like, "I'm not gonna tolerate this behavior, you know. It's a wrong behavior. But I understand that there's something that's bringing it out, you're not just behaving like this because you're just behaving like this. There must be something and you know, I'm here. If you wanna talk about it, I'm here to talk about it, okay". And there's a lot of teens that are like, 'well, I don't wanna talk to you' 'cause most of them think that you're just, doing your job, you don't really care. You have to kind of show some type of sensitivity where you can relate.

The caring help offered by the instrumental adult was integral to all 20 young people's transformation. Through such a relationship, the consciousness of the young person could be further raised, as the adult helped the young person uncover more information about himself or herself, offering alternative interpretations. The relationship also helped the young people assess how they felt about themselves with respect to their involvement in violence, assisted in values clarification, and provided corrective emotional experiences. Prochaska and DiClemente note that a helping relationship significantly influences the potential for self-liberation—the decision to change and the commitment to act. As a whole, the descriptions offered by the study youth on supportive adult relationships did not differ substantially from research on adolescents in varied developmental settings (Grossman and Rhodes 2002; NRC and IOM 2002). The young people in this study experienced the support of such a relationship many times.

Between the ages of 14 and 17, Charo recalls one such individual:

The assistant principal that helped me, changed a lot for me. I don't know if I was just not looking, but the only person that I thought that cared at that point was him, in high school. I was in high school and the only person I thought that cared, even more than my mom. I thought he really cared about me. He was just there for me, he really encouraged me. He said 'You can do this. You're going through this right now, but you can do it.' I don't know if he had some similar issues when he was younger and he just didn't have anyone to be there for him I don't know. It was like something that just brought peace to me. I don't know. He just believed in me so much, too, that I had to be a totally different person 'cause this was the person that said that I am different, so I have to show him that I am and then I could get myself under control, you know. And it was like [sigh] he just made me feel secure.

Charo describes how the assistant principal was able to affect her, calming her fits of rage.

He was the only one who could calm me down after I got into a fight. So they would always have to find him, wherever he was at, whether he was at lunch, or whether he was in a restaurant having lunch outside school, they'd have to actually look for this man to calm me down 'cause I wouldn't stop fighting until he would just come and he would just hug me and like hold me tight.

His belief in her ability to transcend her anger was unwavering, going beyond her expectations of him and perhaps the limits other assistant principals might impose. He did not lose faith in her:

The anger was still there. Nobody really could stop me. Gym teachers and everybody would hold me and I would be like "Okay. I'm okay. I'm fine. You can let go of me". As soon as they'd let go of me, I'd be back to that person, you know. I'd work my way to where that person was, and then I'd be like "You know what? You think it's over now? It's not over yet. I'm gonna see you again. It's like, I'll see you again. 'cause I'll see you outside. It's okay. I'll find out where you live. It's not over yet. This is not it. You started this, so look, I'm gonna end it. Watch." So they would end up being scared. So they'd end up looking for him, and then when he would finally get there and hold me and tell me "it's okay, it's okay, you know. It's gonna be okay." Then I was fine. He would take me to a separate room and he'd be like "Okay, so what happened here, can you talk to me about it, did you beat her up?" He'd be like, "You know what, I'm gonna find a way to get you out of this one". There were so many that he got me out of that it was difficult for him to just keep getting excuses for the principal. He'd be like, "We're not gonna suspend her because of this and that." The next week I'd be doin' the same thing, and then he'd have to get me out of it again. And so, you know, it was like, I knew I was putting his job at risk, I was putting him in a tough spot 'cause everybody was noticing, too. Everybody in school was noticing like, you know, "how come Mr. M does this to her?" And so, he would just kinda treat it as a situation where, you know, "it's okay, these things happen, you know, you're angry."

Helpers in clinical, other institutional and community or natural settings were instrumental in the young person's transformation, by conveying alternatives to problem behaviors through relaxation, anger management and positive self-statements. One of the young participants describes the voice of her youth worker, "it was so soft and calm, it just made me feel safe, just by talking."

In her study of trauma and recovery, Herman speaks to the connections with other people that are so vital to the process of recovery (Herman 1997). In renewed connections to other people, the survivor re-creates the faculties that were damaged or deformed by a traumatic experience, such as the basic capacity for trust, autonomy, initiative, competence, identity, and intimacy. This need to forge new connections was also true of the young people, many of whom had experienced multiple and severe losses due to various types of violence.

The motivation to change can also be atrophied by a clinician, service provider, or other helping person. Unresponsive, fearful adults, who are unfamiliar with the life circumstances of their clients and who are skeptical of the young person's ability and willingness to make a change, often fail to engage that young person, and many withhold critically needed services. As Manolo and Lita note:

A person asks for help to change and you know what I'm saying, they're ruled as a gang banger. He's bad, he's this and that. Why? They try to look for help and they didn't want to give them no help; now they calling them a bad guy, you know. That's what I seen when people look for help, and that's kinda hard. And sometimes a kid'll mess up one time, and then they'll, they'll give up and lose hope on that kid. And that, really, assassination to a person, because if you think about how many times we, as kids, when we were kids we failed and our parents put up with it. Or sometime when we were coming up, up the ladder on the work force and, an uh, we failed miserably and people put up with us, you know. Sometimes we need to think about doing others the way we want to be treated, or the way we were treated.

Other times, the provider was just too overburdened and hardened. When Albert was released from jail:

They could have held my hand sort of when I got out and lead me in a positive direction but it was like you are out and that's it get out. Go see a probation officer, report to him once a week or once every 2 weeks. When I'd go see him I'd expect that he would help me, like maybe like get me in kind of program where I could get back into the mainstream. Some kind of help. If I did have to change my dress code in school that he would help me with that. You know, that he could maybe give me a job placement but they never did that. When I got out it was, "you go see a probation officer" and he tells you basically "if you fuck up you are going back in come see me in 2 weeks," and he'd kick me out the door and that was it. So, they never did nothing which is understandable, they got about 80 to 200 people in the case load and they don't really have time to sit down and speak to anybody individually.

Accessing networks of services and helping to weave webs of positive relationships for the young person was an important role for the helping adult. For those whose lives were more barren in terms of the supports available and safety nets, the presence of one sustained caregiver and care organizer who stood by the young person over time often made all the difference in helping them attain a safe, new, and good life. And that support might need to extend for years, due to deep and varied issues to address that the young person faced. These relationships often recreated family, or filled in as a surrogate family. These helpers were often described as fathers, mothers, big brothers and sisters. For the young people living in extreme situations of violence, longer-term relationships were important. Indeed, youth mentoring research, on youth facing less extreme situations found that longer-term relationships were associated with better youth outcomes, and that relationships that were terminated quickly were associated with decrements in several indictors of functioning. These research findings underscore the importance of communication, respect as well as long-term stability (Grossman and Rhodes 2002).

It Took a Whole Lot of People: One Person is Not Enough

Although one person made a difference, rarely was one individual alone able to provide the caring, education, and guidance required over time to assist the young person through the injury or traumatic event or meet all his or her needs as he or she was reintegrated into the community. For example, in Charo's situation, although the assistant principal cared for her, he would not be the one to teach her the skills and provide the services she needed to deal with the patterns of street violence and domestic violence in her life. That help came from an intervention worker. "He cared for me, but she, she taught me."

The need for help from multiple sources was especially true for the young people who had the least supports in their lives—especially those who were homeless, had the weakest family structure, lived in the neighborhoods that were the most resource deprived. All of these youth identified a series of individuals who helped them move toward a prosocial path. These individuals came from various settings and played varying roles in providing a network of support that many adolescents and adults take for granted, but which was new for these youth. Carl attributes his development to many individuals:

> people in the recreation department. It was some of the nurses. They definitely didn't inspire me, but they helped me. They supported me in any decision I made. Teachers in school. There are certain people that you come close to and those are the people that you can trust with your deepest feelings. And they help you with your problems whatever way is best.

And some of these individuals Carl was not fond of, especially:

> One of my health teachers, her name was Carolyn. She's a teacher. I really hated her guts, but no matter how much I hated her she didn't give up on me. You know what I am saying. She kept punishing me, she kept make sure I was doing what I could to be doing. So I applied and she got me in here, I guess she pulled some strings quick, quicker then most kids would get in here. Why did I hate her? Cause she [pause] I don't know, I hated everyone. It wasn't like she made a difference.

Because of her referral to a specialized school and follow-through, this schoolteacher would enable Carl to continue his schooling uninterrupted, minimizing further interruptions due to medical conditions and transportation barriers. The teacher also held Carl accountable, providing delayed parenting, structure, expectations, and consistency. Carl was 15 years of age at the time.

How He Overcame, It Impressed Me: The Importance of Role Models

The young people mentioned adults who they looked up to and wanted to emulate as important in their transformation. These individuals were often the instrumental adults who took an interest in them and helped guide them along their way.

Albert saw his corrections officer as his role model along with other, older, wise men he met in and outside of jail, from whom he would learn.

I would meet a lot of older people and then they were real educated, real smart and they would guide me under their wing. They wouldn't have paid attention to nobody else. But they would like me. They would like the other youngsters, but they would like me. They knew that I wanted to learn something. You know, they taught me. I remember them telling me "why do you got two ears and one mouth? And then I was stuck on stupid like "what are you talking about?" "Well, why do you got two ears and one mouth, youngster?" You know, that was the first question they asked me and I said "well, I guess to hear better" and they said, "No. In order to acquire knowledge, wisdom, and understanding, it takes a lifetime of listening when one prefers to speak." They taught me to always listen. Just take the time to listen. That's how you are going to learn. You know a lot of us we would get impatient and be get jumpy a lot of the other youngsters they didn't have time to sit down and learn anything from older people. Well, they see that I did and I wanted to learn.

All the participants had at least one role model of the same race and/or ethnicity, gender and life circumstance to look up to, and to help them move along their journey of change. For many of the young people, male and female alike, one of their role models was a mother or grandmother. Erika recounts:

Learned a lot from my grandmother. She's a hard worker. She raised my mom by herself, and she, she cleaned houses, and do yard sales, sell tamales, cater, do a lot of things. And I learned a lot of things from her, the hardworking. And she always would say "go to school. Don't be ignorant. Go to school. That way you don't be ignorant, 'cause when you be ignorant, you get a cheap job and you gotta put up with a lot of stuff."

Others mentioned siblings or other relatives who did not succumb to the life and had the courage to be positive. Carl's role model growing up was his uncle, who went to a private, prestigious university on a football scholarship.

I wanted to be like my uncle, my mother's kid brother, and go to college on an athletic scholarship. He was the only male I knew in the neighborhood who hadn't been shot. Every kid on my street had been. Some of them were killed. Even when I was selling drugs and doing all that. I always went to school. I always got A's and B's, you know, 'cause it was like my parents, well my mother and my grandmother and my grandfather, they always gave me initiative to do well in school, giving me so much amount of money if I got A's and B's, so like I always had the initiative. But then, once I got mature, the initiative was success, you know what I'm saying? The initiative was following my uncle's footsteps and going to college playing ball.

Still others mentioned their children as role models. Cy states,

My little stepson's my role model too, because he always be making sure that he's bright, you know. He likes to ask a lotta questions, and he's something else. Well, the way he carries himself. He's mature. He's seven years old. He's mature for seven years old, I guess 'cause the school that he going to, the school teaches him so much. He knows so much. He knows things that we don't know. Matter of fact, he teaches us some things. There ain't nothing wrong with that. He teaches us some things that we don't know.

Contemporary and historical figures such as Martin Luther King, Malcolm X, and specific authors were also cited as role models, offering "righteous" justifications for walking away from potential violence. These role models were individuals who overcame adversities to which the young people could relate.

For both Flaco and Andrea, the author Luis Rodriguez was cited as a role model, because of the parallels in his life and the challenges he faced growing up in and out of a gang in Los Angeles, chronicled in his book, *Always Running.* Although the book

is talkin' about the gangs in L.A., that book, when I read it, it reminds me of the gangs out here. It talks about the Latin Kings, like the disciples and all that stuff, the way they are run. It's almost the same over here with the kings, but over there is badder than over here. I could get to, read that book and tell people about the book.

For Andrea, the book was important at a time when she, too, had decided to stop running. Having relocated to Boston, and in hiding, she felt that the book offered a road map to a better life.

Delbert, like many of the young participants, saw

Dr. King was a good role model for me, and Gandhi, because they, they had their conscience and they saw that changes could be made without violence. And I think it's the same thing. I mean, I think that sometimes you have to do what you have to do to make changes, but you can do a lot of it without hurtin' somebody or puttin' somebody else down, and I guess King saw this, Dr. King saw this. And so did Gandhi. I mean, Gandhi said 'why are we fighting over salt when we have the whole ocean here?' You just need to find different alternatives to different problems. Dr. King also, he's one of the great leaders. I mean, he would have dogs, and be hit with hoses waters and tear gas, and my man marched on, marched on. I mean, if people just remembered that, if people just remembered how many, how much trouble, you know, people went through for them, you know, instead of taking so much stuff for granted, it would be so good.

Delbert's observations were consistent with recommendations offered by clinicians who work with urban youth, and who report that the philosophy emphasized by Martin Luther King is helpful with angry youth who are victims or who have witnessed interpersonal violence (Ammerman and Hersen 1997,47). According to Kingian philosophy, the act of forgiving must always be initiated by the person who has been wronged, and his philosophy encourages empowerment, making plans and building strategies for future safety, lifting the burden when justice is not a possibility (King 1963, 49-57; Ammerman and Hersen 1997,476).

Theories on the potential protective mechanisms of ethnic culture in the face of risk factors for violence suggest that ethnic cultures provide a range of norms and values that influence behavior and social interactions in the face of stress. They provide a way of interpreting reality, guiding how young people are socialized to overcome social and economic obstacles (Hill et al. 1994). Positive self-reference (and other group) identity can counteract racist and other negative messages from the mainstream culture, mediate involvement in violence in the face of risk experiences, and reduce risk for other self-destructive behavior (Holinger et al. 1994). For the young people in this study, positive ethnic role models and champions from their everyday life and throughout history similarly provided a standard, a range of norms and values which influenced their behavior and social interactions as they strove to make a sustained change in their lives. The ways in which their heroes and heroines acted in the face of stress and repeated insults, the ways in which they interpreted reality and sought to change it served as sources of inspiration for the young people as they sought to overcome the many personal, social and economic obstacles. Historical role models often provided a long view of social as well as individual change:

> I mean, history does have to tie in with violence prevention. And I think the two should merge because you just can't have violence prevention and not educate. You have to have your history, and you have to have your prevention, 'cause in order to see your future, you gotta understand your past.

Role models who had both been in and transcended a violent life were often mentioned as pivotal in the young people's transformation, although not to the exclusion of more mainstream role model choices. George describes one of his role models, Felipe, who

> was in a wheelchair; he was a Chicano. He worked with a project called U-Turn, and one day I seen him in a magazine article which was called Barrio Warrior. And I seen him in there, he was getting a diploma, and in the chair. And one day he came to the church, and he spoke and his testimony, how he overcame, it impressed me, you know. I liked what he was doing.

All the young women in the study identified as role models professional women, of varied race and ethnicity, they met in the hospital, health and social welfare programs among their role models. Lulu remembers her sexual abuse counselor with whom she could speak openly and a person she would later seek to emulate, by becoming a peer counselor. Andrea admired a female physician and academic dean who had power and used it to help others. Ruby mentioned her aunt who had a beauty parlor and was a very good businesswoman, and Erika looked up to her supervisor, a director at the Los Angeles County Board of Health:

> She was a great inspiration in my life 'cause she showed me how to dress, how to conduct my self. And she wouldn't tell me anything, but just give her living example. Because sometimes you can tell people, but if you're not living it... folks look at your lifestyle. They don't even look at your mouth, they look at your lifestyle. She was my role model. She was stable. She was married, and even though her husband was ill, she wasn't wild or nothing. She was stable, and she was more of a mother figure. She was also very professional, very smart, conducted business, you know. She conducted business, but not the way

businessmen do, she wasn't aggressive and muscular. She was still feminine, but she was very smart. She was smart in business, like men do. And she was patient with me, and supportive of me. I really admire that.

The admiration felt towards notable and everyday women who had struggled and transcended echoed throughout the stories of the young women:

I admire certain women that have been through a lot. They themselves know what it is to be on drugs, to be on the street, to be a wayward child, to be abused and everything. And somehow, they have emerged and become great businesswomen, great church leaders, organizing things for the young people, as well as the church. Because a lot of times, you know, the leader or pastor is there, but it also depends on his members, what they do. And I look at that.

The stories of the young women suggest that the indirect gender socialization learned from these women leaders was important to helping leave violence victimization and perpetration behind. These women made them aware of the gendered worlds of family work and civic life they must operate in, focusing on strengthening their pride and identity as strong and positive young women. The influence of these many women persisted as the young women forged and maintained a new, productive and positive life path.

They Were Real: Peer Role Models Were Critical

Peer help, both supportive and critical, was a powerful vehicle to advance change for almost all the participants. The positive peer group or individual provided the young people with mutual friendships that were not based on performance, image, reputation or maintenance of a false self. As adolescents, many of the participants had banded together in negative street groups in order to feel a sense of belonging, they would develop intense new loyalties to these pro-social peers as they rebuilt their lives.

Describing the peer group role models who touched their lives, the young people said it was clear that many of them had lived through similar life circumstances. They were credible role models and helpers, for these peers had been outside the social compact, like them, and they had successfully made the transition to a better life. Andres explains how a group of peers helped him, at age 17, along his path of change:

> Kids from out of the ghetto, these were real. These weren't no fake punks or nothing like that. I've met a lot of them before in my life and I can smell them out. I can smell them out. *[laugh]* So it was like, I got to know them. Basically, I got to know them, and so I saw that they were cool, you know, and I liked what they were doing, so, you know, that was one way out, to rectify my wrongs.

For some of the young participants, forming part of a peer group focused on interpersonal relationships provided an opportunity to practice new behaviors. The peer group offered empathy, while also providing a group that was savvy about street life, that offered a direct challenge and that spoke on their terms. Such interactions allowed the young people the opportunity to discuss their difficult behaviors, and through the understanding and resolution of conflict, allowed for insight and change to occur. Their peers served as role models on how problem situations can be overcome, assessing the medical, ethical, legal, short- and long-term implications of choices and conducts from a young perspective.

> You make a bigger impact on kids if you use their peers, even if they're younger than you. You see, well, he got outta this, and he's like me, so I guess I can do it, too. I mean, especially when you hear the other person's story. If the story impacts you, then you be like, "yo, my story's kinda similar to that and you'd, how'd you do this? How'd you get out?" And they start listenin' to you. [But that young person] has got to be that person who has been through the same shit that that little kid has been through in order for you to change them.

The role of other peers in the transformation of the young people in the study is consistent with rehabilitation precepts underlying the medical and psychosocial rehabilitation of the disabled, in which peer counseling (albeit largely among adults) plays a central function. The role of other peers is also concordant with the dynamics of Positive Peer Culture models, which use an adult-guided, youth-run small group treatment approach (Harstad 1976). The emphasis on the peer group as the primary vehicle for helping troubled youths is also consistent with the symbolic interactionist theory of the self as a product of interaction with significant others in groups (Mead 1934). The young role models created a peer "climate for change," enhancing the young persons' amenability to treatment and therapeutic change.

The themes on peer help that surface from the stories are congruent with recommended treatment strategies for adolescent assault victims. According to an American Academy of Pediatrics report (1996), innovative strategies should also be based on the developmental needs of adolescents, those "for middle adolescents must involve peers, and those for late adolescents must respect their growing autonomy."

The use of young African American men who have been injured or involved in violent episodes and have been trained and encouraged to serve as agents of change has been advocated by Rich in efforts to curb the phenomenon of recurrent violence. According to Rich, young men (and those who have avoided violence in similar contexts) may be uniquely qualified to understand the "underlying logic to some violence, which stems from the context in which these young men live from day to day and the way in which it shapes their thinking" (Rich and Stone 1994). They can offer reasonable and safe responses to confrontation, taking into account the social environment in which they live, understanding the logic and practice of applied violence prevention.

Victims of relationship violence, regardless of the level of trauma, rarely seek professional help. The majority of young women whose experience fits the legal definition of rape do not identify themselves as rape victims, and like many of their adult counterparts, do not report the incident to police. If an adolescent girl does tell someone about the incident, she is most likely to tell a friend. If help is sought, it is more likely that the young person will seek that help from friends (Roscoe and Kelsey 1986). Although Charo did not receive help from peers in order to directly address the relationship violence she was experiencing, partly due to the segregation of domestic from street violence intervention programs, she recommends the use of peers in both intervention efforts and in prevention programs:

> I talk to some of the teens and they're like, "how old are you?" And I'm like, "I'm twenty-one." And they go, "Oh, and do you have any children?" 'cause they kinda ask you all these questions, you know. And I do intakes with them and I'm like, "feel free to ask me whatever you wanna ask me." So I'm doin' the intakes and askin' them about their life, and their childhood, and so on, and some of them ask me, "do you have any children? How old are you?" And, I'm like, "I'm twenty-one, and I have two children" and they kinda like feel at ease just hearing that I have two children, a six-year-old and a four-year-old. They kinda add it all up... "Oh, that means you had your daughter when you was like fifteen or something?" I'm like, "yeah." They go, "Wow! That means you know how I feel." And so we talk about those things and they kinda like open up, at that point, it kinda like makes'em feel at ease a little.

The advantage of using indigenous workers has been well documented in the research literature. The role and settings in which natural helpers have functioned as health workers has been varied and spanned a spectrum of health issues. Where human or economic resources are scarce or unlikely to work with selected groups, paraprofessionals have provided an alternative, and are no less (and at times more) effective than professionals in fulfilling the tasks (Durlak 1979). Often belonging to the community that the intervention targets, they are often seen as "insiders" and serve to minimize the social distance between the agents and the targets of change. Indigenous workers often understand the implications of the social context on individual behaviors and the mentality of the individuals affected. The emphasis on natural helpers, collaboration, and organization is compatible with theories of empowerment, community psychology and community organizing.

A Way to Rectify My Wrongs: Involvement in Social Action

All of the participants in the study felt called upon to engage in a wider world as part of their process of change. The resolution of their involvement with and victimization by violence was not limited to transformation within the confines of their personal lives. Many of the young people identified a social, policy and economic dimension to their violent situation and believed that they could transform the meaning of their personal experience by making it the basis for social action and change. The social action undertaken by the young people took many forms, from one-to-one counseling and peer mentoring of other peers, to involvement in educational, political or community building efforts to prevent others from being victimized and becoming perpetrators. They also participated in broader efforts to address the generative social and economic causes of violence. Much of the activity and social actions undertaken by the young participants were directed at improving the life chances, positive options, and mindset of their peers and younger children. They often sought to provide caring and protective environments that had not been extended to them.

Writing about female survivors of rape, Herman describes the power of social action as a transformative force for a trauma survivor. It is "a source of power that draws upon her own initiative, energy, and resourcefulness but that magnifies these qualities far beyond her own capacities. It offers an alliance with others based on cooperation and shared purpose. Participation in organized, demanding social efforts calls upon the survivor's most mature and adaptive strategies of patience, anticipation altruism and honor" (Herman 1997, 207). As both victim and perpetrator, Erika experienced a similar effect as she participated in social actions. At age 16, Erika would be intrigued by a church, which would serve to bring out the best in her and where she would gain a connection with the best in others.

> They would sit there and feed folks all morning, like from seven 'til one o'clock. And it's be scorching hot and you could just see the sweat and there were *[sigh]*, and um, you know, I just felt the need to wanna go down there and help. When I went down there, I felt useful, and that's something that I had not felt in a long time because I had not been going to school. I had not been working or anything. I had to just hang out, and hang out with a bunch of folks that do drugs. I, I didn't do drugs. I used to drink, a lot. But they did drugs, and as I look at it now, if I would have stayed a little longer, I would have been hooked on drugs big time. 'cause those people were using drugs. They had lost, lights getting cut off, and extreme child abuse. You know, talking about, not child abuse, but child neglect in the sense of no water, no clean clothes, no food, no nothing.

Through similar community activities, the young people were able to transcend the boundaries of their particular time and place, the limitations of their current "negative" peer group. They attained a feeling of participation in an order of creation and social solidarity that transcended their own ordinary and violent reality. They felt part of something larger.

When Sandy was shot at age 12, she had difficulty coming to terms with the trauma she suffered, and her immobility. "I woke up in the hospital the next day, and they told me I had got shot and I was gonna be paralyzed for the rest of my life. I didn't believe it so I tried getting out of bed. And I fell." Part of her recovery and the means of transcending the violence around her was getting involved in

> my own community. Probably because I got shot. I would see on TV a lot of people getting shot, especially innocent kids. And then when I got shot that's when I got to where I wanted to start to do something about it. At first my friends were supporting me, then it was like "Why do you want to stop the violence? That's the way of life." But then it happened to me. That's why I am with this attitude: do whatever you gotta do to help my community. What I like is to go out and take off the graffiti.

Through service to others, the young people were able to enrich their own lives and repair an often stigmatized sense of self. As Albert expressed:

What benefits me is the smile I get from the kids when they see me, and I could go all up into any school that I work in and all the kids jump on me, and they are all over, "hi how are you doing?" They just want to be all over you and are happy to see you. You know, you feel welcome there and it's good see that they accept me there. They know that I'm expressing a positive message and they are accepting it and they are absorbing it and it makes me happy to when a kid come up to me and he'll change his dress and he'll talk to me about getting more involved school or stuff like that. Seeing a change, that is what makes me happy.

Lulu echoes a similar sense of satisfaction with her job as a youth counselor,

To this day I'm not rich, you know. And I don't intend to get rich. My richness is to see young people get their lives changed, that this young person that's in trouble, classified, or statistically or already labeled as a no-good or you're-gonna-die person, has a life change and turns around, turns around and does something with their lives. That's my greatest accomplishment, my greatest richness.

The participation of the young people in this study in a range of service activities demonstrates that Reissman's "helper principle" also applied to their experience of change. According to this theory, the individual helping others is also seen to receive direct benefits (Reissman 1965). Helping others change their perceptions about violence helped the young participants in their own rehabilitation, hastened that process along. Between the ages of 16 and 17, Charo found that helping other "high-risk" youth enabled her to stay in control of her own anger and further her ability to prevent or de-escalate situations in which she was likely to lose control.

I was trying to just make things better for me as well as help other people so they don't have to be in situations I got myself into a lot. I worked with teens and I thought it would be helpful for me, as well, going through what I was going through. I was working. I was doing everything. But I was also going through my experience....

On my way home I would think about how I could help these people, 'cause I had already started changing myself. I started some changes as to where I wasn't getting into fights. I had my daughter and I felt I had to change everything because of her and for myself in the long run. So I used to write things down and think what can I do to make things better and get educated for them so they would stop the violence. I didn't want these kids to have to go the same way, they were young, like 12 years old, 10.

In youth violence prevention we did activities as to where we stopped them from hanging in the streets, something that would be educating for them, like teaching them how to deal with their anger. This violence prevention thing was helping me do my job better, as a teen counselor. It helped me, and it was helpful to them in the way we could talk to them about how to think before getting violent, about teen violence and people just getting killed for stupid reasons 'cause then you end up afterwards where sometimes it's too late—you realize you just killed somebody and it was over something stupid. It's like, what's going on here? We tried to do activities where we could kinda stop that from happening, or limit the situation, to limit where it didn't have to get to this point where it got out of control. We would play a role and we could help each other, you know, kinda figure some other way to do it.

Telling the Truth: The Need to Speak Out

A common trait of the social action efforts undertaken by the young people was their dedication to raising public awareness among younger children, their peers, and adults. Speaking about both their victimization and their perpetration, unspeakable acts, the young people hoped that this would help others. For Martin, as for the other young participants, "telling the truth" was an important part of the success of his transformation process:

Why did it work? It was reality. It wasn't an overnight thing. It worked because I was able to tell my story, tell the truth, and to really see that I was giving some kind of help to somebody else when I told somebody else young, and I told'em the truth, and to see them ask questions and wanna be curious. That was probably one of the things that made it work for me, and that made me wanna keep doin' it.

By retelling their stories, and expressing their challenges and difficulties, the youth sustained the process of change and helped them deal with the natural oscillatory course of change. Albert reckons that what helped him stay positive and sustain his decision to change was:

> This job actually. It helped me a lot cause when I gotten out mentally I had decided I wanted to change I wanted to grow, I wanted to just snap but physically I wasn't really ready. So doing what I do now I made it a lot easier for me. You know I was able to go out and express myself and talk about things.

By speaking out, most of the young people were able to reconstruct the stories of their involvement in violence formed under repeated, inescapable abuse, and to trace with increasing clarity the pathways from victim to perpetrator, to hospital patient or trauma victim to survivor and activist. Through speaking out and by hearing the stories of others, they could also gauge how far they had come. These experiences lend themselves to interpretation, and through their narrative construction of events they vindicated the personal choices made along the way (Mishler 1984, 1986). Among such choices was deciding not to seek revenge, not to see oneself as a hero, better ways of dealing with their anger, and navigating a safe return to community. As expressed by one of the young participants:

> And you let out your experience, and you hear other people, and you don't feel alone anymore… And that's what the teen program did for me, I was beginning to feel, I didn't feel alone anymore. I felt good about myself. I was coming on TV, TV shows, newspaper articles, and not because I want to be a celebrity or nothing like that, but I was able to give up and I seen a lot of girls would identify with me, and I felt like I wasn't alone. And sometimes you would go to juvenile halls and you would hear worse cases that make you feel grateful, and oh well, nothing happened to you compared to this person 'cause this person's talking about losing their virginity by their father, abused by their brother, their sister, their this and that. And I was like *[sigh]*, I done had it compared to you.

> It was important to hear that, to hear those stories because that way when you have a problem, you feel like you're the only one in the world that has it, and when you get to hear that other people have it, have the same problem, you, you feel like you're not the only one. And sometimes that helps you to get help, and it really, really helped. It really impacted me when I went to a conference sponsored by the county supervisor and a couple

black Congresswomen at the juvenile hall where I was at. And it was like me going back where I was at. I was 17... And it really just tripped me out to have the opportunity to go back where I've been *[held the year before when she was 16]* and tell...'cause there was girls that were in custody there.

Sharing this experience with others was often a precondition for the restoration or acquisition of a sense of a meaningful world and their place within that world. The people in whom the young people confided could be the individuals closest to them, a peer group, or the larger community. The responses received from these individuals and the larger community had a powerful influence on the ultimate resolution of the trauma. In victim treatment models, it is well understood that:

> Restoration of the breach between the traumatized person and the community depends, first, upon public acknowledgement of the traumatic event, and second, upon some form of community action. Once it is publicly recognized that a person has been harmed, the community must take action to assign responsibility for the harm and repair the injury. These two responses— recognition and restitution—are necessary to rebuild the survivor's sense of order and justice (Herman 1997, 70).

The public space in which to tell their stories was circumscribed for these young people, as their victimization was often inextricably tied to acts of perpetration, a division upon which victim services ideology is predicated, and which defines which victims are "worthy" of public support. Erika describes how she felt as she began to speak in community settings when she was 16 years old. Although liberatory, speaking out was an often difficult and painful process.

> It dawned on me that, how grown people, when you do bad things, look at you like trash. And after that it stuck on me for months, and I didn't know how to react to it, I didn't want people to look at me as trash. And some times you have to try hard because some times you have a bad record, or some times you have a bad rep *[reputation]*, or you come from a inner-city place. And you have to try hard to prove yourself to, to society that you can do, that you're just as good as they.

There were limited venues available to the young people to explore the circumstances that led to and from their violence victimization and perpetration. The opportunities to speak frankly with health workers were few, and social workers were suspect because revealing too much might lead to Department of Social Services intervening against their families, or by removing their own children. The young people were also largely unable to access the legal system for redress, for they were disadvantaged by the systematic legal bias and the institutional discrimination against them. They were also very fearful of the implications of speaking with law enforcement in terms of their own outstanding warrants, probation status, involvement in the precipitating circumstances, and being perceived as a "snitch." Only the shootings of José and Sandy were brought to trial, and in chronicling their stories, the verdicts did not give them the sense of redress that acceptance of their "truth telling" did in community. In fact, the trials were not mentioned in the interviews at all. As José stated, the man who was put away for shooting him was not so different from him. In other circumstances it could have been José who would have been the defendant. Sandy was shot by one of her neighbors; she was well acquainted with and was even fond of some of the family members of the man who shot her.

Accessing services and seeking legal redress often depended on obscuring the sequence of events that led to injury and violence. Speaking about and reconstructing the events, processes, and personalities that led the young people to and away from violence was liberating and necessary.

Fate Has Given Me a Second Chance: Intervention by a Higher Power

Confrontations with the relentless pressures of life often force a dialogue with (or denial of) issues of spirituality and of faith. For the young people in the study, such confrontations often occurred at very young ages and in extreme circumstances. Both the mysteries and miseries of life they encountered led many, at times, to seek a higher, non-secular meaning and purpose to such events. They raised issues of personal identity, (in)significance of life, and the fundamental aloneness with which these issues must be ultimately met.

> I'm happy that I did, you know, transcend from one place to another. And I'm doing good. It makes feel good that I didn't die, you know. The thing that would most trouble me is if I would died and I didn't have a place, you know, didn't have no type of spirituality. I believe in the afterlife, stuff like that, and the resurrection. And I had always heard that stuff when I was little, so if I would have died, you know—man, you know. I would have that thought. Since I never been dead, but being alive knowing what I know, I've always said that I'm glad that

I'm alive that I can account for certain things for my spirituality before I die.

Many of the young participants were fully cognizant that their lives and traumatic experiences could have been far worse, and that they could be injured more severely or could have died, if luck or fate had not spared them. At 17, José was rendered a quadriplegic, only able to move the upper part of his neck, yet he would describe this event as fate giving him a "second chance."

Many ascribed this luck to divine intervention, and identified a religious dimension to being able to survive their violent situation and involvement. Andres expressed his gratitude:

I'm grateful, I'm grateful that the Lord was kind enough to let me live. Other people who I knew took the bullet, they took the bullet and not me. Basically, he spared me, he spared me for something better, something.

Others transformed the meaning of their personal experience by making this spiritual dimension the basis for personal change. Carl found solace in prayer at a time when he would not allow anyone to get close to him. "I felt like God was the only one that knew the hell I was going through when I was going through it. I was talking to him asking him to help me give me strength through the whole time." George found that "Christianity helped me to change the way I thought. It renewed me in my mind." In looking back at her transformation over a period of one and a half years when interviewed at 17, Erika reflects on her process of transformation:

And I look at myself, I'm a professional. Even if it's nothing to some people, it is something to me 'cause I know how much it took. And I'll never forget where God brought me from, how I was a dropout, how I was a criminal element, how I was a sixteen-year old out of a fatherless house, I don't have my father's name, never did. And I'll never forget how God brought me from nothing, into being something. And that's the main thing I look at myself.

In studies of self-changers, Prochaska and DiClemente note that many attribute their process of change to a mysterious, spontaneous recovery, giving disproportional weight to spiritual or mystic explanations, noting that self-change follows the same processes that are involved in successful change within therapy-assisted interventions.

While also true of the study participant's journeys, it is also evident that all claims to knowledge must ultimately make a "leap of faith" and retreat to basic precepts that cannot themselves be rationally defended.

Like trauma survivors, the young people in this study who "recovered" and who were able to acquire a positive future orientation and change their behavior all discovered some meaning of their experience, whether it was secular or spiritual, as part of transcending and change. If one looks at the odds of their overcoming such barriers and problems, the most reasonable deduction is that they would not make it, underscoring how such matters, as well as the academic investigation of such processes, are never a simple contest between pure or scientific reason and blind unquestioning faith.

Building a Conscience: **The Need for a Moral Compass**

The development of a conscience was described as integral to helping the young people make the change. Albert describes the incremental effect of his "building a conscience" upon his transformation. "I started to care about the accident that I had took in the past, my family, the job." Delbert identifies the love of family as the conscience for one of his friends. He describes how one young man was able to turn himself around because of his "love for his family, and I think that's where his conscience was all that time. I think one day he woke up and he was just like, you know something? I am really hurting the people that I love. And he woke up and he was just like, I think it's time to quit."

A conscience was described by the young people as a moral compass to guide the young people during times they feel like lashing out. It is critical to keep oneself and others safe. As one of the young people describes it:

> Today, even when somebody cuts me off, I don't like to swear at people and stuff 'cause I've been hurt before, you know, where people are puttin' me down and tellin' me I'm no good and stuff, and I hate that feeling, so why would you do it to somebody else? Your conscience tells you this ain't even cool. You shouldn't be doin' this to people. You shouldn't be doin' this to things, to animals, to whatever. Your conscience is there to back you up.

According to the young participants, a conscience can expand possible responses to the narrow range of socially proscribed feelings and responses expected of young minority males. Emmanuel believes that:

Society, today, has basically said that young males, especially minority males, are allowed to show two types of emotions—anger and happiness. Forget about sorrow, sadness, or fear. We're not allowed to show those types of emotions. That's where your conscience comes in 'cause, we act a lot, these days, without thinking. And we would go out and steal something, you know, beat somebody up, and we never think about the consequences. If we beat somebody up, they could retaliate and come back and kill me. We don't think about that stuff! I'm glad I have my conscience 'cause I always think about my actions before I do... you know. And that's helped me a lot.

A conscience is something that can be acquired, fostered, and revived. It is a necessary part of making a change. According to Delbert, "if you lack a conscience, I think that you're one of the most dangerous people out there" because you are likely to hurt yourself and others.

In describing their work with young people, one of the goals, according to Delbert, is to

Try to give 'em a conscience. You try to find something in their life, something. See, I know there's at least two things in their life that actually has a meaning to them—two people, two objects, two something that has meaning to them. If you can tie this thing, this person, this object into their way of life and show them that the actions that they do will affect this thing, then they slowly gain that conscience. If their life is evolved around their girlfriend or their mother, you're like, you know how much you're hurtin' your mother by doin' this? and you show 'em. Don't just tell 'em. You show them, you show them that their actions are hurtin' this person, they start thinkin', they be like, "yo, he's right."

George speaks to the resumption, "connecting back" to the values he held as a child but which were submerged by his will and duty to survive and prosper in a context of everyday violence. As with Martin and other young people whose involvement as aggressor was more pronounced, the abstract, universalist principles of justice, fairness and equality taught in school and the "Christian values" learned at home were supplanted or mediated by concrete, personal, contextual considerations and relationships. Others refer the "connecting back" as remembering one's conscience, and describe having had a "double mind:"

My attitude was Do or Die, a mentality of Do or Die, you know live or die; I don't care. That's the kind of attitude that people have when they get in a gang. That's the code; that's what you're taught. Get money, get with your bitch. That's another one of the mentalities of gangs. So a lot of gangs sell drugs, commit robbery, crimes and stuff like that trying to get rich. But when I was in a gang, I always wanted to be something else, too. I had a double mind, I wanted to be with what the gang was doing and also I wanted to be a family person, I wanted to have a job, a business was what I wanted. I wanted to have a business, a home, a family and stuff like that. But I still wanted the gang to like me.

The building of a conscience or connecting back to one's values at times came with great personal cost. In describing their own and others' transformations, many participants expressed a sense of guilt. Many recalled their friends from the old days who did not make it and who had protected them in the past:

Nobody would mess with me, though. They be like, no, yo, that's Taylor and Darryl's boy, you can't mess with him. So, they had my back, no matter what. So I wasn't scared of nobody. Now, Darryl's locked up, and Taylor's locked up, too.

The guilt could be especially pronounced among the young people who had hurt, witnessed the suffering, or taken the life of others. Emmanuel commented on the transformation of one young man in his peer group and the severe burden of conscience he had to carry, when at the age of 16, the young man began to realize and care deeply about "the dirt" he had done.

He couldn't give back that he'd taken from society, you know. But he had to try. I mean, he moved out of his negative lifestyle, and he came to a different place, and he was trying to give back what he took. And I commend him for that 'cause not a lot of people can do that. Not a lot of people can live with the stuff that he did and live in a sound mind with it. I know he feels guilty, too.

Blaming Others for Your Problems Will Not Help You Solve Them: Personal and Social Responsibility

Cy describes how a sense of responsibility towards his child and wife helped to keep him "straight" and moving towards a positive life. Personal and social responsibility provided a structure and a set of rules to contain him.

> It's so easy to turn back when you don't got no structure in your life, no responsibility, and you just got all that free time. It's so easy. But when you got, you know, your time filled up, married, responsibility, I don't even got time to think about all that. My minds on jobs and takin' care of my family now. But I know if I wasn't married or have a stepson, I probably be right back out there. It's so easy.

Many of the young participants were leaders of their respective groups, and they describe their feelings of responsibility for influencing others in negative ways. They struggle with questions of moral judgment, feelings of guilt and shame for having chosen to be negative influencers, even if the decision was made in contexts with extremely limited choice.

> And sometimes that makes me feel bad, cause all that time I had the authority back then to lead those guys, right? We could have played basketball, played football, did anything other than go and gang bang and commit crimes. But now some of those same guys that I'm counseling tell me "why did you tell us that back then?" And so that kind of keeps me in thought, those types of questions.

Over time, the young people arrived at a reasonable assessment of their conduct, getting beyond the anger and finding a balance between unrealistic guilt and denial of all moral responsibility. Knowing the limits of personal responsibility and acting within those limits was empowering, both for those who were victimized and those who also took a more active role in perpetration. As José summed up, this realization was often tied to a resolution of anger:

> Anger is a natural emotion but it won't do you any good to let it build up inside and not confront or deal with your problems. Anger will make you blame others for your troubles. You hear people all the time or maybe you hear yourself blaming society, the police, or other people for your problems. But blaming others for your problems will not help you solve them. To get

what you want you have to be able to look honestly at yourself
and see what you are doing that is either helping you or is
making it harder for you to succeed. And then—this is the
hardest part—you have to have the courage it takes to make a
change.

In coming to terms with issues of guilt, and finding the right balance
between personal and social responsibility for their actions, the young
people needed the help of others who were cognizant of the moral
complexities of extreme situations and willing to recognize that such
events had occurred. These individuals were also able to suspend their
preconceived judgments, and could bear witness to their tale. Taking on
this role was not easy. Relations of the young people towards each other,
although understandable, were often deeply troubling and disturbing.
Those individuals who assisted the young people along their trajectory of
change were consistently mentioned as playing a key role in the further
exploration of how their problems and behavior affects their community.
Helping individuals assisted in the further development of empathy, in
the "building of a conscience," and in reaching a fair attribution of
responsibility. However, technical neutrality as a helping person was not
the same as moral neutrality, and thinking about both individual practices
and cultural institutions in moral and ethical terms was critical. For the
young people most troubled by past actions, blanket absolutions or
justifications did not help them move beyond this stage.
This process of helping the young people arrive at a fair
attribution/internalization of responsibility poses a challenge for helpers,
program planners, and researchers. The challenge remains to articulate a
standard or various standards on the beginnings of moral and ethical
reflection on everyday and interpersonal violence that takes into account
but is not overly influenced by our own cultural and ethical suppositions.
It also requires that we understand the tangled paths through which a
vulnerable population of children and adolescents, subjected to various
forms and "institutions of violence," are sometimes forced into playing
the role of their own executioners. Addressing such terrible links is risky,
for it can both lead to or be misconstrued as "victim blaming." In
probing such links, the qualities of a negative intellectual worker are also
required, chipping away at the conventional ideological functions of the
medical, social, biological, and life sciences in naturalizing the many
sick-making social relations that lay at the heart of modern violence and
dis-ease.
As children and young adults living in contexts of everyday
violence, their involvement in violence led to active participation in
"spaces of death" in their communities, through innumerable little acts of

aggression that often had injurious and deadly consequences. The often lengthy journey of transformation, during which the young person experienced times of feeling entrapped in the past—with intractable behavior problems, and barely repressed rage—often frustrated those trying to help. If the young people have violated community or moral values there is an added dimension of social condemnation. The complexity of the problem and the solution often results in simplistic explanations that ascribe flaws to personality and moral character. The more extreme characterizations ascribe lesser human status to this subset of youth; many deny them a conscience.

Some clinical and popular conceptions of young people mistake the elemental concerns of survival for an individual's underlying character. Such characterizations are no longer routinely made of released prisoners of war, and domestic violence survivors. Nor are the moral visions and reasoning in such inhuman contexts questioned.

Concepts of personality organization and anti-social conduct, however, are applied to these young people without any understanding of the deterioration of personality and conduct that can sometimes take place in extreme situations. These young people have been described as "manipulative," "crooks," "anti-social," and "sociopaths." This tendency to misdiagnose the other is influenced by our own cultural and ethical presuppositions and shaped by a larger moral order that has suspended its responsibility towards these children and young adults.

You Don't Have to Be Somebody Else: Discovering One's True Self

Finding their true self was a concept that was often mentioned by the study participants. The environment in which they found themselves, with its constant violent/destructive stimuli, buried their inner selves. Part of the change process was realizing that they were more than the violence, more than what others perceived them to be. Flaco described the training he received, and how

> the good parts was when they trained you. But they trained you to be confident on yourself when you do a workshop. How to be yourself. You don't have to be somebody else. They teach you how to be yourself, not to be, how can I say this, not like acting like somebody else. You know, somebody that you're not. Just be yourself.

Lita echoed these sentiments. For her, programs that can give young people a chance to explore and find who they really are

Cause they help 'em realize who they are. You know, they're a
person. They think they're a different person when they're in a
gang, they got different personalities. The youth program helps
them be themselves, not that person in the streets, you know? It
gives'em more head on their shoulders, they're "Oh, this is the
way I am."

Martin ascribes that an influential factor in helping him along the
process of change was the realization that "there was more people out
there like me. More people that was not a hard core person, but was put
into a position to do certain things."

Others see their new self as so different from the old that they are
depicted as an altogether distant individual. Cy talks about this old self
who he has outgrown as a different person who "back there. I left him
back there somewhere. He's on the street somewhere. I can't go back
again. I'm too old."

Carl would sum up how he felt about himself as he looks back into
his past troubles, present circumstances and future orientation.

I feel good. I feel like this is me. This has always been me
inside. It's just that I haven't had the tools to put forth what I
had to, like my skills. I haven't had the opportunity to show
people who I am really. You know what I'm saying. When I
was given this kind of environment to stay in, these kind of
rules, this is how I had to live.

Violence is the Language of the Unheard: **Learning to Speak**

Some of the young people allude to being rendered mute by violence and
describe how they were able to find a voice as part of their rehabilitation
or change process. George describes his "square" older brother who was
killed as his "voice." Losing his brother—his voice—would be the
watershed event that consciously propelled George headfirst into a
violent career as a young adolescent. During this phase of his life, he
would increasingly forfeit speech or opportunities to speak to others
about loss.

I think that's when it really, really got real, real bad was my
brother my oldest brother got killed. When he got killed that's
when I said like forget it. Then I started pulling guns on people
and doing things like that frequently.

He would begin to regain his voice following the second great loss of his life, the death of his mother, an event that made him realize that he was not alone and that others cared.

George explained that he understood how being voiceless, and therefore unheard, had led him towards a violent path and how reconnecting with others helped him find his place once more. He came across a quote of Martin Luther King, "violence is the language of the unheard," that best described his situation.

Ronnie describes learning to speak, articulate his problems, and have a dialogue for the first time when he was in his twenties, in a jail program where "they taught you was how to just share, you know... And they teach you how to say it in a form, the beginning, the middle and the end... Now I try to hold dialogue with my mother." He credits the program and a female counselor, in particular, for teaching him how to speak and giving him a time to speak:

> Learning if I had a problem, just talk to somebody, cause I had a problem with looking at people when I talk. I would always listen. I would look away, but you can ask me word for word what did I just say, and I could tell you what they said... It's not that you're ugly. It's just me. I'm humble, so I don't want to look. And I just can't explain it. I just don't like looking at people. I'm just so shy and didn't want nobody to bother me. And if you talk to me, I'd be looking over here, but I'm hearing everything you say. And then when you finish talking, I can just tell you everything you said. But she said, "you know what? You need to start looking at people then they will understand you. Especially if you're gonna be speaking." And for you to look... and you be like when you say something you can look at them then they be like. They can't look off, cause they know you be looking at them. So you need eye contact, and they taught me how to make eye contact, how to speak loud, make you point and then back up off of it. If you really didn't like looking at somebody, look over them. So they just taught me how to communicate.

It would be Ronnie's neurosurgeon who encouraged him to learn how to read and continue his education. He introduced Ronnie to a world of unknown words, and the desire to "be an educated person."

> he took me to this college group at a hospital. And there was doctors, lawyers and medical people, and they were just speaking so high that I didn't know what they were saying. And

they were asking basic questions, but they were using words I
never heard. And that was intriguing to me to know that there is
a different word, and there is a different word for—if I want to
cross the street. And, I'm like, these dudes are speaking all these
words, and I'm not grasping them, you know. And I must be
dumb, cause they talking, and I don't understand what they
saying. And I'm taking to the Dr., I'm like, "I didn't know it
was words like that." And so I just started coming back out
there, and I told him that I want to speak like that.

Learning More Changed My Whole Thinking: Developing New Skills

In addition to meeting the basic needs critical to survival, recovery, and
"psychosocial health" (safety, self-worth, mastery and confidence,
autonomy/independence, closeness/affiliation and self-awareness/
spirituality) the young people needed to learn other attitudes, behaviors
and skills to help them along their pathways of growth and
transformation. In order to succeed as adults and leave a life behind of
perpetration and victimization, specific "competencies" also needed to be
cultivated.

Awareness or caring alone were insufficient to change old,
entrenched ways of responding to external stimuli in destructive or risky
ways. As many of the young people differentiated, caring was not the
same as teaching, and they recognized the importance of acquiring or
improving additional skills and patterns of connection that would enable
them to prevent, deescalate, or extricate themselves from situations that
contributed to acts of violence. As the young people began to take small
steps towards change, they increasingly relied on what Prochaska and
DiClemente term counter-conditioning and stimulus control, substituting
alternatives for problem behaviors (relaxation, positive self-statements,
desensitization, walking away, and avoiding or countering stimuli and
situations that could lead to problems).

Cognitive development theories state that individuals can "learn new
patterns of connection by which to control their involvement with and
response to social experiences that commonly contribute to violence"
(Pepler and Slaby 1994). The participants in this study, especially those
who relied on violence as a response to insult and adversity most often,
demonstrated the ability to learn new communication and impulse
control skills, and learned that it was not "too late." Some of the young
people learned these skills through specialized violence prevention
intervention programs, while others learned them in natural settings, with
varying degrees of guidance.

Educational interventions that addressed the application of such skills to true-to-life situations faced by young people were very useful at that stage. They had the ancillary benefit of laying the groundwork to question other patterns of connection and response to other forms of violence. Cy found that

> learning more about violence on the streets and stuff like that changed my whole thinking. We used to watch like videotapes about battered women and conflicts, how kids used to fight. Kids be fighting, then they reverse it, how that fight could have been avoided, and stuff like that. And that helped me. That helped my life a lot. I used to think fighting was cool. So I avoid fighting a lot now and the battered women, that's a serious issue too, in a lot of women out here getting battered. So, you know, it's not cool to be hitting no woman. So I watch out for that, too. There's a lot of things I watch out for now because these are real issues and stuff. So I benefit from coming to this program.

The stories of the young people suggest that, in order to expedite the process of change, the young people needed to acquire the coping skills to address various forms of violence and abuse and the abilities to react positively to situations in which they were likely to be perpetrators and/or victims. Given the co-occurrence of various forms of violence and abuse (as outlined in Chapter 5), learning one set of skills to address one facet of the many types of violence in their lives was not sufficient. Charo's story best exemplifies this, she had to learn both how to deal with the rage that led her to commit acts of perpetration towards her peers, as well as the skills to overcome her passive acceptance of victimization by her boyfriend and father of her children. Gendered constructs of violence, in which girls are seen as victims of domestic violence and boys as perpetrators of street and gang violence, were not helpful. The stories of the young participants involvement and cessation challenge such reductionism.

> Whoever was looking at me wrong, being a guy, a teacher, a man, or woman, or a girl, I didn't really care who it was, I was fighting. Physically. And the majority of the time, I don't know if it was like my anger that made me so strong, but I don't think there was a time that I could remember that I got beat up. Well, with the batterer, in the battered situation with my children's dad. I was over here getting beat up and the funny thing about it was that even though he, he beat me up or whatever, while he was hitting me or while he was beating me up, I didn't want to

defend myself 'cause I didn't want to hurt him. But when I was in school, it was like with guys and girls that I had a fight, that I fought, I pretty much got the best out of the whole fight.

The attainment of cognitive and creative abilities, academic achievement and vocational skills, social and cultural competencies were also needed for the young people to leave behind their old lives. Ronnie had to learn how to "hold dialogue" and begin to read, others returned to school to complete their secondary, technical education. Community service opportunities enhanced their social and cultural competencies. The young parents among the participants benefited from learning new parenting skills. All developed their abilities to access services, and to work with juvenile justice services to clear up warrants and outstanding cases. The young people with mobility impairments in particular, needed to learn how to interact with specialized bureaucracies to secure services (housing, medical supplies, vocational rehabilitation, among others). Other skills learned were self-care, taking care of their skin to prevent skin breakdown and pressure sores. Learning how to eat in a nutritious way, develop and stick to a schedule, open a bank account, register to vote, were among the sundry other skills learned. A critical skill was learning how to apply for, get, and keep a job, especially important given the semi-autonomous situation most of the young people found themselves in, often with children or family members to support. At fifteen years of age, Erika needed to find a job to support herself, yet did not know how to go about finding one. She was living in her grandmother's garage, and on days when the money was short, she would scavenge food in garbage cans. The skills to be able to get a job eluded her, and put her at risk:

> I went around my way, and I wanted to find a job so bad. And I was a dropout and you need a work permit, and so much stuff. One time I went to a place and got an application, it was a barbecue place, and I didn't get hired. To tell you how ignorant I was, I didn't even know how to dress for an interview. I didn't know how to answer the question. I went, it was some kind of bam-bam kinky haircut, a clip over my hair, shorts, T-shirt, I think slippers or some kind of funny-looking shoes, and a purse. I didn't really look like I was, for a job interview. I looked like I was maybe standing on the street hustling or something. And when the person came out, the owner came out, shook the other guy's hand. The other guy had a tie on, a nice white shirt, clean haircut, and they were "Oh what school you went to? Oh you went to Dorsey, so did my sister, da, da." I said, "Oh, that's it,

I'm not gonna get hired." And so, you know I would some times jump into people's cars and, you know for money. It is kinda scary 'cause you don't know if you're gonna get out of it alive or what.

Affirmatively meeting the developmental needs of these adolescents and building the functional competencies necessary for adulthood were integral steps in facilitating and maintaining the process of change.

You Have to Offer Them Something: Opportunities and Supports

The essential new skills taught by service providers and other helpers could only be internalized to the extent that opportunities to practice and further develop them existed either through formal interventions or in the community. The provision of opportunities and supports was a powerful influence on the young people. They encouraged change, preventing recidivism, contributing to the civic and social integration, and preparing the young people to be contributing adult members of society.

The opportunities mentioned by the young people included the possibility of becoming actively involved in their own, their peers', and community's learning; the chance to make different decisions, contributions and reparations; the leeway to take on challenging roles and responsibilities and openings to work. As Delbert states, in order to effect a behavior change:

You give them an opportunity,,, ,you show them what else they achieve. Show them the positive stuff that they can do, you know. Not just being out there, chilling, causing trouble, wasting their time. Show them a way to have fun and benefit from that fun that they're having. I mean, show them the Internet. Show them how to play basketball. Show them how to do karate. Show'em how to wrestle. Show'em how to swim, you know. Show'em how to travel. Stuff.

The opportunity to become agents of their own positive development, do things that actually make a difference in one's community, become empowered and exercise increasingly autonomous positive self-regulation was important for the young participants. The opportunity to be efficacious and to make a difference in their social worlds, described as "mattering" in a recent Institute of Medicine research report that integrates the current science of adolescent health and development (NRC and IOM 2002), was also important for the study youth. Opportunities helped shape a positive outlook for the young people in this study and help them assess the costs and benefits of a "negative" versus "positive" life. They were especially critical for the young participants who were young parents themselves, or who provided for their younger siblings or other family members, and wished for a better life for their young.

> You have to offer them something, it's a trade-off. You're gonna tell them I don't want you to do this drug-dealing and this carrying guns and this violent stuff, but what you offering them back? You're taking something away from them, their way of life. And if you take that away from them, then they're void, they're empty, they have nothing to do, you know. Their whole point of being is lost. I mean, this is what they do. They stay on their corners. They sling their drugs. That's how they get by, that's how they live. If you can offer something else, you know, not no McDonald's four dollars and seventy-five cents a hour, which they can't even buy a pair of sneakers at the end of the week... something that they can actually feed a family with. I mean most of these kids who are dealing have kids to raise and have a family to raise. If you want them to do something, offer them something that, you know, that's gonna be there for them.

For the young people, practicing skills in a safe context that offered ample opportunities for youth development was more effective than in reductionist behavioral change settings alone. Yet opportunities were largely place-neutral, these experiences had a positive impact on the positive development of the young participants, regardless of where they took place. Carl described the suburban hospital school he was sent to as "opportunity camp" and told how its pacifying environment helped him make a transition to a new life. The effect of opportunity in a context of safety made his life (and those of the other young people) more adventuresome and more ordinary at the same time. As he connected with himself, Carl felt more tranquil and better able to take on the new challenges ahead. Whereas in the past he may have found ordinary life to be boring, he was now ready to "pull the rug" and begin to live

> I made the change and wanted to make the transition to give it a try at least, and it worked out to my best benefit. They made me shine. Yeah, just like in Dorchester everything that is going on is hazy so it is hard for a young black kid like me to shine. When there are a thousand other ones doing the wrong shit. So why not fit in? Given this type of environment, peaceful, tranquil, opportunity camp, it's like no shit to make you go berserk...

Albert's social worker at the hospital showed him how he could further his education:

> I had a social worker there and she, she's the one that told me that the state would pay for my education that would be fine and that's why I pursue college to tell you the truth. She is the one that let me in on that fact. You know, there are a lot of things that they could tell you about, programs that we could get involved with. You see, we come from low-income families and we don't have the money, I didn't ever think that I could afford college, books, anything like that. I don't even know if there was programs that'll pay for that. There's a lot of other things that they could lead you into that could help you out. The Department of Rehab Housing all that stuff.

As Andres summed up, "kids are looking for something stable, it can be a job, a goal in life, something they can struggle for and have a fair chance to obtain." He distinguishes opportunities from handouts or make-work:

> I tell you this much, because I don't like to take things easy. Anything that comes easy it can't be good and I like to struggle for things to know that I earned it so that within the future nobody would come to say well you know you got it because you're this or you're that. I like to struggle for mine you know and that's what these kids want as well.

Andres' observations on the importance that opportunities extended to youth offer a real challenge, is consonant with research on efficacy and mattering. The psychological theories of Erickson posited that development is a process that young people do for themselves, with much assistance from adults (Erickson 1963, 1965). Bandura's (1994) efficacy theories stipulate that personal efficacy is developed through opportunities for youth to be challenged in challenging, new and imaginative activities. A recent Institute of Medicine report underscores the importance of "mattering"—which combines multiple elements drawn from other theorists and practitioners:

> The importance of having the opportunity to do things that make a real difference in one's community, the idea of empowerment, and the support for increasingly autonomous self-regulation that is appropriate to the maturing individuals' developmental level and cultural background... It must be

emphasized that "opportunity" is not experience as a "challenge" unless youth identify with it: adolescents need to be engaged by opportunities for efficacy and mattering that are meaningful to them (NRC and IOM 2002, 103-104).

With Help, I Can Make it: Supports and Stabilizing Process

It is well understood that change processes are somehow inseparable from and "essential to the order-preserving processes that permit us to function as we do. In other words, it is not possible to speak of human change processes without simultaneously addressing human stabilizing processes" (Mahoney 1991, 5). Sheer will power or resolve can only go so far.

Preliminary research on motivation and predicting risk in offenders under community supervision has found that motivation and need (employment, marital/family, associates, substance abuse, community functioning, personal/emotional and attitude) were related to release failure. "Those offenders rated by staff as low need/high motivation consistently performed better on release than offenders rated as high need/low motivation" (Serin and Kennedy 1999, 2). Those with supports, and lower levels of needs found it easier to adopt and stay on a non-violence course of life development. According to key principles in correctional programming, the intensity of treatment intervention should correspond with offender's risk of recidivism.

> This is because higher risk cases tend to respond better to intensive services, while low risk cases respond better to less intensive service. Once offenders are appropriately matched in this manner, attention should be directed to the sorts of needs that the treatment should address. The need principle distinguishes between criminogenic and non-criminogenic needs. The former are dynamic risk factors, which if changed reduce the likelihood of criminal conduct. In contrast, non-criminogenic needs, which are derived from personality variables such as personal distress and self-esteem, are considered less relevant targets for treatment since their resolution does not have a significant impact on recidivism (Serin and Kennedy 1999).

The literature of trauma and recovery underscores the effect of social supports and the power of the survivor's social world on influencing the eventual outcome of the trauma. Because traumatic life events invariably cause damage to relationships, rebuilding a shattered sense of self "can be rebuilt only as it was built initially, in connection with others" (Herman 1997, 61). The supports that traumatized individuals seek from family and friends and the wider community take many forms and change during the course of the resolution of the trauma, as well as throughout the progression along the stages of change. The young people identified motivational and strategic supports that helped them become connected in new, stable and positive ways to community.

Unlike most young people in the study, and most young people and individuals contemplating the abandonment of habitual behavior, Ruby never slipped or looked back. She completed her high school education that very academic year, left the program and the state to begin a new phase of her life and to go on to college down south. Of all the young people, Ruby had the most resources, order, and stability, as well as emotional, motivational, and strategic supports to enable her to capitalize on the moment of horror when her boyfriend was shot and she was threatened in the aftermath. That event gave her the resolve to change. She would be categorized as high motivation/low need in typologies of offender recidivism risk. Despite her "violent situation," Ruby had a safety shield ready to envelop her, a shield that included a network that reached into many professional spheres, covered many facets of her world as an adolescent, and extended to different parts of the country.

Ruby's mother, in turn, unlike the other mothers of the participants, is extremely well connected to multiple social networks. Ruby's mother is an experienced part-time teacher's aide in an alternative school for adolescents and young adults, is a longtime resident of Boston Public Housing, and has family, friendship, and professional ties to city hall and city health and welfare institutions, street workers, and civil rights groups. She has many years of experience in how to access quality services, circumvent bureaucracies on behalf of her alternative school students and their families, many of whom were involved in violence and gangs. In her younger days, Ruby's mother had briefly belonged to a girls' street group herself. When Ruby started running with a "wild group" and no longer respected her authority or wishes, her mother knew the life and injury risks that would result from Ruby's wild life and was waiting for an opportunity to penetrate a chink in her daughter's rebellious emotional armor. The death of Ruby's boyfriend provided her mother with that opening. Ruby's mother was able to marshal a range of formal and informal resources, calling on personal favors to assist Ruby immediately following the incident and during the six months she would spend in Boston before being sent down south to relatives to begin college and start a new life. Ruby's mother was able to mobilize many people of all ages, family, extended kin and non-relatives to help her daughter. She was a skilled advocate, was perceived by the helping professionals as someone worthy of service, and a person able to hold them accountable if they did not deliver quality services.

In many ways, with so much support and so many resources Ruby should never have gone down the wrong road in the first place. Although her family was eligible for assistance programs for low-income residents in the city of Boston, her family would constantly comment that Ruby "was not like the other, poor kids" in the youth intervention violence support program. And in many important ways, she was not. Although Ruby was raised in a single-headed household and in public housing and had participated in many of the activities other had (assault, dealing drugs, arms sales), she was the beneficiary of myriad family and community supports from her well-connected mother and extended family members (on both her mother's and father's side). Unlike other adolescents, Ruby was immediately able to receive mental health counseling following the shooting, a difficult (and largely unavailable) service for inner city adolescents to obtain. She was immediately admitted into a youth violence intervention project, had safety arrangements made at her school when she chose to complete the remaining three months at her school rather than request a security transfer and not graduate. During those months she was dropped off and picked up at school by relatives, and had her afternoons and weekends after school fully booked with activities with her cousins, extended family, and a new peer group.

Ample evidence suggests that socially isolated individuals, like many of the mothers of the young participants, are at increased risk for poor health outcomes because of their limited access to resources such as instrumental aid, information and emotional support (Kennedy et al 1998). The relationship between violence and cessation for many of the young participants was similarly mediated by their and their family's access to social institutions, informal relations with other community members, and the availability of support networks for youth overwhelmed by such stressors as violence, gang involvement, and poverty. The extent and strength of existing networks influenced the decision to terminate high-risk behaviors and provided the resources needed to sustain a path of positive development. In communities where the extent of interpersonal trust between citizens, norms of reciprocity and density of civic associations that facilitate cooperation for mutual benefit are limited or weak, relationships with social networks are critical because such places provide fewer opportunities for individuals to form local ties and afford few supports (Prothrow-Stith 1987). The stories of the young participants suggest that a violence cessation-opportunity-social institution nexus, in which the relationship between violence termination is mediated positively or negatively through opportunities, supports and access to social (and youth serving) institutions and order preserving processes. These range from family to informal local associations such as sports clubs, boys and girls clubs, community halls to formal organizations such as the health department, church, schools, and police.

Families like Ruby's, the elite in the study group, speak to the need to differentiate between the various strata that constitute the "urban poor" even among a pool of violence-involved youth. Not differentiating or explicitly seeking to reach the least advantaged of the "poor" urban youth population was a concern expressed by many participants, who felt that most violence intervention programs were only set up to help the most resource-rich among their peers of similar socioeconomic status. These programs, of short duration, sometimes only weeks or months, presupposed a short recovery period, and a whole series of supports outside of the program that often were not there or could not be accessed by their relatives and friends.

I Had to Get Out of Town: Change in Environment

Four of the study participants had to relocate to a different state, either temporarily or permanently, in order to stay alive. Others found their efforts to change and those of other young people were impeded or retarded by return to the community. Many community-level factors influenced the outcomes of a young person's contemplation or decision to change, and the situations they were likely to face upon their return or during their attempt to carve out a new life.

Suggestive links to the causes of violence cessation and the maintenance of change can be gleaned from the ways in which individual-level and situational-level characteristics interact with community-level factors. Some of the community level factors that influenced how the individual youth fared when facing or returning to particular situations included (but were not limited to) residential mobility, family disruption, housing and population density, criminal opportunity structures (e.g., levels of non-household leisure activities, gun density), dimensions of social organization (e.g., informal social ties, density of acquaintanceship, supervision of street-corner street groups, organizational density and strength), and the overall ecological concentration of the urban underclass. The quality of policing, availability of transportation, extent of positive peer groupings, and availability of mentors were also community-level characteristics mentioned by the young people as influencing the change process.

Albert remembers an earlier period in which he had contemplated the possibility of change, and how it was not possible to maintain that resolve and access the supports, opportunities, and help he needed to move towards a positive life. The characteristics of his neighborhood, the depth of his involvement in youth criminal organizations, were such that it would have been difficult to maintain his resolve to change. "I don't think that there's any help that could have been offered there. Not much, not much cause I lived in my neighborhood and I was surrounded by my homeboys."

Community and situational level factors also influenced the individual-level changes made by one of Albert's protégés:

A little boy named Nacho and he started getting involved with this gang up in Compton and he went in a school there, he lived close to about where I used to live so it was real easy for me to go pick him up and take him to the meetings with me and spend time with him. So even after work or when I wouldn't work, I spent time with him. Either it was working on my car, he likes to help me work on my car. We'd just go out for drives you know I take homie to the gym where I go work out and stuff like that. We were real close and he started making the change just by hanging around me, just by being with me. I would instill positive things into his head that would lead him away from that I would make him think about things he was involved with and I started seeing a change when he would come up to me and tell me "Look, my mom bought some clothes and it wasn't big old Ben Davis no more, things I was wearing last week." It made me happy to see that, and I was you know that's my boy. I'd always take him with me and my family, he's always around me. I was like my boy, my little boy you know, I felt cool. He was about 14/15 but he was making that change. He wanted to get out. He would tell me he wanted to get out. His family had moved from that area where he was from he was from Compton. He moved to Huntington Park and being away from what he had been involved in, it helped him a great deal. They moved him out and he wasn't around his homeboys no more he was in somebody else's neighborhood and he knew that where he was at so he wouldn't really come out and associate with those gang members around there he would always kick back with me and, and I had him you know he wanted to go back to school he would like I would he would look up to me and he would show me his paper: "Look how much I got in school" and he would talk and talk. He was really talkative and I would always listen and we'd spend time just cruising we wouldn't even listen to my car radio 'cause he would be just talking. And he had a lot to say you know and I would be there to listen to him. So I think he has the potential to change. He wanted to change, then his family couldn't afford the rent there where they were living so they had to move back to where they came from and by that transition I lost him. He didn't even have a phone.

Levels of community education about violence and levels of fear were also influential factors that shaped how easily the young person could access the supports, services, opportunities and helping relationships needed to learn new behaviors and seek a positive life. Youth returning to the community following hospitalization or considering trying on a new set of behaviors and attitudes were often exquisitely sensitive to the degree of support and judgment encountered at home and in their community. They sought the meaning of their encounter with trauma, injury, and death in the stance of the broader community. They needed to know how their actions were viewed, whether they were seen as brave or cowardly, necessary, deserved, purposeful, or meaningless. A realistically accepting climate of community opinion fostered the reintegration into community life; a nonchalant one reconfirmed the cheapness of life, while a rejecting climate of opinion often compounded their isolation.

The increasingly hostile response to crime and violence committed by minors has led even the staunchest child advocates to express rage towards these youth who make their lives feel so much less secure. Community-building efforts frequently do not include semi-autonomous youths on the margins of society, choosing to focus violence prevention and youth development efforts on younger, less intractable children, with greater social supports. In such contexts, the protection of human rights and the extension of growth opportunities to this sub-sector are equated to being "soft on crime."

Policies enacted at state or federal levels had important effects on communities, in terms of determining the developmental outcomes, the aftermath of traumatic exposure, and the extent of opportunities and supports a young person could tap into to aid their process of stabilization and change. One example of such a policy was the 1994 Anti Violent Crime and Law Enforcement Act, which expanded juvenile federal crimes provisions and made joining or recruiting someone into a gang a federal offense.

The act sanctioned the adult prosecution and treatment of juveniles and children over 12 charged with violent crime (murder, attempted murder, aggravated assault, armed robbery, and rape). It established a three-strikes provision; sentenced third time violent or drug offenders to life in prison; and created 50 more new federal death penalty crimes, an over 25-fold increase in capital punishment offenses. The 1994 act rewarded states that upheld truth-in-sentencing requirements and established bind-over programs for violent 16-17 year olds.

In many ways, this act supported state-level policies on interpersonal and gang violence that allowed for more punitive and less flexible responses. The state-level responses and additions to this federal law varied greatly in Massachusetts and California, due to the varied influence of the prison industry and different histories of social welfare ideologies. Yet both states moved towards a more stringent and blanket application of sanctions, distinguishing less and less between adults and juveniles. The flurry of laws shaped the life outcomes of the friends, siblings, and family members of the study participants as they were swept up in the rising number of arrests and number of severely punishable crimes. Many of these individuals were still "perpetrating," but others were caught in the whirlwind of arrests, whether conducted within the letter of the law by the Boston Youth Strike Force, or brutally and criminally by the L.A. gang unit, especially the Ramparts division, which concentrated its activities in East Los Angeles, Pico Union, and South Central, where the L.A. study participants lived. George would describe the role of the police and the gang unit as that of an "occupying force."

The effect of this hardening posture on youth crime and delinquency was felt on Carl's life as he returned to the environment in which these policies were invariably directed and disproportionately policed and enforced. By the age of 16 Carl had left his old life behind after a couple of "backslides." Once he was admitted to the hospital school as a resident, he was exposed to a new tranquil environment, where he was surrounded with opportunities to succeed. At 17, Carl was elected class president of his predominantly white graduating class, comprised mostly of children with developmental disabilities with whom he had little (demographically) in common; yet, he had been chosen to be their spokesperson. At 17, he had been admitted to university, but had to defer, starting two years later, at age 20. A visit back home in the summer of 1996, when the hospital school that he attended shut down for the summer, led to a weapons possession charge which carried a one-year automatic mandatory sentence for juveniles, granting the judges no discretion in sentencing.

Carl had feared the return to his old neighborhood for a variety of reasons, among them the continued involvement of some members of his family in the drug dealing in the community, and the unsettled "beefs" they had with others in the project. But the relatively modern public housing projects offered the only accessible housing option to a young man in a wheelchair; all his other relatives lived in triple-decker buildings from which he would have to be carried down or drag himself, one step at a time, to be able to come and go. A ride in his uncle's car, where his uncle had a hidden weapon stashed away for protection, cost him another year of his life. When riding in the car, he was stopped and searched by the police during a routine sweep of one of Boston's most notorious housing projects. As a juvenile he was automatically given a one-year mandatory sentence for possession of a firearm, despite the letters and testimonies of various teachers, doctors and the hospital school director attesting to Carl's spotless record. Carl would graduate as class valedictorian to begin serving his time. Due to his medical condition, he would serve out his sentence in a hospital prison with adults, and the last four months in another prison hospital where he roomed with two adult convicts who were in the last stages of AIDS, one of them dying during that period. He was not able to continue his education for that year. Carl's biggest challenge was not to fall back into the depression that had once engulfed him, and to stay focused on his goals. He stated that the one-year mandatory sentence was not a waste of a year, but a reminder that he really can't go ever go back, not only to the life, but also to his neighborhood or to much of his family.

Paradoxically, the 1994 Anti Violent Crime and Law Enforcement Act also provided a glimmer of hope for the three participants in the study from both cities who were undocumented persons, brought to the United States illegally as children by their parents. The protection afforded to victims of domestic violence under this act deemed the mothers of the three participants to be victims of domestic violence; as such, the women could step forward and request services, without fear of deportation, and could request resident alien status. Consequently, both the mothers and the children had better access to services and opportunities.

Macro-level changes and policies in specific homicide hot-spot neighborhoods also helped the young people reduce the chances of recidivism as victims or perpetrators and promoted their development. Carl's story exemplifies a few of these environmental influences. A city summer jobs program for low-income residents in the city of Boston gave Carl his next break. Following his incarceration, he took the leadership to start an integrated wheelchair basketball summer league for disabled and able-bodied youth alike. The neighborhood merchants who supported his program with refreshments and donations had been encouraged to stay and invest in the neighborhood and its residents through the municipal main streets small business incentive programs.

THE PROCESS OF CHANGE

The youth who were successful leaving behind extremely aggressive and violent pasts tended to share common experiences, factors, personalities and events that placed them on a trajectory towards non-violence. The journey of transformation violence itself had general characteristics that are similar to and depart from other processes of behavioral change.

It Takes Different Things: Change is Influenced by Many Factors and Processes

The process of significant psychological or consciousness change for the young people in this study does not differ in structure from those experienced by other populations, which "reflect complex, non-linear dynamics. In other words, such change is not a simple and smooth accumulation of small changes, yielding a neatly predictable outcome" (Mahoney 1991).

Delbert looked back on the last five years since he was 13, when he first came to the realization that he needed to "get out of that life," when he failed to live up to his mother's and aunt's expectations. His trajectory away from violence was marked by both perceptible and imperceptible influences and a variety of factors, events, processes and personalities, interacting in ways he does not fully understand.

> Even though I was feeling like getting out of the streets, you know, without my mother and that conversation that she had with her aunt, I would have probably never done it, you know. I mean, it took different things in my life to make me get out. It took that dude getting stabbed, and that, that conversation with my mother. Even, even if, though I was thinking about getting out after that dude got stabbed, I probably would've still stayed. I would've been like yeah, yeah, yeah. And right now I wouldn't have been here interviewing, you know. But it takes different things. It takes some things that you might not even know will affect you to change, but it has a subconscious effect on you.

Although their lives were punctuated by dramatic turns, no single extraordinary event marked the evolution through various stages. The transition experienced by the young people was for the most part, gradual. Little by little, the young people found a greater sense of safety and predictability in their lives, more confidence in ability to protect him/herself as they learned how to control their feelings of anger, what triggers to avoid, and on whom they can rely on help. Andrea explains how she gradually developed a sense of safety and control, along with the wisdom and patience to recognize that "the anger doesn't go away" magically:

> I am not perfect and there are times when I still get into fights. But I try to talk to the person first or I walk away from a fight. It makes me feel good because I know I'm going to see another day.

Summing up his experience, Martin captures the non-linear, multi-leveled dimensions to the process of change experienced by the study participants both in their own personal journeys and observed in the transformation of other young people impacted by trauma whom they, in turn, "helped change."

> I knew once I do something to somebody, it's gonna come back double. Seeing the life, innocent people being wrapped up in my situation. Knowing I have other people who love me and stuff. Those are all things that helped me make this change. I needed to find somebody trustworthy to talk to, somebody who is educated and can help and wants to help. Everything happens for a reason. If a person wants help, even if it's a hard struggle, they'll get it. One way or another, it'll come around, you now. Some doors have to get opened in your mind; some things have to happen in order for that change to happen. I mean, it all boils down to everything happens for a reason. Like me, personally, my doors had to be opened by the things that happened to me for me to see the light. And I didn't die, or nothing. I went through a few traumas, but that was just, basically, payback for some of the things I did.

There Are Ups and Downs: Change is Not Always a Smooth Process

Significant psychological change is generally neither rapid nor easy, especially when the change involves processes central to a person's experience of reality (order), self (identity), and value and power (control). Although many studies of self-changers and psychotherapy outcomes demonstrate the ability of individuals to change, these studies also clearly show that many do not change, or change and relapse, or change only after long periods of time. Several constructs have been developed to explain this:

> Inadequate technology, intensity, or theory are intervention variables that are often blamed. The very nature of change, however, may be part of the problem. Change represents a

movement from one rather steady state or pattern of bei.avior through a transition to relatively stable state or pattern. It is not automatic nor is it simple dichotomous event (Prochaska and DiClemente 1992), 87-88).

For the young people in the study, the process of leaving behind a "negative" life and moving towards a "positive" required momentous and tumultuous change, because for many the change involved processes central to their experience of order, identity, values and control. Also, the forces of stabilization and equilibrium, central to this process, in which "phases and forces of change alternate and intermingle with phases and forces of stabilization" (Mahoney 1991, 18-19), were relatively few in their lives. In addition, the youth in this study had experienced traumatic events that, by definition, overwhelm the ordinary systems that give people a sense of control, connection, and meaning, leading them to experience intense fear and anger, helplessness, feelings of loss of control, and threat of annihilation.

Their journeys were like a river, marked by rapids and reverses, much like other populations undergoing a process of significant change. Albert describes the many falls, and "backsliding" along the way and the motivation to continue:

> They need to go seek help. Put down that pride and go seek some help if they really want to change they will go and ask somebody for some help if they need. If they are not serious, they'll hold it inside and say nothing and, and if he fails he'll just sit his ass down. But if he really wants to change, he will fall and he will get right back up and dust himself and he will go after that 'til he makes that change. And the help would have to come from well somebody that could help him you know, depending what he wants to do with his life.

The stories of the young people underscore that their process and experience of personal change involved conflicts, tensions, and resistance. All experience of change is commonly recognized to involve conflicts in one form or another, part of the dynamic nature of development. In making the decision to change her life and leave her street group, Lulu wrote in her journal about how torn she felt. She expressed great ambivalence, illustrating the dynamics of the contemplation stage described by Prochaska and DiClemente.

> People say that teenagers go through a lot of fazes *(phases)*. That is very much true. I am a 17 years old girl who is going

through a stage that I call confusion. These feelings that I am having are very unpleasant trying to make up my mind and wondering if it was a good decision or was it a bad one. I mean, I now know what I want in life, but how to get it is very hard, that is why I call this a confusioning stage.

Albert remembers the support that the gangs provided him, and still misses some aspects and supports gang life afforded him, even though he no longer "feels like falling in that same drag split."

If you would ask me if I miss some of the stuff, yes, I do. I miss the unity. I miss the friends we had. How we would just all, just care about each other, we were real tight. I miss that. I miss being able to always have somewhere to go and everybody just accept you there. I miss all that.

I've been through times where I've gotten into situation where money is tight, when I'd have nothing, no way out and I would think of going backwards. I would think look how easy it would be for me to go back to my neighborhood and easily accept money from these people that I used to associate with. But it only happens when I'd go through hard times. It wouldn't happen no more. No, I don't even think of that being a way out no more.

According to Prochaska and DiClemente's study on addictions and change, successful change involves a progression through a series of stages, and "most self-changers and psychotherapy patients will recycle several times through the stages before achieving long term maintenance. Accordingly, intervention programs and personnel expecting people to progress linearly through the stages are likely to gather disappointing and discouraging results" (Prochaska et al. 1992, 1111).

Scholars of the process of psychological change contend that some of our greatest strides in understanding and facilitating human change will come from studies of the oscillating processes in human self-organization. Describing the wavering, ambivalent nature of this process as experienced by many of the young people, one of the participants described it as "hell."

I was talking to God; asking him to help me, give me strength through the whole time. It was just, like, at the same time, the devil took over.

Erika describes the natural pendulum swings in her transformation, which, over time, would cease to swing from "negative" to "positive" activities and behaviors, eventually finding a central equilibrium. Her helper, a pastor, would stand by her as she experienced these pendulum swings. He would remain by her side, ready to catch her, if she should fall.

> You can't really be doing good in the, you know, working at a organization, being good at, for a moment in the morning, then in the afternoon, have a twilight or different lifestyle because eventually something is gonna kinda pull you closer. You're gonna give up something. And I didn't realize that and, then after that he was like, "well look, if they put you out, your mom or your grandmother puts you out or what not, come stay with us. I want you give me your probation officer phone number, that way your community service will be done over here."

Similar oscillations took place in relationships to people. The story of one young man's oscillation in Herman's study of Vietnam War veterans (many of whom would have been exposed to traumatic violent events in their late adolescent years) sheds light on the contradictory nature of relationships common to traumatized individuals, and on facets of the study participants' interactions with those closest to them:

> Because of their difficulty in modulating intense anger, survivors oscillate between uncontrolled expressions of rage and intolerance of aggression in any form. Thus, on the one hand, this man felt compassionate and protective towards others and could not stand the thought of anyone being harmed, while on the other he was explosively angry and irritable towards his own family. His own inconsistency was one of the sources of his torment (Herman 1997, 56) .

George describes a similar, complex picture in which trauma both impelled him to withdraw from close relationships and to seek them desperately. His emerging "passion for people" and intense anger made for a turbulent and dangerous transition towards change:

> I think that before I got shot, that I was already changing before I got shot. I was changing, in my heart I was changing. At first, I was cold hearted and my mother died, and when my mother died it was basically me and my brothers and sisters, but I seen a different description of people, what I thought people were at

first, they didn't seem to be that way no more, and, the relationship I had with people changed. I became, in a lot of ways, more vicious toward my home boys, because every body was fearful of me and intimidated by me, and stuff like that, and so I became more vicious towards them, but at the same time I became compassionate, I know it seems like a paradox, but that is how I became.

I'll give you an example. One day my homeboys were beating up on a Hispanic woman. There was two of them fighting in the alley, and I walked up, I thought it was wrong. And so, I ended hitting my home boy, I hit him, you know, and told them, one by one, two of you don't fight like that, I just hit him, my home boy, to leave it alone. And so, things like that, I would kick a passion for people, but at the same time I would be real mean, I still had that edge to do mean stuff, to do bad stuff, and it was lousy even though I wanted to do good stuff, so in my heart I wanted to do good things, but, my actions was bad.

However, among many violence-involved youth, oscillation processes, a natural characteristic of the process of change, are often attributed by outside observers as indicators of lack of honesty, inability to change. The challenge for violence intervention theory and practice is to understand the very natural fluctuations in the process of change as they manifest themselves among violence-involved youth and children in order to facilitate transformation of consciousness and behavior and to set realistic expectations for interventions that foster change.

You Have to Kinda Get There, And it Can Be Far: Change Takes Time

The process of change (from precontemplation, contemplation, preparation, action to maintenance) varied widely among the participants, ranging from a few months with no relapse for two of the young people to several years for most of the other participants. For the change process was characterized by off-and-on engagement. For youth contemplating violence cessation, like people taking action to modify addictions, relapse was the rule rather than the exception. For some, it would take years before they were able to maintain a behavioral goal for six months, successfully altering the behavior and reaching a particular criterion, such as no longer carrying a weapon, no longer associating with a negative peer group, no fighting. Yet their period of contemplation and preparation for change would not be as protracted as those found in a longitudinal study of New Years resolution makers who reported five or more years of consecutive pledges before maintaining their behavioral goal for at least six months (Norcross and Vangarelli 1989). Like successful self-changers with smoking (Schacter 1982), many of the study participants had made three to four action attempts to modify their behavior, experiences or environment in order to overcome their "violence problem." According to Lulu,

> Sometimes you have some cases where the person, the young person will come in faithfully for two, three months. And next thing, the person will disappear and you won't see them 'til six months. Then you still got to be there, you know.

However, among the youth, the sustained presence of a primary helper strongly influenced the likelihood of progression through the various stages and eventual termination of violence.

> Years, it could take, it could, some kids might try at times they just might come in a period of few months but some it might take years. You know, it depends on how caring the person is that really wants to change that child. You want to understand where he's coming from first of all and you need to realize that changes don't occur overnight, it takes a long time. Have patience with the kid don't let them go. Don't let them go astray either though. You got to hold them close to you and help them in anyway you can.

The road to a new life has many detours, and is paved with "mistakes;" therefore, receiving sustained, intensive attention was key in helping a young person stay on that road:

> It is part of the process 'cause that's how you learn, you make mistakes. He's bound to make plenty of mistakes or she and I think you just got get them involved in anything you find that's appealing to them, O.K. I got a little brother and him he's 15 and I hadn't seen him for years. When I seen him he had a shaved head, baggy pants, same style that I was at his age basically, he looks up to me and he remembers me from back when I used to be gang related and stuff and there's not much interest that he does have but today I found out that he likes working on cars. He wants to work on cars. He don't even like school or nothing, but he likes working on cars so I want to pursue that and I'm going to get him involved in some kind of vocational training program where he could work with cars. You know so I'm going to pursue that, I'm going to take that

step and see where that leads. I mean it's also intensity. You need intensity with children cause they've got a short attention span and if you let them flow too long, they might just keep going. So you got to pay them a lot of attention, intensity. And just don't try them to tell them what to do. There's a difference between counseling somebody and advice, there's a difference between counseling somebody and trying to make that person do what you want to do sort of manipulating. I mean you want to just understand the kid.

At 20, Flaco would sum up his trajectory. The first two steps took three months, but it would be another two years before he could say he had his life straight and that there was no going back:

Changing was hard, but I did it. I managed to succeed with it, and here I am. For me, when I think of changing, I think the first step was the decision that I had my daughter to live for, and that I had to leave the gang, and then the next step was to try and get hooked up into a program. The next one was clearing up my warrants. Change is about taking it to the next level, and there are many levels, it wasn't only one thing. It was one thing, but yeah, okay. You've made a decision, but now you have to get the skills, you have to be able to deal with people so that you don't blow up. You have to be able to hold a job. You have to finish school. You gotta do a lot to be able to make that change. You got to keep goin' and goin' and goin' like the Energizer bunny. *[Chuckle]*

Even the young people, who clearly realized that their life had to change, sometimes did not differentiate cessation of violence from the recognition that something meaningful and positive should (and could) be done with their lives. For Andres, it took two years from the date of his first revelation to recognize the latter and another year and a half for his resolution to begin to materialize. Through community public health voluntary service, enrollment in a GED program, assisting other young people who had been shot, he would eventually find stable employment.

In L.A. it was that, it was basically my family that's what it was for me. One day I was sitting there thinking about stuff and it just hit me out of nowhere, to me it was like a punch out of nowhere and I was like, damn, if they don't get me, I'll get them and then *[years later]* in Boston it was like, just sitting one day and thinking, whoa, I was like this is leading to nowhere *[laughs]* I have to change, I'm getting too old for this.

For Cy the process took one and a half years for him to stand on his "own two feet" and leave his former self behind "on some street corner somewhere." Yet it would take another year and a half to deal with the residual effects of his previous life. He had to clear all warrants, complete probation, and have his records sealed so he could apply for a job and be certain that he would not lose it because of past or unresolved criminal activities. At that point, the community and self-perception became aligned.

Martin offers an illustrative glimpse on how the decision not to carry a weapon was achieved, a reduction of one of the main risk factors for homicide victimization and/or perpetration. Stabbed at 14, he would be admitted for multiple stab wounds and head injuries on different occasions.

> I went in on a Thursday and left on a Wednesday, that was like November 20 or 21 and I went back on the 27th because it got infected. I was fighting when I got out and I got hit in it and it infected up, so I had to go back to the hospital.

Martin remembers that the hospital intervention following his first admission had some effect; he developed a safety plan with the intervention worker, with whom he talked:

> about what happened again. And retaliation, and the good aspects of going back and doing stuff to those kids. You know, what's a bad thing, showing its better side than going back into that stuff. Basically just talking cause, you know, at the time I was thinking different, he was just letting me know the choice is up to me, but there is better options. He wasn't trying to make me, he was just letting me know it was best to think about you do stuff. I was just running around in the game room where he came to see me, cause I was mad.

He describes his attitude at the time as "waiting to die. I was saying to myself, I'm tired of waiting to die, I wanted someone to kill me."

Returning to the community was a frightening experience. The young man who had tried to kill him on two occasions was "still out there, he wasn't arrested and then, I was still running into him, like I seen him down the liquor store." It would be on one of those occasions that he would be re-injured, and readmitted:

> I'd be shut up in the house, like I can't, I got to walk around for a few minutes. I got to walk around the neighborhood for

minutes to get out, get rid of the tension. I was afraid to go outside cause you are so able and free in the hospital and everything. Everybody's all friendly and cool. That's why I was outside, and I had another fight and that's when my stab wounds got infected. I had to go back to the hospital.

Once discharged from the hospital, Martin would decide that carrying a knife was insufficient protection, that he needed a gun instead. The safety issues still had not been resolved, even as he stayed with the violence intervention program.

They had a Christmas party and stuff. I enjoyed it, but it really didn't do anything when I was like, out and at home, going out to the bus stop. That's when it's really, that's when it really hits home, when you got to walk down the street, when you got to go to the bus stop, when you got to go to the store. That's when it's really different than being at those meetings. What do you do in real life when these guys are ready to whoop you?

The program lacked insufficient intensity to address the issues he had to face upon his return, and Martin had not yet been able to connect in a deep and trusting way with a helper. He had already made some behavioral changes and some reductions in his problem behaviors, but had not yet achieved the criterion for effective action or reduction of risk factors for recidivism. Soon afterwards, his mother's intervention would set off a chain of events that would enable him to move beyond a preparation stage (in which individuals intend to take action in the very near future and have unsuccessfully taken action in the past year) into a sustained action and maintenance stage.

My mother said I wanted to kill and she found weapons around the house, and she got to get me worried, so she said "Go to the psychiatrist lady." That is how I met everybody, going to that psychiatrist. When my mom found out I had a gun in the house, she thought I was crazy. So they had me see a psychiatrist. And the lady I was talking to, she'd say that she wanted me to talk. She'd say "I know what you need. You need, like a black role model to talk to." So she hooked me up with this other guy, and this guy, he knew what was goin' on. He knew I had court date and everything. And then that's when I talked to Mr. B. And when I started talking to him, me and my friends, we went to his office. We was bringing a gang with us to his office, too, going to talk to him about what was going on. And he came to court with me and, basically, got me off the hook. It was him who got me off the hook 'cause the other guy wasn't gonna, the judge guy wasn't gonna let go. They were gonna say well, my story is not the same, my story is not sufficient. But right towards the end, Mr. B started talking saying that, you know, he had done some work with me, and stuff, and sees that I'm capable of handling myself. And the judge went along with it. So I felt like I owed him something. That's what kept me hooked up with him. That was like the immediate turn around for my life.

Martin was assisted in his resolve to change by the removal from the community of his assailant:

One relief this guy that I was having the main, main problem with, he had been arrested. So that was one thing that kept everything cool. Oh, I still was like carrying little weapons on me when I was the bus station. I used to have kitchen knives I used to hide up my sleeves, and hide'em in my bag and stuff. And then it took me a while to let go of all of that. It took me a while, um, I'd say probably about, maybe about a year to stop carrying. I used to bring the knife with me and stuff, and it just took me a while to say I'm not gonna use it. I'm not gonna put myself in a position to get locked up or something, so why, why carry it? I just gave it all up. I just carry nothing.

It took Martin two years from the time he was 15 to 17 to "kind of give it up" and no longer carry any weapons. In 1994, when he was 18 years old, Martin spoke about the relative level of improvement he had made over the years. In the last years he had had only gotten into two fights, both without weapons and of lesser intensity that his previous fights. He had also begun college, in a different town, to remove himself from his community. When returning home for a vacation, he would learn that the young man who had assaulted him was out of jail. Martin described feeling like he was sometimes "waiting to die again" because on his trips home he would continue to see the young man "basically every week." He was not sure if the "beef" the young man had with him had dissipated, and was fearful. "I don't want to get caught sleeping, you never know, you can never tell. That's the way I see it."

When interviewed at 21, in 1997, Martin considered that he had securely laid his past behind him. The feelings he had in which he had to continue to work to prevent any recidivism and consolidate his behavior and attitudinal changes in his late teen years have dissipated. He is preparing to graduate and working as a residential counselor at a home for emotionally disturbed adolescents, and feels fully ready and prepared to live.

It's All Good: Generalized Benefits of Change

For the young participants, change attained in one sphere resulted in the modification of other problems. The new knowledge and skills gained were applied to new and different situations. For Charo, working with other teens around their and her anger management issues helped her regain the control she had relinquished to her partner who severely abused her. For Emmanuel, learning to control his anger towards his peers helped him regulate his outbursts towards his girlfriends. Learning to walk away from fights helped many of the participants walk way from other potentially harmful situations and better control the ways in which they would react to a series of insults (on the streets, in schools and in the workplace). Learning how to reach out to and interact with clinicians assisted them in accessing other health services urgently needed for the attainment of physical and mental health and well-being. These yardsticks in their health histories included getting a physical, going to the dentist, getting nutritional counseling, getting tests to determine brain damage that might have resulted from violence-related injury. Getting tested for tuberculosis and for HIV was made easier for many of the young people, who had been exposed, and who now found the courage and sufficient future orientation to care about and face the result of these tests. They also were more likely to comply with treatment, if seropositive.

Education about the public health consequences of youth violence and knowledge about other forms of violence (their causes, effects, and ways to control it) helped many of the young people draw analogies between the humanity of one group affected by violence and another, previously derided and dehumanized group. For Emmanuel, gains in his education about street violence spilled over and influenced his engagement in other forms of violence, as he refrained from assaulting perceived or known homosexuals.

Such yardsticks of achievement (both in terms of acquiring new knowledge, applying it to the immediate as well as to different situations) were important to the young people and to their helpers who observed the transformation. They provided an indication of change, internalization, and appropriation of new positive behaviors, and were testament to the potential for growth and development of the young people. Such indicators provided a finer analysis of treatment and change progression than the usual indicators of treatment gains or intervention effects (the number and severity of fights, re- hospitalizations, deaths) and could serve as gauges of overall progress during the difficult oscillation and "slip back" periods.

You Can't get Stuck on Stupid: Moving Ahead with Life

Part of the process of change involved coming to terms with their traumatic past, and eventually moving ahead with their lives. As Erika stated, it is important to not allow oneself or others to become engulfed by traumatic events, but to try to draw positive aspects from very negative events.

> They even told me to go to therapy for me to speak out... and sometimes I tell people to speak out, how they feel about it because they might be angry about how their dad died, how their uncle died, or how their friend died, or they might be angry because they got abused. They need to go and talk about it, and some times, some times there's no therapy, some times people don't have no money for therapy, some they don't know there are services, the nonprofit agencies have long waiting lists, there's a waiting period before you get to one, and some times all you can do is just be the listening say, "I can imagine how you feel." Just pat folks on the shoulder or listen and hand the Kleenex over, get them involved, try to get them to forget. Not to forget, but 'cause you can't forget it, but to bring them out and so they won't be stuck on stupid, on the tragedy. Like after this man got buried, they had a barbecue. All the family members. And it was sad at first because everybody was, you know, stressed out. But it was to bring people out of this so people won't just be stuck on stupid. Because some times when you get stuck on a tragedy, you get like stressed out and you just get stuck. And you can take a tragedy and turn it around by bringing the people, the people that were involved, getting them involved in something... a church program, or to the movies, or doing something, playing a game, a board game, going out somewhere, exploring something different.

Over time, the young people describe transcending their old identities and being able to contemplate their stories as one among many, and place their experience with violence as part of the human condition. As Herman explains:

> Commonality with other people carries with it all the meaning of the word common. It means belonging to a society, having a public role, being part of that which is universal. It means having a feeling of familiarity, of being known, of communion. It means taking part in the customary, the commonplace, the

ordinary, and the everyday. It also carries with it a feeling of smallness, of insignificance, a sense that one's own troubles are "as a drop in the sea" (Herman 1997, 236) .

As the young people were able to transcend their old behaviors, identities, and traumatic experiences, they were more willing to recognize both the damage done to them and to others, and become more forgiving of themselves and others. This was generally achieved when they no longer felt that the emotional and social damage would be permanent, even if some would be permanently injured. Often, this awareness was accompanied by an understanding that positive aspects of self had also emerged from traumatic, "negative" experiences, even as they recognized the high price they had to pay. As Carl explained:

What made me the person I am today? It's just the person that I always been inside me. My mother, grandmother, all the shit I been through, all my friends, all the kids I looked up to, my uncle, my family in general. All that's collaborated together with my support team in school and school in general. The streets have made me street smart and school has made me book smart. These two elements you put together will dominate a young man. And I can't be stopped now that I got those two components. You got kids that only are book smart and don't know what the hell. You know what I'm saying. Once they step out in the big world by themselves they don't know which way to look. You got people that are just street smart and you give them a book and they don't know how to fucking read. Excuse my language. I got two so I'm fortunate. You know I got to be in a wheelchair to use it, but hey, life goes on.

There Just Ain't No Stopping Me, I'm Too Strong: Change and Resilience

Resilience has been variously defined but generally refers to an individual's capacities to endure, survive, effectively cope with, and master severe challenges as from privation, pain and abuse; and to maintain and sometimes enhance the quality of one's psychological integration in the process. A resilient person is able to use treatment to improve coping skills so that later adjustment is moderately, sometimes dramatically, improved. Hardy or resilient individuals have frequently exhibited one or more of the following characteristics: 1) early awareness that his or her parents (family members) were not functioning well; 2) identification and frequent use of alternate persons as sources of security, nurturing, and developmental identification; 3) early identification and refinement of a special talent that opened up new developmental paths and social networks; 4) high motivation to develop, often expressed in unusual tenacity and intensity of activity; and 5) a tendency to experience frustrations and even trauma as challenges and opportunities for development. Other aspects of resilience are a sense of meaning, purpose, or coherence, and a perceived network of caring others—both of which encourage hope, coping, and personal engagement. During stressful events, highly resilient people are able to make use of any opportunity for purposeful action in concert with others.

The theories of resilience are not generally applied to describe the characteristics of young offenders or those who have become enmeshed in a violent lifestyle. Yet these individuals, too, have acquired life skills, demonstrated personal strength and resilience in the face of adversity, although in a manner not circumscribed by the larger society, and not in the traditionally accepted, linear sequence. Charo and Emmanuel describe themselves as having "ganas," loosely translated from Spanish as a drive, a visceral wish to survive, a knack for life, also described by the other young people in the study. Their strength, resilience and talent for life becomes even more apparent "when the going gets tough" and these young people, barely escaping death, experiencing injury or disability, regroup and attain or regain vitality of mind and body. They offer examples of the "Batman syndrome" among the most unlikely candidates. Albert explains:

> I'm brown, bold and beautiful. Just superman. *[laughter]* I feel that just everything I want to be that's, that's what I think, I'm everything I want to be. I want to be this person that could help other people and I am. I want to be proud of what I am doing and I am. I want to be strong and I am. I'm everything, I'm the one that's how I feel. I feel proud of what I am. I am real confident in myself, very high self-esteem. There just ain't no stopping me, I'm too strong. Nobody could touch this, they can't put me down, can ever make me go back into the life I had. I'm real strong willed.

Given their direct exposure to and involvement in violence, to remain hopeful and expend the efforts of existence in the face of such chronic adversity and loss requires a dimension of resilience that other, more protected children, who were able to resist the lure of violence or "the crazy life" (*la vida loca*) may not possess. Cy recognizes that he is strong and admires his ability to bounce back from adversity.

I came a long way. I can't look at nobody else because nobody else was there to talk to me. And I feel like I had to struggle by myself, so the person I admire, not to be stuck on myself, but I learned a lot. I have learned a lot from all the things I went through, but I admire myself. I look up to myself and keep myself focused. I always remember my past so I can get ahead, because I don't want to forget my past. If I do, I'll probably end up back in my past.

Joining or growing into a delinquent peer group, or gang, which paradoxically multiplied dramatically their chances for death and injury, could similarly be interpreted as a coping strategy with dimensions of solidarity as a means to withstand an adverse early environment, strengthening their sense of being. The young participants do not fit the description of the academically or intellectually challenged juveniles engaged in anti-social activities. For Carl, Martin, Albert, Charo, and Ruby there was no discontinuity in their worlds between dealing drugs, being gang involved, and performing extremely well academically in school. Erika was in a program for gifted children. Andres, Delbert, Andrea had been at various times in their schooling careers recognized for their broad intellectual interests, with Andres frequently skipping school at 14 years of age to spend his time reading entries that interested him in encyclopedias at the public library. George and other young participants, with varying degrees of academic preparation, could also be described as forming part of a self-selecting group of young counterculture thinkers.

The importance of experiences in adolescence for later development has been extensively documented, especially as it pertains to the development of identity. Recent research on identity and moral development—some of it inspired by feminist theorists in those areas—has offered new insights into the paradox of the self, more flexible in adolescence than in later periods, and which is experienced primarily through/with others and vice versa (Mahoney 1991). The stories of the young people underscore this.

These young people are made neither of glass nor of steel. Rather, the stories of the youth suggest that like humans in general, they bend with environmental pressures, resume their shapes once those pressures are lifted, and are unlikely to be permanently misshapen by transient insults and traumatic experiences even those that are quite severe. When the environments are improved, these young people's adaptations improve. They are capable of improved and dramatic adaptations through learning, although an individual's improvement depends on that person's being willing to try something else, and the provision of new opportunities and supports over time.

Developmental Needs of Adolescents

The stories of transformation underscore that these adolescents are societal resources and are themselves central actors in their own development, and that all adults who interacted with adolescents along the way, regardless of their familial, program or community connection, influenced their development and process of change. These adult helpers could be positive or detrimental to the young person's positive development. As Zeldin and Spivak (1993, 8) suggest, and the stories corroborate, effective intervention strategies and self-change approaches had the result of "affirmatively meeting the developmental needs of all adolescents and helping them build functional competencies necessary for adulthood." Developmental youth outcomes for healthy and accomplished young people include aspects of identity and areas of ability. Perceptions of self-confidence and well-being and connection and commitment to others (such as a sense of safety and structure, self-worth, mastery and future, belonging and membership, responsibility and autonomy and self-awareness and spirituality) were important to influence as part of the process of change. Among the outcomes identified through the young participants' stories were a perception that one is relatively safe and that daily events are somewhat predictable, the belief in one's ability to make a contribution to others and to self, a perception that one belongs and is valued in the larger community, a perception of some control over daily events and a sense of accountability for one's actions and consequences to others, and a feeling of connection and purpose. The areas of ability that were developed along their trajectory of change included

- knowledge, skills, strategies, and attitudes that enabled the young individuals to act on and respond to other people and events;
- ability and motivation to act in ways that ensured current and future good physical health for themselves and others;
- ability and motivation to respond to adverse and positive situations, to reflect on one's emotions and surroundings and to engage in leisure and fun;
- ability and motivation to think critically and independently, to problem-solve, to learn in a variety of settings, and to gain basic knowledge needed for educational advancement;
- acquisition of career-related abilities and aspirations in order to obtain the functional, technical and organizational skills necessary for future employment, including an understanding of their options and the steps and steps necessary too achieve their goals.

- development of civic, social and cultural competencies were intrinsic to the process of change as the young people developed the ability and wish to work collaboratively for the larger good, and to sustain positive friendships with others, respecting and affirmatively responding to differences among individuals and groups of diverse backgrounds, interests and traditions.

These programmatic recommendations hark to the alternate theories and explanations of Maslow (1970), Fromm (1973), Dewey (1935) and Gil (1996). These theorists stress that the answer to the causation of violence lies in the inability of individuals, groups and societies to meet their inherent human needs and to constructively unfold their potential. Such needs range from biological-material needs, social-psychological needs, productive creative needs, self-actualization, needs and spiritual needs. When consistently obstructed, states Gil (1996), these needs are "expressed destructively as counter violence."

According to Gil, the underlying, fundamental social problems, forms of "initiating structural violence" which lead to interpersonal violence ("reactive counter violence") must be recognized and addressed. "Such an approach," remarks Gil (1996), "is consistent with the public health concept of primary prevention of diseases and destructive conditions, which involves the identification and eradication of sources, rather than mere neutralization of symptoms." Intervening to counteract, buffer, deflect, or otherwise mitigate barriers that hinder developmental factors that are conducive to pro-social development (and the underlying societal processes that erect the barriers) can augment the likelihood that children or youth involved as aggressors, victims, or bystanders will cease to condone violence.

Writing about the underlying assumptions that often drive violence prevention and other youth programs, Zeldin and Spivak note that when adolescents or older children (particularly those of low socio-economic minority status and those belonging to the urban underclass) begin to engage in behavior construed as delinquent or aggressive, they are generally referred to categorical and controlled services. These services are specifically designed to target social, psychological, and subcultural deficits (such as anger management, drug awareness, dropout recovery, homework clubs, detention, moral reasoning interventions). Increasingly, under the rubric of prevention, such secondary and tertiary services are being extended to children of younger ages who merely belong to an at-risk pool or subgroup as part of a primary outreach and prevention effort.

Embedded in this approach, write Zeldin and Spivak (1993), is the belief that such high-risk adolescents do not desire to become contributing members of their communities or that, as a group, these children require re-education. The enriched environment and stimulus necessary for positive development (environments that include sustained interactions with caring adults, relevant learning experiences and legitimate opportunities for young people to contribute in a meaningful way to the welfare of others) rarely constitute the first response.

Numerous reports have stressed the growing complexity of adolescent development, and the particular challenges faced by non-college bound youth and young members of minority groups, especially African Americans and Latinos. The rapid demographic changes, labor market shifts, and socio-cultural transformations have extended adolescence well into the 20s, leading to a heterogeneity of pathways from adolescence into adulthood (Mortimer and Larson 2002). According to the Institute of Medicine's report on community programs to promote youth development, the difficulties for non-college bound minority youth seeking employment are substantial. Summarizing current research on adolescent development and transition to adulthood, the report concludes that unlike many other industrialized countries, there is very little institutionalized support in the United States for the transition from secondary schooling to work. Further, "stereotypes about the competence of African American and Latino youth, along with their lower levels of 'soft skills' (e.g., the ability to communicate effectively, resolve conflicts, and prepare for and succeed in a job interview), along with the loss of employment options in many inner-city communities, have made employment for these youth (particularly males) quite problematic" (NRC and IOM 2002). Programs that prepare young people to face these challenging trends in the decades ahead are critical, as are those that are informed by positive youth development, that assert that "problem-free is not fully prepared" (Pittman et al. 2002), and which transcend remediation and prevention.

WE ARE NOT 'LOST': THE PROCESS OF TRANSFORMATION, VIOLENCE PREVENTION, AND INTERVENTION PRACTICE AND THEORY

The particulars of each individual life in process are truly unique. The experience of change is individualized, contextualized (especially culturally and socially) and cannot be separated from the "experience of the experience." Despite this, abstract principles, stages, and broader processes surfaced from the stories of the young people in this study. The stories delineate some commonalities in the experience of change, with important intervention implications.

It is also clear from their narratives that the private and public are interdependent, and that to capitalize on this window of opportunity, interventions need to understand individual particulars, transpersonal generalizations, and the dimensions of what constitutes the public realm for that young person. A delicate balance exists between what is appropriate to emphasize as within the power of an individual to change (especially among disadvantaged children and adolescents) and what change in the social structures need to take place in order to facilitate this transformation.

The stories and common themes contained in the stories of transformation begin to suggest some contours for our efforts at helping understand the elusive structure of how violence-involved adolescents change.

I Wanted to Stop but Didn't Know How: Natural Cessation and Change

Mulvey and Rosa, delinquency scholars, have described spontaneous and self-determined decisions to stop breaking the law among untreated reformed late adolescent delinquents as the "natural cessation" of delinquency. They found that this behavior change had been preceded in each case by the youths' arriving at a changed perspective on their current behavior and future prospects and resolving to change the former in order to improve the latter. Behavior change followed from arriving at the conclusion that their law-breaking was interfering with their ability of making their way in the larger world. This change was aided by the normative change in previous group identity, loosening of group ties, and the forging of an individual identity (Mulvey and Rosa 1986).

The participants' trajectory towards change suggests that there is a period, often prolonged, between the onset of this weariness and questioning (described by some of the youth occurring as young as eleven), and the later, changed perspective on their behavior facilitated by maturational processes in late adolescence/early adulthood. This period may be becoming longer as youth and children become more exposed to more lethal and injurious consequences of violence (due to the prevalence of guns) at earlier ages. This is a time of limbo, in which these children and adolescents are often forgotten, and which can further contribute to their feeling unsafe and unwanted. The participants of the study survived and eventually "matured out," but they retell the stories of many peers and family members who did not. They describe other young people who were tired and fearful of the cumulative impact of trauma in their lives and in the lives of their families, but who were unable or insufficiently mature to ask for help although they desired it. Many of these young people had difficulty imagining that their life could be other than what it was. Upon returning to their communities, some died from subsequent injuries, others were incarcerated, and a few committed suicide.

The existence of this period suggests that suitable interventions can be initiated earlier, focusing on younger adolescents or preadolescents. The young people expressed feelings of weariness and fear in their earliest stages of active involvement in acts of youth interpersonal and street group violence, suggesting that it is not necessary to rely on the onset of "maturation" for many of the young people to grow out of delinquent behavior. Due to the increased use and improved performance of lethal weapons (semi-automatics and other guns versus knives, bats, bricks and stones) this becomes critical, since delaying intervention will result in the increase of a young offender and victim population. (See Table 2, Fostering change among adolescent victims and perpetrators of violent assault.)

They Just Can't Identify Us, So They Label Us as Lost: Progression and Change

Despite extensive and deep histories of involvement in violence, the young people who took part in this study were able to begin and complete a process of change, contrary to predictors that would make these young people unlikely candidates for change based on their very serious problem histories. Among the young people in this study, change was not due to a mysterious spontaneous recovery, although their experiences with violence led many of the young people to confront and consider the meaning and mysteries of life, sometimes at very young ages. An equivocal concept of "change" as a quality that an individual does or does not possess, and ignoring the quality of the impulse leading to personal transformation, leads to a theoretically difficult position for understanding its process and promotion.

A comparison of the structure of change that surfaced from the young participants' stories with those outlined by Prochaska and DiClemente suggests a number of conclusions that are consonant with and amplify their findings, generating conclusions regarding the process of change for violence involved youth. These findings require further exploration in future research.

The process of transformation recounted by the young people was similar within and outside the various intervention spheres (hospital, community, corrections). The types of supports, resources, and opportunities needed to learn, adopt, and maintain pro-social life skills did not differ. The journeys of change undertaken by the young people also led to a modification of various problem behaviors other than violence and the adoption of many positive, pro-social behaviors along the way.

Table 2. Fostering change among adolescent victims and perpetrators of violent assault

Profile of a youth contemplating change
Defining change contemplation: A young person who has begun to reevaluate him/herself, and is experiencing emotional reactions to the negative aspects of their conduct
Behaviors associated with youth contemplating cessation • Manifestation of fear (actions/thoughts/statements) • Request for help • Consideration of precipitating circumstances leading to traumatic incident • Consideration of alternative behavior • Weariness/apathy • Angry acting out • Guilt, shame
Behavioral profile Key factors to consider: • History of interests and participation • Victimization and perpetration history, distinguishing between the different types of violence • Substance abuse and drug trade involvement
Primary antecedents to cessation of assaultive conduct • Familial involvement • Interest in school and expectation for achievement • Pro social attachments, behaviors • Living in a safer neighborhood • Living in a community rich with child and youth focused resources (boys and girls clubs, recreational facilities, etc.) • Sense of self-worth, of purpose • Religious/spiritual beliefs • Non-discriminatory, effective policing and social services • Living in a community, belonging to a positive group with cohesion • History of participation • Familiar, community, societal disavowment of violence • Social capital of neighborhood
Secondary antecedents to cessation of assaultive conduct • Increased ability to verbalize feelings, thoughts • Decreased preoccupation with enemy or perpetrator • Decreased sense of stigma • Shift in cost/benefit ratio of violence vs. non-violence • Distinction between respect and fear, • Changing assessment of power realities • Wish to contribute to contribute to community, larger society • Emergence of new or buried belief system • Increased sense of guilt

continued

Table 2, continued

Secondary antecedents to cessation of assaultive conduct, continued
- Integration in school and/or community, faith communities
- Cultural enrichment
- Increased ability to access services, quality medical and rehabilitation care
- Involvement/improved performance in school, community activities, work.
- Reinforcement of sense of self worth, sense of purpose
- Sustained exposure to consistent caring, instrumental adult(s)
- Sustained exposure to positive youth role models, who have a sense of solidarity.
- Integration into "new homes" (that provide a sense of belonging (a set of behavior codes and standards ethics). These "new homes" can be secular or religious, groups, in a variety of settings)
- Reestablishment or provision of "safety shields" of security and affection that are provided by family, group, community and society
- Extent of community education about adolescent interpersonal violence

Community life profile
- Feels greater consistent care, support and understanding
- Spends less time hanging out on street
- Increasingly avoids parties where peers are drinking and drugging
- Increasingly avoids areas where violent activity takes place
- Views him/herself as a person worth emulating to siblings, peers
- Keeps busy to reduce stress, flashbacks and lapses
- Increased introspection
- Decreased weapons carrying
- Adoption of new interests
- Increasing participation in community life
- Develops motivation to participate in social, cultural and community settings as well as in schools and workplaces
- Develops abilities to participate in social, cultural and community settings as well as in schools and workplaces

Social services profile
- Exposure to continuous, sustained, easy-to-access social services
- Exposure to helpers who can phenomenologically approximate
- Belief in rehabilitation
- Specialized programs (including safe housing provision)
- Opportunities for non stigmatizing restitution

Community re-entry characteristics/profile
Key factors to consider:
- Level and type of individuals' violence involvement
- Extent of gun, drug, alcohol density
- Nature of policing, gang intervention services.
- Extent of organization of street or gang group
- Level of violence and crime (safety) in community
- Extent of poverty concentration

Table 2, continued

Community re-entry characteristics/profile, continued
- Extent of stable, safe, accessible housing
- Accessibility and quality of specialized social services and schooling
- Availability of jobs and opportunities for involvement in community work
- Social capital of family and neighborhood
- Extent of community education about nature of violence
- Availability of specialized victim services
- Extent of community and societal stigma
- Juvenile offender laws
- Positive peer groups of similar background

Medical care profile
- Exposed to quality, continuous, sustained, easy-to-access health services
- Exposed to helpers who can phenomenologically approximate
- Belief in treatability and preventability of violence

Home/social profile
- Exposure to positive peer influence
- Involvement in community organizations, sports, arts, religious activities higher youth and community worker monitoring
- Increased familial involvement or adoption of new home and family.
- Perception of schooling as positive /desirable
- Decreased involvement with old peer group
- Positive role model /mentor influence and involvement
- Opportunity to practice newly acquired skills
- Sense of purpose

Future orientation profile
- Envisages possibility of a positive future
- Feels that they have a contribution to make as they grow older/into adults
- Develops of a life plan
- Has adults in their lives who can assist they along that journey
- Able to access to information and resources to make life plan achievable
- Has greater confidence that such an opportunity will be given.
- Has greater feeling of controlling life outcome
- Has greater feeling of safety

The stories suggest that the successful termination involved a progression through a series of stages, and that these were not linear. The process of change for violence-involved youth did not differ in this respect from the studies of self- and therapy-assisted changers informing Prochaska and DiClemente's studies, nor were the oscillative processes unlike those that characterize general human change. Almost all the young people "slipped back" on several occasions before stabilizing and leaving the involvement in violence behind them for good. The process of change, like that experienced by other changers studied by Prochaska and DiClemente, is marred with setbacks.

The stories of the young people suggest that there are distinct processes of change among violence-involved youth, and that the time it took for the young people to stabilize and terminate involvement in violent behavior through these various stages ranged from three months to four years. Most young people repeated a progression through these various stages before leaving their old lives and mindset finally behind.

On a practical level, the absence of an accurate and comprehensive diagnostic concept has serious consequences for treatment and for the development of community services to encourage self- or guided change in natural settings. Attempts to fit the patients into the mold of existing diagnostic constructs (the "innocent victim"/habitual juvenile offender), lead to a fragmented understanding and treatment. Programs that are structured to assist similar young people in a linear fashion are likely to yield disappointing results, and the theories—received categories of understanding that inform this—only obfuscate. More importantly, these premises can hamper the natural and assisted internal processes of change among young people in similar circumstances, by pathologizing and labeling them when they do not progress accordingly.

Treatment and Change

The stories reveal that the more "ready for change" a young person is at the moment of intervention, an intervention at times resulting from injuries induced by a traumatic event, the more likely the individual will move along the process and terminate the behavior. The premise that traumatic experience and violence-induced disability automatically create change and treatment readiness, preparing young people for action-oriented programs, is likely to generate disappointing results.

Treatment and community alternatives for young people involved in violence need to include a variety of strategies and approaches depending on the change readiness of the young person. There was not a single trajectory or intervention that was best suited for all the young people interviewed and the many others they counseled, underscoring the need to acknowledge and respect individual differences and develop programs that allow for varied approaches. Treatment approaches to overcome perpetration and victimization proclivities needed to address the contextual reality of their situation.

The age of the child or adolescent, their life circumstances, and the general complexity of the causes and motivations of violent behavior require helpers in and out of programs consider a broad range of factors. The myriad individual, situational, and community level influences on the causation and prevention of violence require deeper consideration than the behavior change interventions of other health problems, on which Prochaska and DiClemente's theories are based. Further, the range of ages at which many young people find themselves enmeshed in violent behavior and begin to contemplate change (including preadolescent children) encompasses various stages of child and adolescent development. This suggests variation even among violence-involved youth about the relative weight of certain processes over others.

Solely focusing on deficit remediation as a means to prevent violence recidivism among adolescents was insufficient in fostering a process of change. According to Zeldin and Spivak, deficit remediation foci "reinforce faulty societal assumptions about adolescents generally." A concurrent youth development approach should be integrated alongside such programs. Such an approach, argue the authors, "requires that policies and programs be directed toward meeting the fundamental development needs of young people and demands that treatment, service and community providers seek to help adolescents develop a full range of competencies" (Zeldin and Spivak 1993, 6).

Treatment models need to recognize the resiliency of their youth participants, even though they are violence-involved. Resiliency theory, which implicitly drives some facets of primary and secondary youth violence prevention programs, was developed to explain why one-third of "at risk" individuals did not develop psychological or developmental problems, despite facing many obstacles. Despite experiencing moderate to severe perinatal stress, being raised by parents with little formal education in a disorganized family environment, living in chronic poverty, experiencing desertion, divorce, or the effects of parental alcoholism or mental illness, some children and youth had individual or environmental characteristics that fostered an adaptive outcome. Associated with a sense of hope, of spiritual purpose, and a belief that negative life odds can be overcome, the characteristics of resiliency, combined with external support systems or protective mechanisms (such as the presence of a caring, supportive adults, opportunities for involvement in meaningful activities, task accomplishment, and high expectations) modify the individual's response to a particular risk factor (Gabriel et al. 1996; Bernard 1991). The stories reveal that a greater program and research emphasis needs to be placed on the capacities, resiliency, and the agency of youth who have been impacted by violence, acknowledging those who not only survive but who also select and transform their social and physical environments.

If hospitalization provides a teachable, susceptible moment, it is in the larger social unit of community settings that the "steady barrage of interventions that erode destructive behavior over time" can effectively take place (Prothrow-Stith 1987, 141). Programs need to recognize that it may take a prolonged period of program involvement, often over a period of several years, not only to unlearn destructive behaviors but also to attain competencies (such as academic, and vocational development) to enhance their social, economic, and academic status once the young people have left behind acquaintance violence. Thus, treatment strategies should be linked to natural or deliberate interventions in community.

Helpers and Change

The stories reveal that numerous practitioners from different disciplines encountered by the young participants over the years emphasized different processes when working with their young clients. They rarely transcended the boundaries of their disciplines to address the full spectrum of risk factors, nor were they able to harness all the resources and provide the supports and opportunities for the young person to develop to his/her fullest potential. Nevertheless, helping relationships were a critical component in the young people's transformation. The primary helper, encountered in a variety of professional and other settings, often engaged the young person intensely, playing the dynamic role of primary motivator, often over a protracted period. Their success in influencing and guiding the young participants underscores the interactional and interpersonal process of change, behooving clinicians and others who serve youth to motivate and commit to work with their young clients.

The stories suggest that there are particular characteristics to effective helping for this segment of youth. Both professional and non-professional helpers, regardless of background, needed to be able to phenomenologically approximate. Styles of helping and modes of treatment, services, and opportunities must be closely matched to the preferred learning style and abilities of the young people. Due to the importance of sustaining motivation in the process of change and the primacy of the helper in facilitating and encouraging this process, matching clinicians and helpers with the individual youth is also important. Peers played an important role in assisting young people along a process of change.

There is little research on the impact of professional and natural helper characteristics on violence intervention treatment. This is a much needed area of research and monitoring, since clinicians and other providers working in a common setting and offering the same treatment approach often produce dramatic differences in terms of outcome. Even though responsivity and motivation are widely recognized as key factors mediating the success of treatment programs in correctional interventions, and described anecdotally by the young people and youth workers as critical to success, few professionals have the experience to be able to intuitively assess responsivity and change readiness. The signs are often contradictory. The stories also suggest that attitudes of clinicians and other youth workers that do not believe in, or match the aims and content of, a program may lower treatment intensity and reduce its integrity, and that the results can be extremely noxious.

Studies of health professionals indicate the demoralization of many professionals giving up on their clients' ability to change. The single biggest obstacle to getting physicians to help their patients with health behavior problems is the physician's pessimism about people's ability to change. In one study of health promotion among primary care physicians, two-thirds of the physicians were pessimistic about people's ability to change. Demoralized by the many patients who fail to change, rather than inspired by those who achieve it, the primary care physicians equated change with successful action, not fully appreciating how much they could further the process from a pre-contemplation stage to one in which the patient is ready for action (Orleans et al. 1985; Klar et al. 1992). As recommended by one of the young people in this study, "don't get hung up about successes, because successes are one by one. Because some times your success might be stopping by, and touching them, but we don't know."

Evaluation Implications

The adolescents in this study achieved significant psychological change as they progressed through a series of distinct stages (from pre-contemplation to maintenance), employing a variety of change processes. (see Table 3). Recovery from violence traumatization and the development of pro-social skills and attainment of adult life preparation competencies were integral parts of the transformation process for this population. The challenge remains to integrate these constructs into a model to guide the development of an assessment protocol for use by clinicians and program staff in non-health settings.

Their stories suggest that the assessment strategies to determine treatment or intervention effectiveness must measure these different strands and dimensions in the evolution of change. The paucity of standardized measures for these three dimensions (violence cessation/change, trauma recovery, youth development), often designed for a population other than the persistent adolescent victim/perpetrator, suggests a need for a new assessment strategy. Simple compilation of existing tests, premised on other received categories of understanding, will not capture this phenomenon.

Table 3. Change processes employed by study participants: variations and amplifications of Prochaska and DiClemente's typology

Environmental re-evaluation
Assessing how one's conduct, particularly through the effects of trauma, affects community, and loved ones, especially younger children and mothers. Observation of consequences of drug trade, weapons carrying.

Self re-evaluation
Assessing how the young person feels and thinks about oneself with respect to a problem: value clarification, imagery, corrective emotional experience.

Self-liberation
Belief in the need, the ability to change, and then choosing to act.

Helping relationships
Being open and trusting, being able to "tell the truth" to someone and to groups who care; therapeutic alliance, social support, positive peer self-help groups.

Dramatic relief
Experiencing and expressing feelings about one's problems and solutions, grieving losses, role playing. This was done privately and publicly (through organization of peace march, eulogies for peace at funerals, public statements made through art, music, literature, poetry, theatre).

Consciousness raising
Increasing information about self and both problems and potential; observations, confrontations, interpretations, journals, "bibliotherapy" through stories of life transformation such as Luis Rodriguez's "Always Running: Mi Vida Loca," history and stories of other peers.

Counterconditioning
Substituting alternatives for problem behaviors, relaxation, "keeping one's eyes on the prize," thinking of children and mothers, younger siblings, thinking of themselves the way their role models see them.

Stimulus control
Avoiding stimuli, people, high-risk situations that can lead to revictimization and/or perpetration; restructuring environment (removing weapons) or leaving one's environment (safehouse and relocation).

Reinforcement management
Rewarding one's self and being rewarded by others or a positive group for making changes.

Social liberation
Increasing "positive' alternatives for violence involved, at risk youth, advocating for rights of other victims and communities, oppressed groups, empowerment, policy interventions focusing on risk factors (guns, education), and social change.

There are a host of factors such an assessment strategy should address. Among these is the recognition that intervention participants are not at an equal departure point, that change is not a linear process, and that delays in recidivism and the mitigation of the seriousness of the relapses are additional valid measures in determining program effectiveness. Similarly, the strengths, skills, supports and opportunities available to intervention participants are not equal.

Further, the adoption of new skills and competencies have a generalizable treatment/change effect, indicating that these should also be legitimate measures in determining program effectiveness. Developmental yardsticks and the attainment of competencies needed for adult life are integral to the attainment and restoration of health for children and adolescents. Assessment strategies need to address the progress made towards the establishment of safety (from unpredictable danger to reliable safety); remembrance and mourning (from disassociated trauma to acknowledged memory); and reconnection with ordinary life (movement away from stigmatized isolation to restored social connection).

Accurate assessment of motivation and responsivity is also critical in order to attain maximum effectiveness. The symbiotic nature of change and the primary importance of helpers suggest that the interaction between the helper and the young person is central to the progress of change, and evaluation measures should also attempt to determine the relative contribution of this factor to progress.

Interdisciplinary Approaches to Fostering Change

Changing involvement in violence is a complex process, both as an individual and in program and community settings. The challenge for violence intervention theory and practice is to understand the natural fluctuations in the process of change as they manifest themselves among violence-involved youth and children in order to facilitate transformation of consciousness and behavior, and to set realistic expectations for interventions fostering change.

The themes and processes of change identified by the young people through their individual and collective stories have varied theoretical origins from competing disciplinary systems. Processes from cognitive, experiential, and psychoanalytic traditions were especially useful during the pre-contemplation and contemplation stages. Also, insights and techniques from existential and behavioral traditions helped the young people take concrete steps towards change. Social change processes and community organizing traditions were useful throughout all stages. Community and societal change accompanied individual change.

Rather than being the result of a reduction of one or two risk factors or behavioral conduct disorders, the termination of assaultive conduct and movement towards prosocial development and integration resulted from a number of psychological, developmental, social, economic, and historical processes shaping the lives of the young participants and their communities.

The stories of the young people suggest that processes from competing theories of change (and by extension, of underlying violence causation) can be integrated within their trajectories of change. The young people in this study were remarkably effective in finding practical means of integrating powerful change processes, even as the practitioners they interacted with often had narrow disciplinary approaches. The stories illustrate the need to develop a framework for change for violence-impacted youth that transcends both the narrow categorizations of violence as well as the gendered constructions of victimization and perpetration.

Research has soundly documented the importance of caring relationships to overall development. Indeed, resiliency research—the study of children who have "beaten the odds"— points to the presence of a caring adult as the pivotal reason why some children who should have succumbed to damaging life circumstances have thrived. An emphasis on people, as well as services, formally linking youth to adults in one-on-one supportive relationships was also important for the young people who took part in the study, suggesting that the provision and enhancement of such influences in health (and other) settings is important to enhancing the process of change among young people who have experienced violence-induced trauma.

Part of the process of unlearning reliance on acts of "counterviolence" required not only change at the individual level but a reasoned analysis of and involvement in altering the deficient role of social systems in addressing the unmet needs and potential of this sub sector of youth and their communities. For the young people who were contemplating the adoption of new behaviors, community action was an integral part in maintaining that momentum and resolve, thus reducing their odds of recidivism. A recent study of violence prevention and young adolescents' participation in community youth service with seventh and eighth graders in large, urban, public schools in New York found that

> When delivered with sufficient intensity, school programs which couple community service with classroom health instruction can have a measurable impact on violent behavior of a population of young adolescents at high risk for being both the perpetrators and victims of peer violence. Community service programs may be effective supplement to curricular interventions and a valuable part of multi component violence prevention programs (O'Donnell 1999).

The findings from the stories suggest that interdisciplinary approaches to, and investigations of the cessation of violence need to broaden their focus to include less proximal causes, and to move beyond analyses that favor individual and situational deficits.

On a deeper level, the challenge remains to articulate a standard or various standards on the beginnings of moral and ethical reflection on everyday and interpersonal violence that takes into account, but does not privilege, our own cultural and ethical suppositions(Shepherd). It also requires that reflections on everyday and interpersonal violence go beyond a focus on private life and on interactions among individuals to encompass a broader focus on public life and on relations between children, citizens and state polity. How we understand the often troubling and disturbing actions of some of our young, make sense of them and respond ethically ourselves, with compassion, are larger questions the field of violence prevention needs to address.

CHAPTER 7

Health, Hospitals, and Nonviolent Development

What could the schools have done to help turn you around to the person that you are now?

Well that's kind of hard, 'cause the school tried to, and I avoided. It's like my homeboys had more power over me than the school did.

How about the juvenile justice system?

That just got me smarter. That just like builds you up to be more destructive.

So what turned you around?

The hospital, I mean the gun. The shot, man. Getting shot and thinking about it. See, if I never would have got shot, I never would have been here.

—Manolo

All the young people in this study cited interactions with health and hospital institutions as providing an opportunity to reach other young people like them, provided they can get youth to open up to them and address the underlying circumstances that brought them there. The situations prompting youth and children to seek care for their wounds afford health and hospital programs a variety of unique opportunities to intervene in the cycle of violence, and to encourage and support nonviolent development. Among children who are at risk for victimization or perpetration due to bullying or community and peer group situations, health and hospital programs can treat and provide a departure point for intervention efforts. Such settings play a critical role in the prevention or redirection of a delinquent or injury career, assisting those who have become enmeshed in violence to extricate themselves, and reaching those who are maturing out. Programs in health care settings can help young people move through the various stages of change and help traumatized patients heal. In a broader sense, health and hospital settings can serve as an entry point to sustained, intensive youth development services in the community.

Risk factors for acquaintance and street violence recurrence have not been well described in public health literature, but may include gang involvement, poor academic achievement, poverty, psychiatric disturbances, and alcohol or other substance abuse (Sims et al. 1989; Goins et al. 1992). Recent research reports that hospitalized survivors of gunshot injuries report significant long term declines in physical and/or mental health at eight months post discharge. At a time when performance should be closer to normal, the health of the young victims was worse than before their injury with more than 80 percent reporting moderate or severe post-traumatic stress. Many of the patients interviewed report not having received even a consultation for mental health services eight months after injury (Greenspan and Kellermann 2002). A prospective study of symptoms of acute stress reported by violently injured youth in the emergency department suggests that early detection in the immediate post-injury period may offer clinicians the opportunity to connect with high-risk youth in family, community and professional support that may prevent long-term psychological ramifications (Fein et al. 2000). Another study by Mount Sinai and the Chicago Boys and Girls Clubs in Chicago found that young victims of violence ages 10-24 can change their lifestyles to avoid becoming repeat patients to emergency departments for treatment of gunshot wounds and stabbings, and that change can be initiated by the physicians and emergency department staff who choose to do more than "treat them and street them" (Zunz and Rosen 2003).

WE JUST BEAT AROUND THE BUSH RIGHT NOW: TOWARDS A MODEL APPROACH

The challenge of a violence-induced injury presents an intervention opportunity that has largely remained untapped except by a few large urban pediatric trauma and acute rehabilitation centers. Most of the existing hospital-based programs employ intervention strategies that develop nonviolent problem-solving skills, such as mediation and negotiation, challenging the beliefs that encourage violent resolutions, and providing referrals with varied degrees of institutional articulation between the health care system and social service agency. The Boston program, the first of its kind in the country, is currently undergoing a second evaluation effort in order to correct for gaps in the program design. The first evaluation showed disappointing program results due to the difficulty in tracking and enlisting the support of the young patients, suggesting a promising although methodologically weak program (De Vos et al. 1996, 5). Other cities such as West Orange, New Jersey; Chicago, Miami, Wisconsin, and New York have begun initiatives similar to those in Boston and Los Angeles, incorporating many of the same program features while adding unique components of their own.

The young participants also expressed a concern that most violence prevention programming is directed to youth and children who may not be at greatest risk:

> Most violence prevention programs preach to the converted, at some degree. You have a whole bunch of these kids in there, who are not even on the streets, you know, and you're still preaching and talking about we need to stop the violence. These kids don't do shit violence in their lives, you know. And when the violent kids out there who are dealing drugs, carrying a gun, they stay away from them.

Like juvenile delinquency prevention programming, violence intervention efforts have resulted in a paucity of efforts directed at those who need it most. Hagan and McCarty describe this tendency:

> North American criminology also neglects street youth. Despite the adversity of street life and the prevalence of crime, contemporary criminology concentrates more extensively on youth living at home and attending school. This focus limits the study of more extreme social and economic situations implying that the influence of such adverse backgrounds is exaggerated and that problems of crime are sufficiently represented by the experiences of more ordinary young people (Hagan and McCarty 1997, 1).

Reflecting on the current lack of knowledge informing health care interventions for youth involved in violence. Delbert describes the dilemma:

> The ideal program, I wouldn't know what it is 'cause it hasn't been invented yet. A lot of programs are just beating around the bush right now. We're just, now, finding out how to deal with

these things. We've been talking about it too much, and we're now starting to do something about it, finally.

Developing a Comfort Zone: Getting to Disclosure

The stories of the young people in this study suggest that a young person who was ready for change and reached a stage of contemplation could greatly benefit and move along the process of transformation if the right approach and supports were offered. Studies carried out and reviewed by Prochaska and DiClemente on intervention-assisted changers note that "if clients progress from one stage to another during the first month of treatment, they can double their chances of taking action during the initial six months. The data demonstrates that treatment programs designed to help people progress just one stage in a month can double their chances of participants taking action on their own in the near future." (Prochaska and DiClemente 1992, 1106.)

Prochaska and DiClemente's studies found that the more patients progressed into action early in therapy, the more successful they were in attaining the behavioral objectives by the end of treatment. For the populations studied by these investigators, the stages of change were the second best predictors of outcome, better than age, socioeconomic status, problem severity and duration, goals and expectations, self-efficacy and self-support. The only variables that outperformed the stages of change as outcome predictors were the processes of change the clients used early in therapy. While the course of action and progression of change of the young people in this study suggest a similar relationship, the more complex risk factors for violence, characteristics of trauma and the age of the young patients involved added other dimensions to this process, creating unique challenges to the promotion of healthy outcomes for this population.

In order to reach and engage the young people in treatment effectively, and encourage termination, hospitals and other health settings need first to create a safe, secure space. The creation of a secure "comfort zone" was integral to that process, and needed to be established in the very first contact with the young person. Initiatives for other victim sub-populations (sexual assault, domestic violence and middle-class victims of crime) have long recognized the need to minimize re-victimization that results from repeatedly asking about the precipitating circumstances leading to admission. The negative effect on the individual and family who are forced to repeatedly relive and re-tell a traumatic incident has resulted in streamlining this process, so that in the best case scenarios, the victim recounts the incident once, and is accompanied by an advocate thereafter. Young people who are admitted for acquaintance or street violence-related issues typically do not receive such consideration, even in hospitals with current state-of-the-art programs. Mo speaks for many in the group when he remembers getting shot and losing the use of both his legs on the scene. While incurring an injury considered to be among the most catastrophic, he, like the others, would be subjected to a battery of questions again and again:

> I answered them truthfully. But, I mean, I got tired after a while, you know. I got mad with them. Yelled at them. It was just aggravating after a while. You get mad, 'cause I mean you just—they constantly asking you the same questions, and you giving them same answers, which is the same situation with coming in on the ambulance, you know. And with the police being on the scene of the crime, you know. There, the police are asking you these same questions, you know. Then you got the ambulance drivers asking you these same questions. And then when you reach to the hospital, you got the doctors and the nurses there asking you the same questions, you know. When it's all right there on the paper, you know. I don't know why they ask so many questions, you know, why they ask the same questions over and over.

Reliving the incident only heightened the anxiety, fear, and despair, expressed as anger and creating feelings of insecurity for both the young patient and the staff. As Martin states, when he was admitted at age 14 for stab wounds:

> You had to keep telling stories over and over, that was something they kept doing. Why can't they just, like, write it down like that? Every time a new nurse came in, tell them what happened. I got tired of telling the story. Like in the ambulance, I had to tell them, and I had to tell three fellows, and I had to tell the nurse, then I had to tell the other nurse, and I had to tell all the people in the trauma center. I think they should write it out.

In the interest of being able to reach the young person early in order to expedite treatment, the provision of a victim advocate with experience dealing with young people would be helpful. The advocate would follow the young person through the hospitalization experience and the return to community. The service would be in keeping with the emerging standard of care for other populations impacted by violence.

Another dimension of a safety or comfort zone is reducing the possibility and/or perception that the victim would be re-assaulted in the hospital. Carl was not alone when he expressed his fear that the person who had shot him would come back to finish the job. Albert recommends that young people admitted for gang and acquaintance violence-related injuries have visits by other gang peers curtailed, even if they do not pose an immediate threat. When he was hospitalized, the frequent visits by his fellow street gang members made it difficult for him to sustain doubts about his former lifestyle. Curtailing peer visits may also help foster the exploratory, contemplation time often stimulated by a traumatic event and its aftermath.

Hospitals and rehabilitation center staff need to be able to distinguish, or have means to find out, if the young people visiting the injured patients are harmful (Daane 2003). Clinical staff need to be able to discern actual versus perceived risk, or have ready access to individuals who can, and must be credible purveyors of such knowledge and safety to the young people. They need to be educated about the co-occurrence and characteristics of various forms of violence. A safety protocol based on accurate perceptions of risk and change possibilities is critical to promote a sense of safety for all. A study to assess emergency department clinician attitudes and behavior regarding identification, assessment and intervention for youth at risk for violence found that although clinicians recognized the need for evaluation of those at risk for violence, they are often less able to perform risk assessment and guide patients to appropriate follow-up resources (Fein et al. 2000).

An understanding of the dynamics of violence is critical in creating a space in which the young person discloses the precipitating circumstances, thus helping to identify strategies to prevent recidivism. For victims of violence, a critical component of recovery from trauma is a shift from unpredictable danger to reliable safety. When Charo was 16 she would be seen at the hospital for domestic violence-induced injuries, one of over 20 visits she would make to emergency rooms and health clinics from the time she was 14 to 20, including a visit at age nineteen for an especially brutal rape. She would also suffer a miscarriage due to blows sustained when she was 19.

Despite the severity and frequency of her injuries, she never felt safe enough with the clinical providers; they were never able to engage her in a conversation at a level where they could provide a referral to a battered women's shelter.

> Nobody else ever gave me the number. I mean, I never really knew really what was domestic violence, I really didn't know it was an issue. It was more like I believed it was just something that was going on, and it was normal. And nobody changed my mind about it because nobody really told me that it wasn't really, like normal, at the hospitals or the police.

She admits that probably those efforts "wouldn't have made a difference, I was stubborn." Still, in retrospect, many of the exchanges were very flawed from a practice perspective, and might have placed her at further risk if she had disclosed the violence when she was accompanied by her abuser. When she was admitted at 16:

> They asked me, as well, what happened. And I said that I fell, I fell and I hurt myself. And I got some stitches, and that was that. When I went more to the hospital where it was like I was black and blue or whatever, that's when they were more concerned and they were like, asking, and he's like, right there. And of course I'm not gonna say there was something wrong when he's right there, you know. I'm already scared enough as it is, and so I didn't really say anything. Sometimes the police did come to where we lived, and as soon as they got there, even though I was like, bleeding and everything, I would be like, "Oh, it's okay. There's nothing wrong. Nothing's going on."

She believes that she might have been reached earlier:

> maybe somebody that would've been in a similar situation. Somebody that would've told me, "You know what? I know what you're going through, even though you're over here saying that nothing's going on, that everything's fine, everything's cool." Somebody who would've made me felt safe, even if I talked to that person about it.... "It's gonna be safe, and it's gonna be okay, you know, I went through this, and I've lived through it and you can live through it, as well. If you want to, you can choose that."

> I guess it all really depends how ready you are to listen to what's bad and what's not. Basically, you have to start by creating a relationship with a person. You can't just like go there and start talking about well, you're going through domestic violence and this is not right, and this is not normal. Whatever. Start to develop a relationship in which she can feel comfortable where she can open up. Or violence in general, with teens, where they can open up and tell you what they're feeling. You have to really know how to separate issues that you have to deal with. It depends what the situation is.

Some of the specialized staff of domestic violence interventions and clinical practitioners she encountered lacked sensitivity and were often cold and were not able to connect with her:

> They weren't sensitive, like you know. We were more like projects to them. It's like, you know, I did something and it was like they would watch our every move or whatever. There were a lot of resources that they could've offered; there were a lot of things that they could have done. They would have groups, and then all these meetings and it was like more to learn from us, really, as to actually help us. They needed to be more sensitive; they needed to create a space where we could feel comfortable with them, so we could help them help us.

Clinicians at times fail to appreciate the urgency and importance of such encounters, the gravity of the precipitating circumstances, and the missed opportunities:

> You know, it's like I said before it's like, if you die, you're dead. You can't change anything when you're dead. You can change things while you're still alive, you know, while you're still here. I feel like if I would've found someone who had gone through that experience and would've felt freer, would've felt that they could talk to me, would've felt the freedom to talk to me and tried.

Establishing trust, which can take longer with this population, becomes an ever more urgent task as managed care pressures hospital and rehabilitation facilities to shorten stays. The "window of opportunity" to establish a bond, a comfort zone, and a discharge plan that takes into account social and environmental risk factors is ever narrower due to changes in health care delivery and financing systems.

Find a Way of Communicating: Clinician Proficiency

Research on behavior change states that external factors (such as clinicians) interact with the characteristics of the young person to affect (assist or impede) responsivity. Thus, it behooves adults who work with and encounter similar young people in a myriad of health and hospital settings to motivate and guide the young person affectively to facilitate the process of change. In the treatment of offenders, it is widely accepted that behavioral, cognitive-behavioral and multi-modal intervention strategies produce the best outcomes, yet a well-designed program is not a sufficient requirement for effective intervention. Like correctional interventions, health-based programs must consider the characteristics of the young person and then match the styles of the young person and the service provider. This is fundamental to the principle of treatment responsivity, a term used to describe client-based factors that influence the likelihood of positive treatment effects.

The stories of the young people underscore the importance of health workers in helping them initiate, sustain and maintain a process of change. Reaching young people during the earliest stages of admission following a traumatic incident required specific skills on the part of the health workers in order to capitalize on that window of opportunity. As one young patient commented, many do not know how to approach and speak to young people. "The first time I was admitted, I guess there was all youths, kids and stuff, and some of them don't really have what it takes to talk to the kids, they don't know how to talk to them" (Table 4).

Table 4. Ways of communicating: questions to engage children and youth in health and hospital settings

How are you feeling?
What can I/we do better to improve how you are feeling?
What can I/we do better to improve my/our work?
Is there anything you would like to ask me?
What kind of music, movies, TV shows, comics, and books do you enjoy?
Where do you like to go and hang out?
What are your hopes?
What would you like to achieve in your life?
What gives meaning and purpose to your life?
What are your hopes for your younger siblings, your children?
How can we help you to achieve your goals, dreams?
What do you need to achieve them?
Who can you turn to for advice, to talk?
Are there things you have no one to talk to about?
How do you get through difficult moments, times?
How do you feel about school, work, activities you are doing?
Tell me about your community, your friends, a typical day?
What things or people make you happy?
What kinds of things give you strength?
How would you describe yourself?
Who do you admire, look up to?
If you could change three things in your life, what would they be?

This young patient, hospitalized at 19 due to violence, would have appreciated having

> Things to do, like how I would change myself, what else can I do differently, how I can avoid what happened again. Things like that. It doesn't have to be somebody like a psychiatrist; it could just be somebody that understands.... You want to understand who the people are, don't use some psychology term on them. We're not that old, you know, I mean, we really don't have that much experience in psychology but we watch TV too. You know you don't want to just seem like a psychologist, you want to seem like a friend.

Helping the young person make a change requires both the patient and the health worker to believe that change is possible. Health workers need to be educated about the stages and processes of change among violence-involved youth as part of their preparation to interact with their young charges. They must be encouraged to reason by analogy when attempting to encourage behavior change with an unknown illness or public health problem, as they do with other health challenges. If reasoning by analogy that violence is a "disease," they need to do it fully, and not allow considerations from other frameworks to cloud the perception of what services can or should be offered, or determinist notions of patient intractability.

Even if a patient does not take steps towards behavior change because they are not ready yet, the clinician can consider it a successful clinical encounter if a comfort zone has been created. Clinicians also need to be able to understand something about the life circumstances and realities faced by their young clients, and what obstacles will be encountered along the path of behavior change, as well as some general insights about how to assess readiness for change, for the signs are often contradictory. As Carl states, the clinicians he encountered on the floor when he was 14:

> didn't know shit about me than what was on that paper that they had in front of them. They didn't know nothing about my background. They didn't know nothing about what I had to go through growing up. They didn't know shit other than my name and my diagnosis and probably where I came from and that's geographically where I came from not mentally.

Clinicians treating youth and children who have sustained a spinal cord injury due to violence should not make treatment decisions and outcome expectations on the superficial category of etiology. A young person's underlying history of violence involvement, education and employment appear to be the most important factors, beyond actual impairment or disability (Adkins et al. 1997). Further, the younger the gang or violence-involved spinal cord-injured individual, the more difficult community reintegration becomes. Evidence surfacing from collective clinical experience suggests that the age and maturity levels of this population and the subcultures of violence in which many of them live pose further obstacles to existing treatment and integration models.

According to the study youth, health settings and professional and university training programs can actively recruit individuals who can understand the life situations and pressures faced by their young patients, and thereby train and equip staff to comprehend and acquire the skills to address the young patients and meet their needs in a more expedient manner:

> They need to hire somebody who's been where these patients have been. You know, who can say I understand what you're going through, 'cause we done been through it. Some of the therapists used to come to me and say "I know how you feel." I would say "No you don't. You don't have to stick you finger up you butt to use the bathroom, so you don't know how that feels. So for you to tell me that, don't say it. because you don't know. I appreciate you saying that. That's saying that you have sympathy for me, but you don't know how I feel. And you come in here smiling like everything's ok. But shit ain't funny, you know."

> When I used to tell them that, I guess they thought I was a mean guy, but I was telling them how I felt, you know. My back used to constantly hurt. But once I eased up and calmed down and told myself I need to cool out, and learn what they're trying to teach me. 'Cause once I leave, I'm on my own. And I can go back and ask them, but if I've been an ass the whole time I've been they not gonna tell me. Well some of them will be obligated to tell me, but I said let me just chill out and just be cool.

All the staff that come into contact with these young clients need to overcome the fear of those they serve in order to provide effective treatment:

There are both parallels and differences... between the roles of the psychotherapist and of the medical emergency professional. In both roles, professionals cannot be optimally efficient in providing services if they are terrified or emotionally traumatized by the pain and trauma of those they serve. The analogy is limited, however in its application to the mental health professional: that is, to be optimally helpful, psycho-therapists must also be able to phenomenologically approximate and be emotionally present to the experiences of those they serve (Mahoney 1991, 323).

Focus on the Positive: Counseling and Education

Once a comfort zone was established, clinicians were able to uncover the areas of behavior and life circumstances requiring specific interventions. Besides allowing for a correct diagnosis, creation of a comfort zone also encouraged the young patients to try something new, intrinsic to the process of change.

As suggested by the youth, the challenge is to immediately "create like a comfort zone where they can feel comfortable as to where they could speak about things, based on a program that would be focused on like having positive feelings, positive potential." The clinician's focus and approach should be:

> looking for everything that's positive on this teen, you know. Maybe they need help with the anger, or they need help maybe with the parenting, or they need help with this or that—just look at the positive side. We can work together in these other sides where we can make things better. Give you parenting classes. Give you other classes. Make you aware of things that aren't normal, that you might think that are normal. And we can make it better together. And it's not always perfect, but we can make it together, you know, I'm here to help you. I'm here, I'm here if you need me as a support.

Viewing violence as a public health issue can foster critical thinking on violent circumstances and provide opportunities through counseling and education to reconnect young people (or link them for the first time) with positive adults and pro social peers. Such a perspective also can lead to the creation or re-establishment of internal and external "safety shields" protecting the young people, educating them about how to diminish risk factors and avoid the spaces of death in their communities and provide entrance to spaces of health and development.

However, such a framework needs to go beyond analyses and proscriptions at the level of interpersonal change alone, and should incorporate an understanding of the many forms of violence (not minimizing structural forms of violence) and their interplay with interpersonal violence. Similarly, clinicians need to understand alternate theoretical explanations on violence causation beyond the dominant deviance- and pathology-centered perspectives of social and individual breakdown, learned orientation, and relative deprivation theories. Broader perspectives include families of theories that attribute greater weight to solidarity, collective action and resource mobilization factors, and those in which violence is seen as the result of structural changes that can indirectly inhibit or unleash patterns of resistance and protest, as well as shape the response of social control.

Everyone's Different: **One Size Fits All Will Not Work**

The life histories and perspectives underscore that there is no such thing as a generic "violence-involved youth" or street group member. Adolescent victims/perpetrators of violence are not a homogeneous group. One treatment strategy cannot be expected to meet all these young people's needs.

A violence intervention program should take into account varying levels and types of victimization and perpetration, the differing individual and social costs to continuing or desisting from certain injury-prone activities or lifestyles, and the individuals' characteristics and immediate environment. Characteristics and strengths of the young person must be considered when assigning or referring them to treatment programs. Similarly, the journey towards change of behavior has multiple paths and obstacles, and interventions focusing on promoting change should address the various processes and the varied stages of change.

A differentiation according to risk and need may further increase the precision by which intervention and treatment can be applied and lead to a more comprehensive assessment of responsivity-related factors. The field still needs to develop a multi-method assessment protocol of treatment readiness, responsivity, and participation to enable clinicians to answer the question of how they know if, and when, a particular young person will respond to treatment. The experiences of the young participants outlined in the previous chapters suggest some general indicators that may apply to health settings. Both the general literature on behavior change and the stories of the young people underscore that treatment planning should consider motivation, readiness for change, and responsivity to achieve the maximum effectiveness of treatment programs. Overlooking these antecedents to violence cessation leads to ineffective prevention efforts, stereotypical descriptions, and an increase in the general feeling of hopelessness towards these young people.

Cessation of violence has multiple causes, manifestations, and pathways. Uniform and time-limited assessments and interventions will not address the diversity and longevity of the restoration period. Prevention and intervention efforts must be tailored to the developmental level of the child or adolescent, and must address the critical influences of children's social (and economic) milieus at various stages of development.

It Has To Be Multi-Dimensional: The Need for a Comprehensive Approach

The causation of violence cessation that emerges from the stories of the young participants suggests that it is a multi-leveled process influenced by many factors and forces. Although violence cessation had common themes among the participants, each young person had an individual experience. A comprehensive, holistic approach was often needed to help the young to achieve a change in outlook, behavior, and life circum-stances. Such an approach encompasses such interventions as medical (treatment and rehabilitation), cognitive and behavioral (education on violence and its prevention, journal-keeping, stress management), interpersonal (building a therapeutic or helping alliance) and social interventions (community support, gang mediation). Elements of trauma recovery also need to be included. Efforts to encourage violence-impacted young people to transform their lives need to recognize that violence prevention/intervention and o trauma recovery alone are not enough, and that an effective way to reduce recidivism and prevent other tragedies in adolescence is to pursue the highest level of youth development possible.

Medical workers need to be part of a social service network of other providers whose objective is also to reduce the incidence of this "new morbidity" and without whose help this chronic, recurrent disease cannot be "cured" or prevented. Health workers must also be linked to youth development programs and opportunities to help their young patients achieve the full range of competencies required for a transition to healthy adulthood. Assessment and treatment must address individual needs, recognize the reciprocal relationship among the levels of an adolescent's ecology (family, neighborhood and community, public policy and cultural factors) and focus on context-specific challenges and opportunities faced by the youth following exposure to violence.

The categorical fragmentation of youth programs is not helpful and can be detrimental to the process of change and pro-social growth.

Greater coordination and even centralization was suggested by some of the Boston youth study participants:

> The ideal program would be one program branched out to different communities. I really do think that we need to branch out. I mean, we have this one program in Dorchester, one program in Roxbury, and if these programs would only wake up and tie together, you know, become one program, you know, throughout the whole city of Boston, maybe we can get some work done. But if you have one program dealing with violence prevention, the other one dealing with STDs, the other one dealing with history and you're just only educating somebody in that one subject, in that one area. If you have a program that deals with all subjects, in all these areas, that would be good.

The young people also mentioned cultural diversity as an important feature of a program, because part of violence prevention is learning respect for others, and that requires a lot of contact:

> A good program needs to be multi-dimensional. That also means you see different people of different nationalities involved with it. That's what I like about this particular program is that we have different nationalities. The majority of the programs here in Los Angeles are not like that. They're either all Hispanic or all black or all white. Those programs have failed miserably. Because you don't have the cultural diversity there. So a good program I think would have to have cultural diversity, and also someone that has really, really been there, someone who could relate to the experiences that these kids are going through. That's basically what I think that you would need to begin with.

The theories of proactive socialization which undergird ethnocentric prevention models, in which ethnic youth are consciously socialized to understand and be aware of the varied cultural realms they must operate, focusing on strengthening cultural pride and identity. These emerge as an important feature for intervention programs (Holinger et al. 1994). Yet all the young people who had been exposed to a variety of programs with varying levels of diversity stopped short of endorsing approaches that were limited to a single sex or single race or ethnicity. The varied demographic composition of the young people (mixed race and/or ethnicity) and the increasingly diverse neighborhoods in which the young people live often curb the extent to which an ethno-centrist critique could explain violence causation or harness the resources for its prevention. The "balkanization" of service provision in neighborhoods and by institutions was often anachronistic, as it was based on an outdated demographic conception of who lived in a certain area, which differed from an increasingly multicultural urban youth culture. The young people often required social and economic inclusion opportunities, connections, and services that extended beyond the reach of a single community, ethnic or racial group's sphere of influence.

You Got to Hold Them Close: Intensity and Consistency Matter

Intensity matters in any intervention, regardless of what entrenched violence-related behavior you try to change. Emmanuel draws an analogy with important implications for practice:

> You just can't make somebody change their mind. If somebody's a white supremacist, you really, really have to work at them for them to see that other backgrounds and races aren't that bad. I mean, you have to work with them like, every single day and put it in their minds, have them be with these people, chill with these people, have them over their house, you have to work at it. You can't take a kid off the street, and put him in a program for one day and think everything's gonna be better, you know. You can't give them an hour meeting at their school and think everything's gonna be better... oh what, they heard this man for one hour, what the hell's that gonna do? You have to work with them. Day, after day, after day for like, a year, for two years, get them involved with their community. Show them that even that one little bag of dope that they deal plays a bigger part in this whole circle of destruction that we live in.

Consistency is another key component in a program, both in terms of the approach of individual staff and also in ensuring that the instrumental adults in the program do not leave. The high turnover of staff in youth programs was a concern to many of the young people as they reflected on their and others' feelings of having been abandoned by health workers who had come to symbolize surrogate family.

Erika describes one violence prevention practitioner who embodied a quality of consistency and offered a sense of permanence and engagement, despite experiencing great personal adversity:

> But one thing that I look back now, as I look at my life experience and what helped me change was that when you work with young people, you have to be consistent. You have to be consistent and patient. He was consistent and patient. He's

never left the corner he's at. And even though he lost his daughter, his daughter got killed outside a church by a stray bullet and everything, he hasn't left that corner. On the contrary, he started a youth center named after his daughter.

As the process of change could take up to several years, efforts to reduce injury and violence recidivism need to be structurally and formally linked to stable programs in the community, that have the staying power to a accompany a potentially lengthy change process. Such programs are few. In an evaluation of one of the most comprehensive programs for post-discharged young victims of violence, which provides six months of case management in the community, the study concluded that six months may not be enough time to change the attitudes of young people who have lived years surrounded by violence. The program plans to provide case management for at least one year, to be able to achieve a greater intervention effect in victimization reduction, change in youth attitudes and strengthening effects on the social relations of the youth (Mitka 2002).

The young people interviewed for this study noted that there are many partial, poorly supported "true prevention" efforts, and these were often built around the tireless efforts, and at times the traits, of a charismatic provider, with important short-term, but often little long-term impact. The right programs, states one of the young people, are programs structured like the Boys and Girls Clubs, or Big Brothers and Big Sisters programs that do not give up on the youth, and that have longevity in the neighborhood. His observation is validated by evaluation findings that found such initiatives among the few that "work" in preventing violence (McGill et al. 1998).

It's time we actually do something about it. Everybody's heard, yeah, "we got too many gangs and too many drugs" and "I had a dream." We've heard that before. We heard it like, six times, you know. It's time that we stop saying it's time to make a change and make that change. Making a change is going out to these street corners and offering these kids something to do with their spare time. There are a couple groups out there who actually do it. One of them who I think up to a lot is the Boys and Girls Club and Big Brothers. They help people. They get them in there. They get them off the streets, keep them busy, in groups or in one-on-one as they grow up. They use a lot of sports, activities, to calm anger and aggression, and it's one of the few groups I've seen that does it.

Prevention and intervention programs must not only be built around the consequences of violence but alternatives to it. Manolo described the difference between an unsuccessful intervention in which former gang members came into his secure juvenile facility to educate about gangs, and another, later successful peer-based intervention in his life:

> They didn't tell me what's the right from wrong. They told me you have to do better things in life, but they didn't explain to me what it meant.

In addition, those who have been more deeply impacted by violence and with the least supports and inability to return to their communities need specialized services to supplement other efforts. Such initiatives require a partnership between health, victim services, youth development and restorative justice approaches, which have yet to be deliberately formulated. Such a program would continue to support these young people through young adulthood and as they gain the necessary competencies to attain a secure place in a mainstream world.

You Have this Beautiful Child: Build on Child Centeredness

Health and hospital programs can capitalize on the child-centered concerns of this subsector of the population. Many of the young people in this study expressed a terrible fear that their children will experience a fate similar to theirs and are able to bring to the fore protective and caring abilities that they did not extend to themselves. They often took great risks to doing so, going to great lengths within the universe of available options. Indeed, a substantial body of research disproves the commonly accepted notion of a "generational cycle of abuse," noting that most survivors of violence neither abuse nor neglect their children (Kaufman and Zigler 1987).

Based on their experience as mentors and advisors to other young people, the young participants suggest appealing for behavior change among youth by focusing on their children or younger siblings. It is also important to focus on the assets and strengths any individual possesses. Charo states that:

> You have to be thankful, the way I see it, for everything you have. And that's another thing that I show the women that I work with. It's like, look at your child. You have this beautiful child. You're intelligent. You're young. But you're intelligent 'cause I see the way you parent. You're being a parent to your child. And, you know, it's like you're so intelligent. You're so

young, you're just really gonna do good. You're gonna end up doing really good.

Engaging young parents in parenting classes, organizing activities with the young people for their younger siblings, involving them in health and hospital programs for children who are witnesses to violence, or who experience serious health conditions, are some of the ways to reinforce child-centeredness as an aid to prevention, and influence an individual's process of change in indirect but potentially powerful ways.

We Need a Year Round Thing: Keeping the Young Person Healthy

The challenges to stay healthy and move along the process of change require programs that are not only consistent and intensive, but that can keep the young people involved year round. This is especially critical since many are out of school, unemployed, and outside the mainstream youth programming. Further, many of them are socially and economically semi-autonomous, having to provide for themselves, their siblings or families at very young ages. A positive example are the summer jobs programs for low to moderate income youth provided by some municipalities as a youth development and an urban security measure, keeping teens busy during the high homicide summer months when they have ample free time and often not enough to do. The young people would like to see this type of program extended year round, allowing young people to be of service while earning an income and struggling to make a personal change. It is also an area of violence prevention research that is understudied.

The issue of payment was a source of some discussion among the young participants, raising issues of how sincere the participants in such a program would be if they should be paid. Carefully screening youth who are "serious about change" to take part in such opportunities in health settings was a recommendation made by all the young people, with the caveat that youth do slip back often on more than one occasion. The material necessities, however, underscore the importance of receiving some form of compensation:

> We need a year round thing, select those who are serious about change. But you need people who are going to be serious, and I think these kids would be more serious about it if there was cash involved in it. Although it's like, although some people might say you know there's money is involved in it maybe their hearts not in it, but what would you have them rather do? Go out and sell drugs and kill people and mug people?

There is So Much We Can Do: **Reinforcing Change Through Health Opportunities**

The steps taken early in treatment, relationships made and the strength of post-discharge safety net established by the clinic can significantly enhance the progression along the various stages of change and help reinforce the processes that drive the transformation in community. Health and hospital settings can bring new resources to broader community efforts, a sense of legitimacy and a unique perspective that transcends the false perpetrator/victim dichotomy. Symbolically, such settings can create a space that allows for the young person to speak and validates their intimate knowledge of injury, violence, and death. A health focus underscores the chronic nature of the problem, and can offer a competing diagnosis of violence as one other than an acute problem in which surgical interventions that remove offender from community are sufficient. As a field of action health can bring its resources to help create a more supportive and protective environment.

Health and hospital settings offer unique opportunities for active participation in specialized service, youth leadership, and youth organizing experiences that meet actual community needs and are integrated into the young person's life and rehabilitation plan. The stories of the young people suggest that social mobilization and consciousness-raising should be considered as an integral approach to services and violence prevention. Such settings can provide multiple and varied opportunities for engagement for young people, a critical dimension of the process of change, and can sustain the young people through the natural oscillatory process of change, providing continuity, guidance, and reinforcement. They can provide access to and encourage young people to take pro-social risks, facilitate their re-enrollment in educational activities, assisting in the development of a future orientation, and provide young people with opportunities to practice decision-making, communication, goal- setting, self-assessment and self management skills, as well as reinforcing anger management. Through opportunities for service, youth leadership, organizing, and civic engagement, health organizations can foster the development of a citizenship ethic among young people, in keeping with theoretical models of the development of social competence and social skills critical to risk reduction.

Health-based youth violence prevention and intervention programs need to address factors that can increase school retention, improve alternative school programs, remove barriers for youth reentry, and generally enrich the school experience. Partnerships with job training programs, community service, and comprehensive community initiatives are also vital since they can provide positive community opportunities as the youth re-enter the community. Street outreach and peer recruitment efforts are also important as a means of reaching the mostly out of school, highly mobile, high-risk youth who are not involved in school or community organizations.

Health settings can help prepare violence-involved youth for adulthood through training programs, preparing the youth to be marketable in specific health and other related employment niches. The ability to speak and write other languages, including street languages, and the knowledge of how to interact with different groups (race, ethnicity, nationality, sexual orientation, youth with disabilities, language, gender, class and life circumstances) are assets than can be actively cultivated in health settings (see Table 5).

Table 5. Trauma intervention framework

1. Non-judgmental early outreach and modeling (peer counselors, clinicians, youth workers, supportive peer group)

2. Counseling and education, including dialogue on other forms of violence (not minimizing structural forms of violence and their interplay with interpersonal violence)

3. Peer influence (positive peers as role models in social rehabilitation and in community)

4. Opportunity-taking (taking pro-social risks, enrolling in school, work, development of a future orientation, collectivist ethos). Opportunity to give back, for some to do penance.

5. Reinforcement (peers, family, society, jobs, schools, view of self as contributor to society)

6. Mature out of violence involvement with a new set of marketable skills, formal sector employment, social, civic and political participation.

7. Mature into a consumer of routine, preventive care (transitioning from sporadic, emergency room-user profile)

8. Contribute to the diminution of the more general risk and causal factors in high-risk communities,

9. Increase in general prevention (protective) and development factors in high-risk communities.

Helped Me Heal a Lot of Wounds: Towards Restorative Health

Participating in health programs gave young people in this study the opportunity to heal many different types of wounds, not only the physical lesions sustained due to incidents of violence, but also to help heal those wounds inflicted on others. As both perpetrators and victims of trauma, the young people needed to reconnect with ordinary life, moving away from stigmatized isolation. Such reconnection is a critical dimension of social and medical rehabilitation and recovery. When asked what benefited them the most along their process of change, one of the participants remarked:

> Benefits? It may sound selfish but it was, it was basically to help me heal a lot of wounds. To help me heal a lot of wounds. I know that I had admitted to what I did in the past but I can never go back. I can never go back and, and all those, the lives I did take. I can't get, you know, for me it was a way to give back and that was one thing for me that's what, that's what probably benefited me the most. I was looking for something to do and I saw that as a, as something to do to help out, to pay for the wrong I had done.

The youths' experiences underscore the need to develop creative programs that raise the "social costs" of violence. For example, education about the true costs of violence can be carried out with groups of positive peers, or by other members of the community who are respected by these young people (such as grandmothers, mothers, and other relatives, elders, older rehabilitated youth) who view the young offender as worthy. Health-based service experiences can offer opportunities and alternatives akin to those provided by restorative justice, by offering nonstigmatizing alternatives. They can provide these young people, viewed as too experienced to be children, and too young to be citizens, with challenging, protected environments that offer a nonpunitive way to redress past injuries to others while healing their own injuries. Violence is not only an offense against another individual, but also an action that both affects the well-being and is shaped by the general health conditions in the community.

Health settings can foster change processes integral to behavior change, including environmental and self-evaluation. Manolo describes the effect a hospital-based violence intervention program and the education on drug education as reinforcing his decision to change:

> Helping me just think about it. I don't want to get in trouble no more. I don't want to go to jail no more. I want to be a different

person. I want to be helpful; I don't want to be destroying. 'Cause to me, people who sell drugs are destroying people, they keep coming back. When I used to sling, I used to feel bad, 'cause people would come back to me bringing their house stereos, bringing their tape recorders, bringing any little thing just for a piece of rock. A piece of crack. Give me anything. They use to say "Give me anything, I just want to get high." I felt bad you know.

Program activities that raise the social benefits of nonviolence go beyond the scope of traditional, disease-oriented public health approaches. They contrast with other approaches in which the young person can be viewed as an individual with personal or behavioral problems, with limited participation in the definition of the problem but bearing much of the individual responsibility for both pathology and change. The individual focus offers the point of intervention at which to examine and begin to control risk factors. However, ideally, program efforts should promote attainment of health, which encompasses greater physical, social and economic well being; positive social and environmental conditions, such as adequate housing, nutrition, employment, health care, and personal security; and inclusion in the web of healthy relationships between people and institutions that bind (see Table 6, Restorative health framework for victims of youth interpersonal violence).

Deal With Personal Issues: **The Need for Specialized Programs**

Some youth who do not have a home to return to, or those whose home environments might foster continued perpetration and high-risk behavior, may need small, residential facilities with surrogate fathers or mentors with very special sets of skills and life experiences. Much like shelters and transitional housing programs for battered women, which provide safety, guidance and allow a woman to establish herself, find a job, establish a credit history and save for school or an eventual apartment of her own, specialized residential programs are needed for some of the young people, who are discharged from the hospital, attended to in clinics, and served by community public health programs. Such a need exists for both able-bodied and disabled youth, as well as for youth who are being discharged from other institutions such as juvenile or adult correctional facilities.

Table 6. Restorative health framework for victims of youth interpersonal violence

Victims:
- Receive treatment, assistance, and services
- Receive victim compensation funds
- Receive restitution, other reparation from the offender
- To be involved and encouraged to give suggestions as to how to repair the harm done
- Have the opportunity to face offender, other youth or community and tell their story
- Feel satisfied with the justice process, receive equal services
- Provide guidance and consultation to medical, rehabilitation public health and allied social service professionals on planning, advisory groups, coalition-building and policy initiatives
- Have an opportunity to take part in prevention, revictimization prevention activities and education.

Citizens, Families, and Community Groups:
- Support the young person to leave behind harmful behaviors and increase competencies
- Become involved to the greatest extent possible in health, community and justice initiatives that serve such youth
- Work with other adolescent impacted by violence on local community health and service projects
- Provide support to youth as mentors, employers and advocates, holding youth accountable
- Provide service opportunities for youth that allow youth to make meaningful contributions to the quality of community life and to offer restitution to the victimized or affected communities.
- Raise social benefit of leaving violence behind as both victim and perpetrator
- Advise public health and play an active role in program and service design

    Some young people need to leave their area in order to stay safe. Depending on the level of involvement and of gang organization being left behind, or in cases of multi-generational gang membership, the young people may require services/assistance/linkages that extend beyond a certain neighborhood or city and that integrate features of a victim assistance/relocation program, such as safe houses, as well as some characteristics of foster homes, especially for some of the younger victims. Andrea was taken in by a loose, ad hoc network of safe houses—volunteer providers working with violence-involved youth—for three months while the former street group with which she was associated was looking for her. Such programs offer acceptance, guidance, discipline, a routine, and a secure environment where the young person can establish a life plan and begin to learn how to achieve it. Some of the skills such volunteer providers have taught their young charges are as basic as dressing for a job, basic hygiene, and how to set an alarm clock.

    A range of complementary, specialized initiatives would help sustain the violence-involved youth as they begin a new life or start to participate in the limited, traditional existing community service programs. As noted by the participants, the community service programs available in their neighborhoods are scant. Although situated in inner cities, they offer few openings to inner city youth as a whole. The young people from the inner city neighborhoods who do take part and complete such programs, are often the elite in the community, and rarely include violence-involved youth. The programs often presume that their young participants' lives are relatively stable, and offer few extra-program supports to those who face more extreme social and economic circumstances:

> My criticism about that program is that you go out, work for the community, and do community service work, but they don't deal with your personal issues and stuff like that. You gotta get out there, do a community service work, look out for other people, but then when you got a issue, it's not about you. When you got an issue, personal problem, they don't got time to deal with it, but they got time to deal with people that they don't even know.

    Some of the issues faced by young people while participating in such programs included having to regularly look for food and make regular rounds at food pantries towards the end of each month, or by mid-month, in a tighter situation, on behalf of their families. Other problems encountered were homelessness, the inability to move freely in the neighborhood, spotty school attendance, evictions, hospitalizations of relatives, and run-ins with police due to their past violence involvement. The young participants recommended that specialized, complementary programs acknowledge that many young people like them are living in extreme situations and should recognize the need for "memberships for food pantries, insurance, everything."

In the absence of such programs, or other alternatives, some young people choose an even more marginal and transient life. If homeless or precariously housed, they "break night" (sleep in fits and starts on the street) with occasional stays with friends and relatives, who themselves are in crowded apartments, often in violation of their lease or occupancy conditions. Living on the street, moving from place to place becomes a risk factor for further victimization or offending. Other times, the young people might carry out criminal activities in a way that will facilitate apprehension, thus securing them a stay in a correctional facility.

An example is Mario, age 17, a young man who had been recruited into a health-focused violence prevention program by other peers who had left his gang. He had been in and out of juvenile facilities in Puerto Rico, Chicago, and Boston since he was eleven, had been hospitalized on three occasions for gunshot wounds, and most recently, for trauma to the head, in addition to several emergency room visits for stabbings. When he came into the health- based violence prevention program, he had been homeless for three months, working intermittently as a bagger in a local supermarket while sleeping outside. No residential program for street youth would take him, because of the risk he presented due to his gang affiliation and heavy family involvement in organized gang activities. Due to his upcoming birthday, he was not encouraged to seek Department of Social Services (DSS) assistance by agency staff. In addition, he had a series of outstanding warrants and probation violations, and he was afraid of being turned over to the police. He was being considered for admittance into the home of a Nation Of Islam member, who was willing to take him on, once a room was vacated by another young man who had "made it" and was ready to start out on his own, starting college in January. However, in November as the weather grew colder, he was fired for tardiness, and he decided to rob a taxicab and walk along the highway after the event, so he would get caught. With his previous convictions, he faced charges of aggravated and armed assault. Mario knew he would be assured a place to stay for the next couple of years, perhaps in an institution that might offer him limited protection, depending on whether many members of his gang were also there.

I'm in a Wheelchair, but Life Goes On: Addressing Violence and Disability

The structure of service delivery in the U.S. health care system affects particular subpopulations with greater intensity, affecting their ability to obtain care and a reasonable quality of life once they are discharged.

Minority and economically disadvantaged youth are among such populations. The young victim of intentional violence (regardless of injury severity and permanence) is generally reticent and unable to secure ongoing primary and secondary health services. Unstable residential histories and residence in resource-poor neighborhoods are further complicated by a risk-taking lifestyle and the generally young age of the patient. For the subset that sustains a spinal cord injury or other severe disability, the consequences of health service delivery gaps are magnified. Of the 20 study participants, 9 sustained a spinal cord injury, and their efforts to regain their health and vitality offer important lessons for both rehabilitation and other health providers.

Studies carried out on health and community support services available for such individuals noted that spinal cord injury model systems have had the most success in the acute care and inpatient rehabilitation periods, but that the post-acute, community-based service needs of the general spinal cord injury population have yet to be addressed (Whiteneck et al. 1993). The young, uninsured or Medicaid-insured, many of whom comprise the new wave of violence-related spinal cord injuries, have an even greater challenge in obtaining quality medical care post-injury and the assistance in securing a reasonable quality of life post discharge. Individuals with spinal cord injury who are members of racial and ethnic groups, those who are economically disadvantaged, and from traditionally underserved groups, will likely face a further set of barriers to health.

These barriers are multileveled, ranging from individual, situational, and community-level obstacles to impediments due to larger structural factors. Part of the difficulties experienced by the young people in this study, and the young spinal cord injured patients they counseled, were the poor housing, transportation, and street maintenance conditions in their respective neighborhoods and their inability to secure services available to other patients with a spinal cord injury. The Technology-Related Assistance for Individuals with Disabilities Act of 1988 was legislated to correct the lack of access by many individuals with disabilities to information on assistive technology devices and assistive technology services needed to function in society in accordance with their abilities. Yet, traditionally underserved minority groups have less access to and receive fewer resources from the public and private sector. Obstacles such as discrimination, poverty, and inadequacy of specially trained professionals mean fewer resources directed to these groups. Many were never informed that such devices and services were available. Differences in language, literacy, and cultural beliefs may also present significant barriers to the dissemination of information on assistive technology.

Further, assistive technology is often cost-prohibitive. Individuals who are unemployed are not likely to be able to purchase the expensive new assistive devices. Most private and public insurers strictly limit the type of technology devices they will fund, generally favoring the funding of devices that address a particular medical concern to assist patient recovery, as opposed to devices that will improve level of independence and quality of life. For immigrant legal residents (and the individuals with spinal cord injury among them), the limited public funding for these devices and other social support services and information dissemination is further reduced. Securing these services for undocumented youth like Manolo depended on the commitment and resourcefulness of his providers in California, who were willing to circumvent policies when needed for him to obtain what he needed.

Despite the passage of the Americans with Disability Act, a National Organization on Disabilities survey carried out in 2000 determined of all working-age people with disabilities (ages 18-64), only three out of ten (32 percent) are employed full or part-time, compared to eight in ten working-age people without disabilities (81 percent) - a gap of 49 percentage points (NOD and Harris 2001). Many remain unemployed because they would lose income, health care coverage or other benefits if they worked full-time. Full integration, the right to meaningful work and independent living has thus been circumscribed for large segments of the disabled, including individuals with spinal cord injuries, in part due to existing health care delivery and financing models.

Young violence victims with spinal cord injury have even fewer incentives to seek employment: many have not completed school, and they lack the skills or job experience to command wages much higher than the minimum wage. A recent study to determine employment outcomes of adults who sustained spinal cord injuries as children or adolescents compared with the general population found the high rate of unemployment among adults with pediatric-onset spinal cord injury a cause for concern. The study found four factors associated with employment: education, community mobility, functional independence, and decreased medical complications. Other variables significantly associated with employment included community integration, independent driving, independent living, higher income, and life satisfaction. These risk factors associated with adult unemployment provide guidelines for targeting rehabilitation resources and strategies (Anderson and Vogel 2002).

Health professionals also need to assure that existing facilities serving children and adolescents with disabilities and complex health care needs remain open to or begin accepting violence-involved youth, and are responsive to the post-discharge needs of an emerging pediatric population with disabilities. Rehabilitation centers in Chicago have found that the traditional hospital schools, serving mostly youth with developmental disabilities from birth, do not grant admission to gang- or violence-involved youth out of concern that these young people are a threat to others. These semi-autonomous youth, many of whom are risk takers, pose a threat of a different order, since they are not docile patients, nor have they been socialized by such total institutions since early childhood as have many of the other children there with developmental disabilities. The violence-involved youth often challenge the staff and culture of the organization as well as influence the other youth.

Similarly, youth development programs that traditionally serve able-bodied adolescents need to be inclusive and accessible to youth with disabilities. Among the youth facilities that are accessible, only a few possess the means to transport youth who use wheelchairs. Violence prevention programs generally need to acknowledge the existence of a growing subset of young people impacted by violence who become temporarily or permanently disabled and who need to access their services and participate fully in their programs. Inclusion through youth development is important as a means of reducing the likelihood of re-victimization or retaliatory perpetration, but also may minimize secondary disabling conditions and related hospitalizations.

Keep Moving and Stay Strong: Preventing Secondary Disabling Conditions

The control of pressure ulcers, the leading causes of morbidity for spinal cord injured people, suggest the likely intertwined benefits of medical and social rehabilitation. Pressure ulcers are the most common of the skin complications that occur after a spinal cord injury and are the most frequent cause of re-hospitalization. They are among the costliest complications to treat. Between 59 and 80 percent of people with spinal cord injury will develop a serious pressure sore at least once during their lifetime (Rodriguez and Garber 1994). Approximately 40 percent of spinal cord injured patients in acute hospital care develop pressure ulcers, with the risk continuing following discharge. One third of all community residents who have spinal cord injuries have pressure ulcers at a given time. All the young people who were disabled by violence and who participated in this study had experienced at least one of these debilitating sores.

Ulcers lead to long, costly and painful treatment, lengthy and repeated hospitalizations. They can lead to secondary infections, demoralization and depression as well as forgone educational, employment and recreational opportunities affecting both independent living goals and general quality of life. The costs for treating pressure ulcers range between $30,000 and $50,000, and can be as high as $195,000 per individual ulcer, these costs not including follow up outpatient or home treatment (Wharton et al. 1987). Risk factors associated with pressure ulcers are immobility, malnutrition, aging, and systemic illness. Psychological and social factors also affect the likelihood of developing pressure ulcers. Among outpatients, the risk for pressure ulcers correlates with dependence on others for skin care, self-reported satisfaction with activities in life (educational, vocational employment group activities, living arrangement, sexual activities), and, to a lesser extent, self-esteem. Pressure sores are least likely to occur among individuals who maintain normal weight, return to a work and family role, and who do not have a history of tobacco use, suicidal behaviors, or self-reported incarcerations, alcohol or drug abuse (Krause et al. 2001).

Among outpatients, African Americans are more likely than those from other racial and ethnic groups to have more severe ulcers. One interpretation of the data suggests an association between the socioeconomic disadvantages of African Americans in the United States, as manifested by poor access to quality health care and socially-valued, productive activity and an ulcer's developing from superficial to deep. As more data surfaces on the pressure sore profile on individuals with spinal cord injuries due to violence, an increased prevalence of pressure sores among this population is being documented (Waters and Atkins 1997). The length of subsequent re-hospitalization among those with spinal cord injuries sustained due to violence also tends increase over time (Zafonte and Djikers 1999).

Additional innovative treatment approaches are needed to prevent unnecessary death and further injury to victims of violence-induced spinal cord injury. The challenges for the young sustaining spinal cord injury due to violence are similar to those experienced by their able-bodied counterparts, who can walk away after violence-induced injury, although they require a greater (but ultimately cost-effective) intensity of services.

Violence Prevention and Preventive Care

Fostering prevention behaviors among the young people in this study often resulted in greater general public health awareness, and accessing preventive care for other health problems (HIV/AIDS testing, condom use health check ups, dental visits). As the young people participated in health programs they realized the benefit of shifting from sporadic, emergency room care to routine, preventive care. This shift increases the chances that their children will follow a pattern of receiving preventive health services.

DEALING WITH THE LARGER PICTURE: ADDRESSING SITUATIONS AFFECTING VIOLENCE-INVOLVED YOUTH

Health care settings provide unique opportunities to address risk factors and foster cessation processes among youth impacted by violence. In doing so, the influence of the more extreme social and economic situations in shaping the outcomes for this segment of the population should not be minimized. This implies actively seeking to extend effective preventive and remedial intervention services to all the youth and their families including those who come from different cultural traditions, regardless of legal or insurance status; those who have differing degrees of family and community cohesion and organization; those who experience varying degrees of economic dislocations; and those who have varying levels of violence and gang involvement.

Health and hospital initiatives can also address the more general risk factors in high-risk communities, conditions that also place their young patients as well as their older neighbors, parents, and younger children at risk for involvement in violence. The presence of ethnic, racial and class disparities among minority adolescents appears to mirror those encountered by the adults, relatives and neighbors in their communities, as well as the conditions encountered by their younger siblings, and younger neighborhood children. Health and community partnership efforts can focus on strengthening protective factors and the overall development factors in high-risk communities, conditions that may also positively affect the life chances of young people impacted by violence, as well as those of their neighbors, parents and other children.

DEALING WITH THE LARGER PICTURE: MANAGED CARE

The structural characteristics of current health care delivery systems can circumscribe the implementation of the general approach and components of a model program that surfaced from the youth accounts and recommendations. Public mission advocates are concerned about the increasingly competitive nature of the health care system. The disappearance of cross-subsidies and cost-shifting, common in the past, and the growing inability to allocate costs across payers to treat Medicaid and uncompensated care recipients have led to institutions either reducing the amount of uncompensated care they provide or finding other sources of revenue (Gornick et al. 1985). During the course of this study, both the Los Angeles and Boston hospital and rehabilitation centers scaled back the amount of care given to the uninsured, and the public mission of Boston City Hospital would be transformed as it merged with a private, not-for-profit teaching hospital.

These realities require a more concerted effort by health care professionals and their allies in community, professional, and policy circles to provide equal opportunities for access. Managed care programs, in their myriad forms, are emerging as an increasingly popular cost-cutting health services delivery and organization system. Operational and ethical concerns about the appropriateness of managed care health delivery and financing systems is an issue that has been raised in the general literature of health care policy, and is a central issue of debate in the literature relating to patients with spinal cord and other chronic disability. The potential economic costs presented by these users may provide incentives to withhold or scale back services in the interest of increased profits. Managed care provides an economic and system rationale for reducing levels and scope of services to those who need more.

Some advocates fear that the organizational dominance of managed care within the health care system will lead to blatant or covert discrimination against individuals and groups of patients such as the seriously disabled, for, with their high health care costs, they could become suitable cost-cutting targets. Similar ethical and operational concerns have been voiced by health activists of inner city and community hospitals across the U.S., the main purveyors of free care and medical care of the uninsured, the institution of last resort where many patients are "dumped."

Indeed, escalating incidents of violence involving shootings and stabbing have been described as an economic missile speeding toward the heart of the health care system (Prince 1993). All trauma presents a big drain on health care system costs, but the costs are significantly increased for patients who require rehabilitation and those who become paraplegics or quadriplegics (Smith et al. 2003). Spinal cord injury is an increasingly costly health problem, consuming a large portion of the healthcare budget of the United States, resulting in an annual expenditure of $4 billion (Tyroch et al. 1997). The direct costs of firearm-related spinal cord injury (actual expenditure of funds and costs associated with care) can be divided into acute care, rehabilitation costs, and lifetime care costs. A study of adolescent patients with spinal cord injuries caused by gunshot wounds, in a cohort whose average age was 17, found a direct cost of $142,710 for the mean hospital stay of a patient with quadriplegia and $87,750 for patients with paraplegia. For 79 percent of the patients, payment was made with some form of tax revenue (Medicaid, Medicaid eligible, or Crime Victim Compensation Fund; Carrillo et al. 1998). Another study of direct costs of acute care and rehabilitation for spinal cord injury caused by gunshot wounds from 1980 through 1991 treated at Rancho Los Amigos Medical Center in California estimated the average per patient cost to be $137,118 in 1991 dollars. For these patients, some of the highest medical costs will be incurred following discharge. The total cost of such injury treated at this center during this 11-year period was $78 million, and after factoring this in as a 20 to 25 percent estimate of the total lifetime care costs associated with spinal cord injury, the cost of gunshot injury wound treatment at this center was between $312 and $390 million in 1991 dollars. It is estimated that 66 percent of approximately 8,000 injuries that occur yearly are preventable (Garland and Wharton 1994).

The costs of care for this subset of injured youth are such that financing rich youth development programs can be a cost-effective alternative. While the cost of comprehensive youth programs for this segment of the injured population has not been estimated, the average community-based youth program costs about $500 per youth annually. Intensive supervision programs, such as Multi-Systemic Treatment (MST) models for serious and violent juvenile offenders, which would more closely approximate the intensity of services and guidance needed for some of the young people more deeply involved in violent lifestyles and injured by violence. MST is a home-based client focused program with a therapist ratio of 4:1, and its net direct cost per participant has been estimated at $4,748 in 2000 dollars (Aos et al. 2001). The program recognizes that individuals live within a complex web of interconnected systems, and emphasizes the provision of treatment in naturally occurring contexts such as the home, school, and community (Henggeler et al. 1998). A study of the comparative costs and benefits of programs to reduce crime in 2000 dollars, found MST's net benefit per participant to range between $31,661 (where only taxpayers' benefits are included) and $131,918 (where taxpayer and crime victims' benefits are included). In addition, the study found that programs that can deliver even modest reductions in future criminality can have an attractive economic bottom line, provided the programs can be delivered at a reasonable cost (Aos et al. 2001).

The young people who have been able to break the cycle of violence, re-injury, and re-hospitalization offer many compelling reasons to invest in programmatic alternatives. One of the many young people who benefited from such a program was Manolo, who was a shooter for one of the most organized and lethal West Coast gangs. Brought to the U.S. illegally as a child of 3, he was uninsured. He received intensive emergency medical services, as well as gang and violence reduction intervention with psycho-educational and vocational components and a relocation service. Staff and community members determined to make the existing health services, assistive technology funding, and financing system work for him. As a result of these efforts, he was able to leave the shooter life behind.

Benefits of a different nature have accrued to society as a result of the positive activities and societal contributions made by Manolo. He worked as a volunteer peer educator of other at-risk youth for three years, and has served as a role model and counselor to other young people who have chosen to terminate their violent behavior. Manolo has also influenced his younger siblings and relatives to stay positive.

Health and hospital-based programs for adolescents have not developed to the "market-like" stage of criminal justice programming, where net value, net benefits per participants and rates of return on investment have been calculated. Health economists can begin to quantify the costs and benefits of health intervention programs, and understand the cost-benefit of promising approaches and programs to assist in the transformation of violent behavior. (See Table 7, Promoting cessation among youth in health settings: towards a model approach, p. 234.)

Affected Youth as Change Agents

I strongly believe in what I'm doing right now, I made that change. I do believe that violence can prevented, that's why I'm so passionate when it comes to my work. I get real excited, energetic. I give it all I've got because I believe in it, just like when I was loyal to my gang. But now I'm loyal to this and I feel that violence can be prevented we're not a lost generation, we just need to be shown, guided right by our adults.

—Albert

There is some debate about whether children and youth living in extreme conditions of violence can or should be involved in violence prevention community projects. The stories of the young people in this study suggest that such activities were important to their transformation to a positive life. Their voluntary engagement, and their opportunities to address their priorities and those of their peers, family members, and communities, resulted in exemplary and often lengthy records of civic service, and for some, led to eventual career choices in health. The length and type of involvement in such health and service activities ranged considerably among the youth. Some of the young people were involved in health and hospital programs only as a temporary, purely therapeutic endeavor, which enabled them to move on to pursue other interests and activities. For others, these voluntary activities led to the discovery of a life purpose and sense of mission.

Book Knowledge and Street Knowledge: Education and Community Service

Given the educational profile of this population, education and literacy are important goals as a means out of poverty and towards full participation in society. It can be argued that interventions should seek to place the young people in schools as one of the priority steps. For some young people whose ties to school have not been severed, returning to school should be an immediate goal. However, the priority of schooling for many of the young participants, who were estranged from schooling, was often only fully understood as a result of health and social justice community service. Community service activities in general are often relegated to the voluntary and after-school hours of traditional and alternative public school programs. Yet for these young people, the opportunities to learn more about the health and rights of their communities, while exercising their rights and responsibilities and improving health, were much more powerful than the traditional education programs that often tacitly accept these children's dire economic and social circumstances. Many of the young people came to realize that acquiring literacy and education skills was necessary to deepen their knowledge and roles and to give voice to their "subjugated knowledge." Schooling and literacy became an important goal because education became fundamentally relevant to their lives and advancement of community. Work and service, often in health settings, were the precursors to education, unlike the traditional school-to-work paths for the majority of youth.

With the exception of Ruby's mother, who had obtained a post-high school training certification program to work as a teacher's aide in an alternative high school, the parents of the youth in this study had not completed high school, and many had not attained middle school. To date, 18 of the 20 young people in this study have completed their secondary education, graduating from high school or obtaining their General Education Diploma. Ronnie is learning how to read, and his peer educators and chief of surgery serve as his alternate tutors. Manolo, who dropped out of school before the 6th grade, has just recently obtained his high school diploma in a specialized hospital program linked to a community college for young disabled athletes. Mo has decided against completing his GED, after two failed home-schooling attempts following two lengthy hospitalizations for pressure sores and bouts with depression. Erika, Lita, and Sandy, completed an associate's nursing program at a community college. Carl, Emmanuel, enrolled in four year programs. Delbert, Albert, and Ruby completed their undergraduate degrees in psychology and are applying to graduate schools. Martin is currently in graduate school.

**Table 7. Promoting violence cessation among youth in health
settings: towards a model approach**

Clinical Settings:
- Streamline admissions to prevent re-traumatization.
- Provide youth patient/victim advocate on admission.
- Establish safety protocols.
- Train of all clinical staff on stages of change, working with adolescent and young adult populations, theories of violence causation and termination.
- Hire diverse staff.
- Match clinician and young person's styles.
- Develop assessment tool of responsivity related factors.
- Improve access to assistive technology, social services, and victim compensation.
- Train and support young people to serve as paraprofessionals.
- Provide volunteer and paid internship opportunities for youth.
- Involve youth in program design, implementation and evaluation and in the development of protocols for care.
- Provide home visitation health services for violence impacted youth.
- Develop strong linkages to local, state and national social welfare, community based health, education, recreation, youth employment, street gang worker programs and victim assistance organizations, hospital schools, disability and other advocacy organizations.
- Ensure that hospital schools and other specialized programs for children with complex health care needs and disabilities serve violence impacted youth.
- Place greater effort on diminution alteration of deeper violence risk factors, addressing situational, community and structural factors through partnerships.
- Share resources with community based efforts to promote violence cessation efforts.

Broader Community Initiatives:
- Conduct street outreach.
- Develop specialized food pantry programs, safe house networks, and transitional housing and relocation programs.
- Involve youth in comprehensive community initiatives design, implementation and evaluation.
- Develop work-to-school programs in conjunction with other community partners.
- Broaden community mobilization efforts to transcend particularized efforts/activities.
- Provide specialized assistance programs for young people 18-24 who are attempting to change violent behaviors.

Table 7, continued

Broader Community Initiatives, continued

- Include violence-impacted youth in community and social mobilization initiatives, including youth with disabilities.

- Collaborate with local, state and national social welfare, community based health, education, recreation, youth employment, street gang worker programs and victim assistance organizations, hospital schools, disability and other advocacy organizations.

- Place greater effort on diminution, alteration of deeper violence risk factors, addressing situational, community and structural factors.

As a Discipline and Field of Action:

- Adapt or restructure health systems so that an ongoing, quality personal relationship with a child patient is maintained through childhood, preadolescent, adolescent years as the child enters young adulthood.

- Monitor and publicize impact of changes in health delivery structure, and social welfare policies on vulnerable populations.

- Advocate for patient management structure that provides client-centered services.

- Encourage engaged practice in medical school, health training programs and in service.

- Promote the development of health personnel through non-traditional programs.

- Support increased supported employment programs.

- Encourage clinician-client joint advocacy initiatives.

- Monitor compliance with Americans with Disabilities Act, Technology-Related Assistance for Individuals with Disabilities Act, and other legislation that forbids discriminatory health practices within varied spheres of practice and influence.

- Reiterate belief in equal opportunities for access to quality health care regardless of race, ethnicity, gender, race, nationality, insurance status, violence involvement, life circumstances and disability.

- Revisit mission of trauma, rehabilitation care and the public health as it pertains to violence prevention work in the current social and policy contexts. Include the eradication of practices such as needless incarceration and the death penalty within scope of violence prevention work. Lobby against tying prevention funding for youth violence intervention programs to laws that will further increase incarceration, increased juvenile eligibility for the death penalty.

These big markers in the life chances of these young people were preceded by a multitude of little, but meaningful and difficult achievements. Among these were the certificates of health education obtained in violence prevention, HIV/AIDS education, gang and drug prevention, and other health and community service programs, the awards and thanks received for community health service projects and completion of street fair and education workshops; and the many interactions with young people whose lives they transformed as counselors, peer educators, mentors and friends were other significant manifestations of the social benefits reaped due to their own, deeper shift in world view.

The youths' stories also suggest that the recovery process from violence victimization is also helped by meaningful engagement in health efforts. Part of their individual process of unlearning reliance on acts of "counter violence" required change at the individual level but also involved a reasoned analysis of and involvement in altering the deficient role of social systems in addressing the unmet needs of other children and youth, their families and communities. In follow-up studies of rape survivors, women who had made the best recoveries were those who had become active in the anti-rape movement. They became volunteer counselors at rape crisis centers, victim advocates in court, and lobbyists for legislative reform (Herman 1997) .

Power of Positive Peers: Youth as Agents of Change in Health Settings

Involving other young people may be an important way to reach young patients who live on the margins of community. For many of the young participants, the term community often did not refer to the usual concepts of geography, race or ethnicity. For many, their first community of reference was their peers—other children facing similar circumstances, from various "hoods." Many of the young people had grown up in families that were highly mobile and fragmented, others had been homeless or were precariously housed, and were not incorporated into other neighborhood organizations (such as school, boys and girls clubs, or a religious organization). Service, leadership and organizing opportunities in health settings, and the relationships that sustained them often became the new community, the new homes of these young people.

> The teen group is my community now, 'cause they did a lot of stuff for me. They gave me a job, and for me you know, I don't have no papers. It's hard to get a job out here. I'm glad this turned out to be a job for me, because I ain't saying I'm getting paid all that, but you know its something to help me out. Keep me off the street from selling drugs.

The stories of the young people suggest that peers can play many complementary and important roles in a young person's recovery and prosocial development, as well as in larger health initiatives. Research on peer influence shows that influence towards positive behavior (finishing school, excelling at something) is much more common than influence towards deviant behaviors and that peer modeling can be an important motivating force in participation in service activities (Scales and Leffert 1999). For the young people in this study, the health-based or linked peer counselor and group served as a pro-social, adaptational construct, in the absence of, or complementing, other private or public interventions. Peer groups provided credible role models:

> Those were things that could really help, sometimes when teens see people that were actually injured. "I was just like you. You know? And look at me now. I'm in a wheelchair, but I'm going on with my life. I can do something, even though I'm like this." Or they don't necessarily have to be in a wheelchair. They're just a person that has gone through a lot of violence in their past, and gangs and all that, and "Here I am moving on. Here I am making a name for myself, helping you guys. You know? Trying to help you guys. Trying to get to you where you could make it better for your children or the other generation."

The peer group or counselor offered ancillary support to a young person during a time of crisis and in medical settings that were generally short staffed, thus reinforcing the work of the adult staff.

> And then they referred me to violence prevention, which was great. I mean, it didn't only open my eyes to my situation, as to where I could have moved on, but it also opened my eyes to how to teach me how to deal with all that I was dealing with. And so, you know, it was like, was a learning experience. It was really helpful for me. I remember that. And I remember the support that I got from the teens there and from the staff person, a lot of support, support that I needed at that time.

Peers in health and hospital settings can also help institutions that are encountering new patients whose life circumstances they do not fully understand and who are not being served due to the limitations of current practice and knowledge. Adolescent victims of violence have only recently begun to be studied by rehabilitation researchers. Despite the rising incidence, very little published information exists on specific events that lead to spinal cord injuries caused by violence, or the characteristics of those injured other than age, race, ethnicity, gender, and rehabilitation outcomes (Waters et al. 1996). No widely accepted

protocols of care currently address their rehabilitation needs (AAP 1996).
Ronnie recognizes this demographic shift in the patient pool in the rehabilitation center that treated him in Los Angeles. He notes its impact on the providers, and the special role peer counselors can play in mediating the chasm between the clinicians and their clients:

> The majority of the people here—I don't really know the percentage—from what I see, who gets shot are Hispanic gang members, or black. There's not that many Asians in here, but its especially Hispanics and blacks. The white people are in car crashes, diving in swimming pools, things like that. They [therapists] can say, if they're having a problem with them two and the therapist can't understand them—which half of them don't, half of them go home with headaches, and they be over there crying, 'cause the patient is over there dogging them out, you know—they can call the youth counselors and say, "can you send one of your members over here and talk to this guy?"

Delbert, now 23 years old, coordinates a full service "wraparound" adolescent development program at a neighborhood health center, where he supervises some of his former adult youth workers. At 23 he has 9 years of "youth work" experience behind him. He has served as a youth leader and volunteer since the age of 14, when he first began his journey of change and became a peer violence prevention worker at the local public health department. At 17, he was among the first group of teens to serve as peer counselors and part of the rehabilitation psychology team at the regional spinal cord injury center. Interviewed at age 18, he reflected on the different types of peer health work and degrees of difficulty in carrying out such service

> I mean, anybody can speak about a certain subject if they really believe in the subject they're speaking about. But counseling is one of the hardest things for me, though, especially counseling at the hospital to paraplegics and quadriplegics because you're sitting there and you have no choice but to think about these kids who get shot. It's really sad and shocking. At times you'd be thinking, damn, I would hate to be in that situation. And then at other times you'd be thinking I wonder how he feels, and then at other times you be like, "Yo, he's really lucky that he's not dead, or he's really lucky he's off the streets."

He is clear about the benefit of this work for him and for the young people he works with, and in his ability to relate to them as an equal, as a human being and not as a subject. When interviewed at 18 on the impact of his work, Delbert stated that:

> I really do feel it helps them 'cause you have to get that pain out of your system. I mean if you keep it inside too long, it's like a kettle. If you keep the steam in there too long, it's gonna erupt, it's gonna burst.

> I feel it has a therapeutic benefit because the bond that I made with certain people in the hospital has lasted. And when I first went in there and I saw these, these faces with like, no hope on them, with these, these eyes that look like they want to pop out, you know, just want to break down crying... and then you see them a couple more times, and a couple more times and they start to look better, and they start to get happy, and it's, it's like it makes you feel good 'cause when you first walk in there and you see this person for the first time and he knows he doesn't have his legs anymore, or she knows that or know they can't move beneath the neck anymore. It's sad, you know, for both persons. And then when you talk to them and they get their stories out, and then they start talking, you relate to them as a human being and not a subject, you know, they come out, they gradually accept their situation and I guess it has some good benefit 'cause everybody I've seen looks really good now.

The peer counseling is often difficult work that takes its toll on the young people, underscoring the importance of preparing the young people and supporting them in this work.

> I would like to say it doesn't affect me personally, but it does. I can't say that I just go in there and I talk to these kids and I forget about it until I go back to work. It's just constantly on my mind like, damn, I wish he had done something differently. And when they tell me their stories, then I feel like, you know, at the point that my eyes get watery hearing how they could've got out of the situation if they had done this or this, or just haven't been in that certain spot at this certain time. It's like both of us just be there [at the counseling session], and the mood is just silent and, I can't really explain the feeling that comes over me and that other person, but it's not a good feeling.

The young peer counselors like Delbert had received extensive training in youth and gang violence prevention, disability and spinal cord injury issues, and basic peer counseling skills in preparation for their work. They had also traveled to the Los Angeles and other hospitals to learn about the nature of the peer counseling work done there and to meet and learn from other young people and their adult program staff about how to develop a program.

The one-on-one and group skilled peer counseling interactions provided opportunities for issue-focused discussions and positive peer social interactions that challenged the young patient's emergent cognitive capacities and stimulated perspective-taking. This was an important service because the more a child or youth participates in a positive peer social group, the more opportunities he or she has to take the social perspective of others, offering opportunities for mutual role-taking opportunities essential to moral and social development. Group activities with their peers also served to promote more equitable, democratic participation, a positive group identity, through dialogue, and by encouraging the young people to construct their own solutions to tasks. In research with adults, the establishment of group identity has been found to be a factor of great importance in the development of social cooperation (Dawes et al. 1990). The opportunities and support for the young people to build this sense of group identity through participation in health and public service activities provided was an important contributor to their democratic development:

> It is now a generally recognized theory that people acquire patterns of action and interaction, not merely discrete behavioral sequences. Children and adolescents become more aware of their own and other's perspectives in disputes with peers and attempts to convince others, as well as through differences of opinion which emerge in topical discussions. These reflective abilities can inform future interactions. (Hart 1997, 34)

Their own struggle for change was the focus of their action and research into the causes of violence. These young people responded well as they were asked to remember their peers as they pulled themselves out of their difficult conditions. By analyzing their own options for their future, they also served their community better. While building a sense of identity and self-worth through the promotion of individual rights, fostering a sense of responsibility towards others is important to address both the victim but also the victimizer aspects of their conduct. The stories of the young participants suggest that the theory of "natural helpers" from community social networks also holds true for youth who have been affected by violence, and that it can inform programs to foster change in health and hospital settings.

The stories also suggest that for children and adolescents living in situations of chronic violence who lose contact with the networks within their community, or who may be stigmatized by that community, positive peers can provide the interactions needed to foster moral and social development and other critical youth competencies. Stevenson's study of youth living in neighborhoods with high rates of community violence found that emotional adjustment was enhanced when there was a high level of social capital within the neighborhood, and that communities that engage in discussions that include their children's and youth's opinions and ask appropriate questions to stimulate growth assist in the moral development of their young (Stevenson 1998). Positive peer groups in heath and hospital settings can provide these opportunities and pose questions to stimulate growth, health, well-being and civic strengthening, and promote both bonding and bridging social capital (Putnam 2000). They can reinforce the identity-driven reason for the youth group struggling to effect change, reinforcing purpose, ties of loyalty and support, and can lead to a sense of pride, uniting a group and help a given community draw together to help itself emotionally and socially, encouraging community development and promoting public health. In addition to the bonding function, peers can promote bridging experiential, demographic and social differences, leading to more information diffusion and acceptance, the development of a broader identity, and more multilateral behaviors.

GIVING BACK TO THE COMMUNITY: YOUTH AS COMMUNITY CHANGE AGENTS

I make something positive out of every negative experience that I've had. I learned something from it. I have like this urge, "ganas," like I'm on a mission, the way I see it now. I didn't think I was capable of this much. I believe more in myself, now. And I believe that I can make a difference and that the help that I needed, I have to make it available to other women. And I have to let my community know what is right, what's wrong and what you can do to make things better, you know. There's the way you were taught to do things. Not only on domestic violence. Violence in general, and the way we bring up our kids 'cause there is a lot of families that don't beat their kids but then they do the verbal abuse, that sometimes end up much worse than just beating.

—Charo

Many of the study participants gave back to their communities in highly specialized ways, reinforcing health messages or reaching populations outside the reach of traditional health education or youth programs. They performed in roles in which others who lacked their life experiences may not have been so effective. The young people generally approached their work of violence prevention without the categorical divisions that demarcate one type of violence prevention from another. The usual gendered distinctions that are prevalent in the field were often challenged by the young people, with a lot of crossing over boundaries of expected practice.

George served as "an advocate, a mentor, a community organizer and community outreach" worker before starting his own program with his wife in 1996, working with violent juvenile offenders in secure facilities and with street youth from his neighborhood. He summarized his early work as a substance abuse counselor with a spinal cord injury as also having been beneficial:

> I've done mentoring and help some youth that were in gangs. There have been certain youth that had been contemplating suicide; they didn't kill themselves. Some of the things that I have organized have helped people. I helped start the drug rehab for paraplegics. I basically did all the organizing and all the outreaching. That benefited the people that came into the center. It helped some people that had drug habits, you know, in the community, in a wheelchair smoking on dope. So that helped them, but as for the community, that helped decrease homelessness, you know, so that helped keep people off the street. I've been an advocate. I guess I've helped push different issues around violence prevention.

Emmanuel's history in community health service dates back to when he was 17 years old. Starting as a rapper who educated about HIV and violence through his music, he worked as a peer educator for the health department, serving street and other high-risk youth in correctional settings for three years. His first formal health job, after several years of youth violence prevention and adolescent health education volunteer activities, was an HIV/AIDS outreach worker in "crack houses" handing out condoms and bleach kits. He now heads a street health outreach program for young black and Latino males, and was the first male health worker to introduce a breastfeeding support group for the partners of pregnant young mothers. He is now training as a social worker.

Now studying part time at a university, Carl was elected student council president of a largely white student body in a suburban hospital high school when he was 17. Despite the difference in backgrounds and the very distinct, often passive disability culture of children with developmental disabilities as opposed to risk taking, often oppositional and defiant characteristics of youth injured by violence, Carl would be elected and looked up to by staff and students alike. When interviewed at 17 he described his role in that capacity:

> Yeah, I'm the president right now [of the student council]. This is my second year on student council. I was treasurer last year. And I got some hands-on experience with accounting. And got some on the front-line, directing orders, taking responsibility for the whole council stuff like that. Showing my leadership skills, playing that role model I'm supposed to be.

> The student council gives you a role of leadership no matter what position you are on the board. Because you are representing the whole student body and you have some say on what goes on, what affects you and your student government.

He would be the leader of the Spinal Cord Cartel, a group of five youth from inner city Boston injured by violence (most of whom knew each other, or were linked by one degree of separation) and their "little wing man," a young boy several years their junior with spinal bifida who was the smallest of the young patients at the hospital. The other youth who arrived after Carl (and who are being referred to such schools in greater number due to the increase in the number of youth with severe violence-induced disabilities) found this institution a strange one to navigate and succeed. Carl was their guide and at times succeeded in retaining them, but many would be expelled due to behavior problems. At 21, Carl led a recreational program for the city that integrates able-bodied and disabled youth in a wheelchair basketball league. He has been commended by the Mayor for all his efforts and contribution to youth services in the City of Boston.

Andres worked as a peer educator with youth in secure facilities, educating them about gang and violence prevention and teen dating and domestic violence. He worked with gay and lesbian youth programs as a liaison to the city health department, and assisted in the training for clinicians, establishing programs for youth injured by violence in health settings in cities across the U.S. He also served as a peer counselor for youth with violence-induced disabilities. Andres volunteered up to thirty hours a week for months at a stretch, volunteering over a period of three years. Domestic violence work would be his passion, and his means of fully reintegrating back into society. The outrage he felt due to the beatings and abuse experienced by his mother, and understanding acquired about domestic violence as a social phenomenon, enabled him to generalize the empathy felt for his mother to other abused women, and eventually to other groups of the victimized, including his former enemies. In looking back to his gang involvement between the ages of 11 and 16, he "saw the worst of human nature" and understood the underlying root of much of his rage. He decided to reach other young men like himself in community settings:

> I had learned from my father that women were there for you and only you. He taught me that women were nothing but bitches and the only way to deal with them was to beat them. I never saw any truth in what he was saying and I always told myself that I would not turn out like him. I started to see that it was not right what we men were doing to women. I saw that there was nothing for women who were battered and women in general. I decided that I would try to do something about it or at least try to change the views that my friends and other youth had about women... and to try to slow down the violent cycle that is domestic violence.

Paradoxically, Andres' involvement in domestic violence work enabled him to see a police officer as a human being, and as a person worthy of trust. The nature of policing as practiced by the Domestic Violence Unit in Boston was altogether different from the policing in the street in Boston and Los Angeles, two cities in which Andres had lived. Over time, his work would include initiatives with the city's community police around domestic violence. Andres' street reputation made him an effective speaker with young males with high-risk backgrounds and an unlikely but helpful partner to law enforcement efforts to curb domestic and dating violence. The popular, although poorly documented, theory of the intergenerational effect of violence on ongoing violent behavior between intimates (Widom 1989a), and the framing of the issue as almost exclusively a problem of male aggression, results in few opportunities for young males to work in this area, making Andres one of the early pioneers in this work.

After working in youth programs for a period of three years, Charo worked as a hotline advocate and a child services advocate in the battered women's shelter that took her in as an adolescent. At the time she was interviewed, Charo supervised the volunteer hotline workers and led a group of young battered teen mothers. She describes the zeal that drives her work as:

> knowing what I can provide, and I feel that I'm really there to help, and I feel that I could make a difference and feel that I am gonna make a difference. It's like I'm on a mission right now.

One of the most important aspects of her job was to help women make safety plans. Even if the women do not leave or go back to the batterer, Charo does not give up "because fifteen, eighteen times I left him, and I ended up going' back before the last time I left him for good." Her activities at the shelter focused on:

> Safety planning as to what they're gonna do, if they're not ready to go now, let's find something for when you are ready to go. There's what you're gonna do: start saving up money, all your documents, your important documents, take them to somebody else's house, yours and your children's. Take them somewhere where when you leave, you can have them. If you have to just walk out the door, you can go pick them up somewhere else. Car keys. Money. Start saving at least a dollar, fifty cents every day.

> We tell them that there are support groups available for them, where they can talk and listen to other women. If they're not ready to leave yet, they can listen to other women and that will help them realize that it's not right and it's not gonna stop. That's a way to teach them. To come into the shelter, you know. And we provide legal services. There are a lot of legal things that are available. There's a lot of women that stay in these situations that are immigrants, that are not here legally, don't have their papers, and so they're married to this man, and they're trying to get their residency type of thing here in the United States with this person that they're married to, and this person beats them and they feel they can't leave them 'cause then they're not gonna get their green card or whatever the situation is. There are laws now, you can get it anyway. You can leave. And if you guys are married and he's a resident or a citizen, you're gonna get it away, as long as you're not divorced by the time you get it done, you know? So it's like there's a lot of laws that a lot of women aren't aware of, and we kind of make that open to them. And child services, we provide services for children. If you're not ready to leave, well we provide services where you can have your children in so your children

can feel better about the situation and talk about things and you can see how it's affecting your kids.

Charo also supervised childcare activities for the teenage mothers in her battered teens group. One of her jobs was to create "safe spaces" at the shelter for children. Many of the children have "difficulty relaxing." They remind her of her daughter in the early days following their arrival at the shelter.

But it's just how I love my job. And you know, when you love something, you do it. So that's how I feel about my job and about the kids. I feel that they're my kids, too. I also see my daughter in a lot of them. And, you know, it's like I feel like, wow, my daughter was just like this. She's so intelligent, and she was so intelligent at that age. They're just really reacting to what they're seeing. So it helps you understand. One of the mothers came in and she's like, my daughter's never, never been quiet in this childcare room, she's been coming here for a year, and she's never stopped crying. And now she doesn't cry anymore.

Charo completed and then led a training course to "teach teenagers how to become parents and how to become adults and how to get their life together, really, basically how to get a job, an apartment, how to manage money, being parents, food. It's training about being an adult, really." It is a course that many young people, regardless of the type of violence they are experiencing could benefit from, and a program she would like youth programs in general to offer.

Charo's goal is to go to the Dominican Republic, "where I'm originally from, and make it a point there, educate the women there and show them that there is so much more to life, there is so much more you can do, for your children, for yourself. Like, you can live by yourself, without having to depend on a man." She would also like to start a support group here for the "Dominican community, for Latinos in general, all Latino women. There are a lot of them here, that are living here, where there's all this help that's offered to them, and they're not aware of it. And they're still kind of really stuck in the old ways, and how it was, and they're still thinking that it's got to be that way, with the domestic violence." Charo has since completed college and is now working as an elder abuse caseworker for the past two years. She describes the elders as a "forgotten group, like children, and there is so much that we need to do for them."

Erika works with her husband in secure facilities for serious and violent offenders, as part of an outreach effort to recruit the young men into a community-based violence prevention program once they are released. She deals with "a lot of young people committing murder, a lot of young people ... they start off with an armed robbery, snatching purses, which becomes killing a person because one thing leads to another. It's not a planned crime. You don't plan to kill a person, but what it is that the person might fight, like the carjacking issue. The person might not want to give up their car."

> I sometimes go with my husband to juvenile hall, and I have to deal with kids that murder folks. And we have to tell them "How do you feel about it?" They say "Oh, I don't feel nothing about it." Then sometimes we'll take them graphic, sometimes you have to bring awareness to these kids. "What is it that you're doing? Look at what you're doing! Because you're a child, you're foolish, and you don't really think about it. Sometimes when you take lives, or see a person dying or something. How do you feel? What if that was you? Okay, you're the perpetrator, but think about the victim. How would you feel that somebody took your life, and you lay on the floor, and there's no hope for you, and you're going to die, and you feel the life just bleeding out of you. Just think about his person. This person never graduates, and this person will never see, have, or will see their children grow up." And I don't say it in a reproaching manner. I'm just saying it in an awareness manner.

Erika has been involved in many other initiatives, such as AmeriCorps, Vista volunteer and serving as an advisor on an after-school film on children and guns. Along with other peer counselors, she has offered guidance on how to depict the situation and its aftermath in a realistic but uplifting manner.

> It was a Disney movie called *Under the Gun*, something like that, where the kid brings a gun in school, and the consequences of it. And so we had to sit there and say no, he should lay down this way, no, no, no, he should lay down the other way. He should be [re-enacting moaning], that kind of thing, so it was, it was funny. But I think that's another way of getting people out of a tragedy and a way of bringing them out, you can't just stay there and live on it, just lock up on that. You have to kind of turn it loose.

Erika is currently working as a geriatric nursing assistant and is taking courses to "get into the field of counseling. And right now I'm

nursing. I like nursing and counseling. I want to, by the time I'm thirty or
forty I want to become a nurse practitioner and I would like to go places
like Rwanda and then war places and then do medical things. Right now,
I want to go into the counseling field and help a lot of children, a lot of
young people that's incarcerated or out in the street, with counseling
because I feel that, that a lot of people need counseling and don't get it."
    Martin worked in a residential home for children ages 6 to 11 and 11
to 18 throughout most of his college years. He is studying "community
health and adolescent health. What I've been working with is what made
a change in my life, and what I like to do. So that's what I chose to do."
He voices similar concerns for his younger charges as those he had when
he had to leave the security of the hospital to return to the community,
and speaks about the paucity of services for young people once they are
released from institutions:

> While they're in the residential program, you know, we do our
> best in providing services and giving them everything that they
> need to keep them safe, but it's the after effects when they leave
> the residential program. Once they leave, if they leave out of the
> program, what's going to happen then afterwards? What is
> going to be their outcome? What's going to happen if they are
> trying to change? The next program might just be a bunch of
> staff members who just want to get paid, and don't really care
> about the children.

    He recently spoke at the graduation ceremony for youth educators of
the city's adolescent health program about his transformation and the
challenges for young people ahead. He is pursuing a master's degree in
counseling psychology.
    Lita and Sandy began work as nursing assistants and have now
become licensed practical nurses, Sandy is working with children and the
elderly.
    José died in late 1996 at the age of 21 due to complications from the
1991 gang-related shooting that paralyzed him form the neck down when
he was 17 years old. Youth workers and program administrators from all
over the city and state, recognizing his contributions, attended his
funeral. José had served as gang mediator and peer counselor, advised
national funding collaboratives on violence prevention, developed public
service announcements for the city, and was a disability activist and
educator. His cousin, who is now head of police and youth relations
board and the executive director of a neighborhood recreation program,
eulogized him, remembering how it was José who was the positive
influence in his life and helped turn him around when he was finished his

last 6 year prison sentence. José was lauded posthumously in the Boston Globe for his role in crime reduction efforts in Boston, which included a 35 percent drop in the homicide rate and a sharp drop in gun-related crimes:

> It is certain that the new partnerships among local, state and federal law enforcement officials and the diminishing of budget and turf battles among agencies have enabled police and prosecutors to focus on recidivist criminals, the group that elevates serious crime rates. That great initiative, however, could be easily undone by the presence of just a few unenlightened police chiefs, federal agents, or district attorneys. It is the personal insight gained by young men like the late [José] Ojeda and the continued support of their counselors that will lead to lasting amity (Boston Globe 1997).

Making it Happen: Working with Youth in Health Settings

Young people are important, albeit underutilized resources in efforts to improve treatment of young victims of violence, and as change agents in health initiatives in the larger community that seek to and reduce violence. The study participants suggest that health programs can tap into the potential strength of the cooperative/ collectivist ethos among many youth in street groups by linking them to adult, guided, positive peer groups working toward a peaceful neighborhood. The existence of abundant social capital and vibrant informal networks is evident among urban youth, even as the primary networks (crews, posses, gangs) and their forms of associational life are not approved by the larger society (Sullivan 1997).

The greater degree of reciprocity and flexibility in positive peer relationships provided opportunities for the young people in this study to test their understandings of violence and cessation and adapt them to the requirements of ongoing interactions and life circumstances. Research experiments carried out in the 1970s and 1980s where young people were diverted from the juvenile justice court to prevent the youth from being labeled as delinquent, employed "change agents", usually college students, matched by race and gender with their assigned youth. The "change agents" worked with the young people in their environment to provide community resources and initiate behavioral change, employing both advocacy and behavioral approaches. In an evaluation of program effect on males, a comparative cost-benefit study of programs to reduce crime found an effect size for basic recidivism sufficient for taxpayers to gain approximately $5,270 in subsequent criminal justice cost savings alone for each program participant. The typical average cost of ADP per program participant is estimated to be about $1,138. Adding the benefits that accrue to crime victims increased the expected net present value to $27,212 per participant, which is equivalent to a cost-benefit ratio of $24.91 for every dollar spent (Aos et al. 2001, 19).

Our society can benefit from developing and training groups of young people to whom others can turn for advice and support. Intervention programs in health and hospital settings can help train formerly violence-affected youth as paraprofessionals, as change agents and role models for the new youth entering the intervention programs, and as youth partners in the training of health professionals. A study of the effects of a violence-screening education program on pediatric residents and medical students comfort level and skills in the identification and management of violence risks found that involvement of teen educators in the training improved the participants' self-reported violence questioning, increased perceived comfort and importance in violence screening as well as improving their identification and management of a standardized violence-related scenario presented in an adolescent clinic setting (Abraham et al. 2001).

Research on civic engagement among youth identifies five varied paths, all of which can be offered through hospital and broader health opportunities, in addition to the counseling, peer group and mentoring roles. The paths of policy/consultation, community coalition involvement, youth organizing and activism, and school/community learning settings had three overarching qualities in common to be successful: youth ownership, adult-youth partnerships and facilitative policies and structures (Camino and Zeldin 2002).

The young participants in this study noted that incorporating peers in clinical and other health settings requires that youth-adult (as well as lay-professional) interactions undergo some transformation. Administrative policies and structures need to be conducive to this. Research suggests that by early adolescence, children's relationships with adults are capable of being transformed from mere authority to reciprocity, as the individuality of both the adolescent and the adult emerges (Youniss 1980, 36). Such developments vary greatly according to culture as well as the extent of opportunities offered. To provide such opportunities in health settings, institutional structures often need to undergo some changes. The great divide that often exists between the young person and their community and the large health organizations that make decisions that affect their health can be minimized through institutional or strategic alliances with youth empowerment organizations, consumer advocacy groups, community organizations, and local governments.

Although the young participants in this study cited the guidance of adults as necessary, they also recognized that successful peer groups or counseling initiatives to promote change should be encouraged to construct their own ground rules and codes as much as possible. As Youniss (1980) notes:

> A successful group will be encouraged to consider alternative suggestions from different members when discussing an ideas or deciding how to go about tasks, and to be respectful of each other's contribution. The successful group's activities will be designed expressly to reflect the values that the group members are interactively learning: reasonableness, orderliness, respect for other's feelings, equality, freedom to take risks, and the capacity to listen.

Young people should also be involved in efforts to improve community and social conditions, program development, advocacy, organizing, changing organizational practices, coalition building, research, and efforts to influence macro policy decisions. The individual, or target of the intervention services should also be seen as a potential advocate, and as a person with the power to effect change. Such efforts generally require greater decentralization, and fluidity and designs that stress youth leadership, community citizenship, strength and participation.

In one example of the use of a teen-centered research methodology to develop municipal adolescent health initiatives, a study in Philadelphia was conducted with in-school youth to give local teenagers in an area of concentrated poverty a voice in determining how resources intended to benefit them would be allocated (Ginsburg et al. 2002). While the advisory panel that included city officials, school district representatives and community members concluded that violence and teen pregnancy were the most important problems affecting youth well-being, this study sought to determine from a cohort of urban youth what factors they believed could make the most difference in influencing whether they could attain a positive future. In developing a methodology that allowed adolescents to develop, prioritize, and explain their own ideas, the investigators developed a process that engaged youth to build solutions to within their communities. And since their insights were used to gain additional funding for programmatic activities, the young participants in this Philadelphia study may have gained a sense of empowerment. These young people presented different priorities than the adults, and expressed their belief that supportive solutions would do more to enhance their likelihood of reaching a positive future than would attempts to reduce "negative" behaviors or disruptive environments, suggesting that "research and policies should consider how best to augment the protective influences of education, employment, meaningful use of time, and connection to adults."

Give Us a Chance: Invest in Youth Impacted by Violence

An Institute of Medicine study found that a significant number of young people—especially those who are living in poverty and in high-risk neighborhoods, and who are disproportionately likely to be members of racial and ethnic minority groups—are in particular need of support. These young people often experience repeated racial and ethnic discrimination, and have substantial amounts of free, unsupervised time. According to the report, other young people who are in need of more community youth development programs include youth with disabilities of all kinds, youth from troubled family situations, and youth with special needs for places to find emotional support. Community programs for youth are being increasingly looked at as one way to redress the social inequalities that currently confront the United States (NRC and IOM 2002, 29).

Addressing the disparities in youth development opportunities will likely require deliberate efforts to involve and retain youth at most risk in such programs. According to Spivak and Zeldin, "skimming" of the most-likely-to-succeed (or investment in the most-visibly-resilient) youth, which some programs do, puts higher risk youth at even greater jeopardy by further isolating them from positive options, and supportive environments and attachments through which they can strengthen their personal, social, and academic competencies. The call to focus violence prevention efforts on ever-younger children also represents a maximization argument of sorts. Developmental psychologists are increasingly advocating that programs start with young children, thereby maximizing the chance of pre-empting or curbing subsequent violence. Where prevention dollars are scarce, many perceive that younger, more easily impressionable children are seen as likely to yield a larger prevention payoff. The state of California's spending on youth exemplifies a ubiquitous fact across the country—outside of the basic cost of schooling, it spends far more on younger children than it does on youth. At a local level, however, Boston serves as an example of a city that has expanded the quantity and quality of after-school community programs for youth (NRC and IOM 2002, 283).

The decision on whom to spend the limited funding for youth development is often influenced by prevailing "risk" interpretations of violence causation, and assumptions about which young individuals constitute a good "risk" on their return. Adolescents who have engaged in interpersonal violence are seen as poor social investment, and opportunities are not extended to young people from the most disadvantaged communities (or from those in the high homicide hot spots within specific disadvantaged neighborhoods). As stated by Zeldin and Spivak (1993, 9), as long as these adolescents are

> seen as lost causes, the question "why invest?" continues to linger. As such the U.S. invests its "youth development dollars" almost exclusively into those adolescents deemed at "low risk." Specifically, it is the low risk young people who are consistently engaged in relevant and challenging tasks, such as those found in internship, peer leadership, cooperative and experiential learning and community action programs.

Building a Conscience: The Engaged Health Provider

If the therapist went over there and says, "I can't deal with these kids," and then its like, they're bad, and then they want to send them away… I used to crack jokes. But they used to be scared of me, 'cause I was kind of big, you know. And I used to never smile. I used to always keep my shirt up; I got tattoos everywhere, and then when my homeboys use to come here, they use to be scared to come up. Afraid we're gonna do something to them.

—Ronnie

It is also necessary to acknowledge and address three myths that have been obstacles to the understanding of and the appropriate health care for adolescent victims of violence: (1) adolescent victims of violence are "bad kids"; (2) it is dangerous to treat adolescent victims of violence; and (3) it is hopeless to treat adolescent victims of violence.

—Task Force on Adolescent Assault Victim Needs (1996)

The participants in this study relate encounters in health and public hospital settings in which nurses, psychologists, and other staff actively participated in the normalization and institutionalized social indifference to violent victimization of urban, generally minority and poor adolescents. The young people describe a range of responses from health personnel that include summary dismissal, with no attempt to diagnose or treat the underlying causes; fear; discrimination; and withholding treatment. Ronnie, now a staff counselor at an SCI unit, remembers one such incident. It involved his cousin, who was still "in the life" and was shot during a drive-by, witnessed by Ronnie. His cousin was taken, in full gang attire, still alive but with multiple gunshots to a busy, underfunded and understaffed local emergency room, where he had to await treatment, as other, less severely injured or "more deserving" patients received priority care. According to Ronnie, the staff described his cousin as "just another gang banger" while they ushered in other patients ahead of him. The cousin died awaiting treatment in the emergency room and had no one beside his cousin, a man of very limited means, to request an autopsy to determine the impact of the (delay in receiving) medical care on his eventual death.

Ronnie stated that his cousin was injured pretty badly and that he might have required an expensive and lengthy hospitalization and perhaps rehabilitation, depending on the nature of the injury. Looking at the general cost-cutting thrusts, the institutionalized inequality of health care services, and the increasingly harsh climate towards children and youth who are involved in acts of intentional violence, Ronnie wondered if the life of and treatment possibilities for this young man were valued equally to those of other patients in the emergency room. He questioned if the emergency room staff used the practice of triage as justification of postponement of treatment.

Indeed, dismissive attitudes are prevalent in the trauma and rehabilitation field:

> Violence etiology connotes that individuals injured by violence may possess certain attributes, which might cause them to respond less successfully to rehabilitation than those injured by other means. Indeed, among some it might be held than those injured by violence versus other means bear a greater share of fault or guilt, or are somewhat more accountable for their injury and therefore perhaps less deserving of the benefits of rehabilitation and have poorer long term outcomes (Waters et al. 1996, 5).

The stories told by the young people about their health experiences are congruent with critical pediatric expositions about the state of treatment for adolescent assault victims that describe how "many people—including some health care providers—think that adolescent victims of violence are uniformly bad kids who probably deserved what they got" (AAP 1996, 1998). These young brown and black bodies, at times scarred and tattooed, are viewed as dangerous; the perceptions of these health workers are likely colored by the pseudo-speciation that is pervasive in much of the public and policy discourse on violence.[9] Some of the youth's experiences recall the culture of institutional efficiency and indifference described by Basaglia's study of state mental hospitals. In this study, Basaglia describes the efficient nurses, conscientious hospital workers, cautious administrators and psychologists, who tolerated, enforced, and monitored the brutal treatment of those confined not for what they had done but for acts that they might possibly commit (Scheper-Hughes 1992). Scheper-Hughes recognizes how "ordinary people" (like Basaglia's technicians of popular knowledge and popular consensus) enforce practices "against categories, classes and types of people generally thought of as 'deficient' and therefore in all likelihood as 'better off dead.' The profoundly mad have often fallen into this category, along with the mentally deficient, despised ethnic minorities, female infants, and severely disabled or disfigured children." (Scheper-Hughes 1992, 890)

These injured adolescents, perceived as beyond rehabilitation, and undeserving of care, also incur exorbitant medical costs, in an era of cost-containment, privatization, and lifetime caps. Such representations of the violence-involved youth as an economic liability and a burden proliferate in the popular culture. They are compounded by disembodied images in which they personify runaway health care costs and the crippling costs of firearm injuries. Such depictions are among the more extreme expressions of the declining societal value of marginal children. In cross-cultural studies of childhood and children's rights, Scheper-Hughes and Sargent describe how adult-centered, post-industrial, neo-liberal consumer societies

portray children—other people's children, of course—largely as a danger and a threat to societal order and to adult economic and personal security. A citadel mentality predominates in which fears of engulfing hoards of unwanted children (all those "dangerous" HIV-infected and drug-addicted babies) and their irresponsible parents ("impossible" teenage mothers, post-welfare "losers," and deadbeat Dads) have coarsened the political discourse (Scheper-Hughes and Sargent 1998).

Doctors, and other health personnel whose "expert" knowledge maintain the commonsense definition and order of things, can either misidentify or choose to correctly diagnose the situation of the young at the margins of society. As healers, they can challenge assumptions about their young patients and conventional responses to the problem of youth violence. The vitality of practice and their direct engagement with the injured young in a broad range of health settings can challenge experience distant assumptions and coarse discourses.

A study of level I and II trauma center directors and their associate directors and their involvement in violence prevention, revealed strong support among trauma surgeons for violence prevention programs and the integration of such programs into trauma centers. The study explored the attitudes and knowledge of trauma surgeons about victims of violence and the need for trauma centers to engage in violence prevention research. Although only a small number of surgeons are actually engaged in violence prevention activities, most were willing to become personally involved. Perhaps they see the carnage along with the vulnerability of even the most "hardened" patients at a time of crisis and near death. Many trauma doctors, like Manolo's Dr. M, have been the early champions of this work in health settings. In the study:

> Trauma surgeons overwhelmingly disagreed with statements that the majority of homicides are gang related, or the majority of victims are hardened criminals, or that gang members cannot be rehabilitated. These are responses corroborated in the National Crime Survey, from professionals who see this crisis every day and can make astute and clear statements to a relatively uninformed, but attentive, public. According to the study, 'the discrepancy between actual involvement in, and general support for, violence prevention efforts may be explained by a lack of established roles and previous experience for surgeons and by limited guidance outside of existing programs.' (Tellez and Mackersie 1996)

Many of the young people in this study were fortunate to encounter some of these concerned practitioners. They speak of interactions that were life-giving, not only from specialized surgical interventions that removed a bullet or repaired the damage, but from support that gave them a chance at a new life. The young participants saw these caring providers who delivered beyond categorical service guidelines and established protocols as critical in their process of transformation. These were health providers who "correctly diagnosed" the fuller problem, although they might not have fully understood all aspects of the social malaise. Often, the providers went beyond the boundaries of their roles to help the young patients. It mattered that providers believed that they were "equal, and worthy of help."

Recent efforts to define competencies for health professionals in youth violence prevention and control have begun to delineate levels of skills and expertise across the span of emergency medical training, from emergency medical services academic training to postgraduate continuing medical education. These competencies range from a generalist level, which should be obtained by all health professionals, a specialist level, which should be obtained by health providers such as emergency medical providers who have frequent contact with populations affected by violence, to a third, or scholar level, to be acquired by health professionals who wish to become experts in care, research and advocacy. Level three skills emphasize greater skill at eliciting nuances of patient history in an effective, a compassionate manner, and expertise in the interconnections/spectrum of violence. Being skilled change agents in the health care system, and in political and social advocacy are other important specialist level skills identified (Denninghoff et al. 2002).

They Cared about Me: Concern, Dismay and Humility

The young people describe health personnel who were pivotal figures in their process of transformation: neurosurgeons, psychiatrists, primary care physicians, nurses, emergency medical technicians, researchers, social workers, public health and gang intervention workers and counselors, hospital school sports coaches, medical secretaries, hospital intake workers, dietary aides, hospital janitor and health center security guards. The individuals who were able to reach the young people in this study displayed concern, they were compassionate in their interactions with them, without pity or immodest identification. These were individuals who could be present and respectfully accompanied the youth as they struggled to regain a sense of safety in their lives. Dismay and even outrage on hearing the multiple insults that the young people faced often propelled these providers into action, giving voice to the pain, grievances and needs of their young charges. The humility to recognize existing gaps in services and a certain modesty that recognized the limits of existing knowledge was also a characteristic of most providers.

The strong personal bonds and solidarity of the health care champions of the young people were predicated on seeing their young charges not as objects of dispassionate interest, but as human beings and collaborators in a shared cause. This type of closeness and mutuality can be difficult to foster and sustain in a clinical and research culture that values professional distance and edits out sentiments, since unbiased treatment and observation are deemed to require a distant and impersonal stance. Without close personal ties, however, the possibility of an authentic understanding is severely diminished. Especially where children and young people face extreme social and economic conditions, providers' distance can seem a passive or heartless endorsement of the status quo, a sign of tacit approval of structural violence.

Such engagement, however, can come at a personal and professional cost. When a young patient is already devalued or considered unredeemable, the most traumatic events in his or her life exist outside the realm of socially validated reality. The health worker who challenges this socially validated reality can also find their credibility challenged:

Clinicians who listen too long and too carefully to traumatized patients often become suspect among their colleagues, as though contaminated by contact. Investigators who pursue the field too far beyond the bounds of conventional belief are often subjected to a kind of professional isolation (Herman 1997, 9).

Hearing stories of violence, recognizing the paucity of services and the difficult road to recovery can overwhelm health care providers and lead to feelings of despair, rage, and terror. The psychological literature describes this phenomenon as vicarious traumatization, which can lead even experienced clinicians to feel suddenly incompetent, "de-skilled" and hopeless in the face of a traumatized patient. Health workers who work closely with youth affected by violence can benefit from an ongoing support system to deal with such intense social and psychological challenges. Such support is needed at the practice level, but also needs to span a range of prevention activities that address individual, situational, organization, community-level, and policy factors. The opportunities to take part in such activities should be provided to the staff and volunteers of all ages who work closely with the young people.

LOOKING AHEAD: EXPANDING THE UNIVERSE OF HEALTH

The health community needs to revisit its mission of trauma and rehabilitation care as it pertains to a growing segment of the populations it treats, and the changing social and environmental contexts.

During the 1960s, urban violence increased and hospitals saw more patients who were injured by gunshot wounds and stabbing. They were challenged to revisit their practice and mission in order to serve this growing segment of patients. The concept of a trauma center, like that of rehabilitation center, evolved out of the need for a systematic approach for specific types of care, and out of the recognition that treatment approaches were failing to prevent unnecessary death and disability (Cales and Trunkey 1985). Initially, early rehabilitation, one of four features of a trauma center, received less emphasis than the other three: prehospital, or emergency medical care, operative care and intensive care. Increased attention to rehabilitation, in both trauma and rehabilitation centers, grew out of the need and desire to return the victims of violence and other trauma patients to a productive life. There was also the fiscal incentive, as multiple studies concluded "that most trauma patients can be rehabilitated successfully and that rehabilitation costs far less than custodial care." (McKenzie et al. 1988)

By the 1970s a new, expanded role for the field of trauma began to surface: to properly address trauma, surgery and other specialties needed to broaden their focus to include social, environmental, and political disciplines that had not previously been considered a concern of clinicians. The surgeon, like other clinical staff, needed not only to treat the patient but also address societal issues. In the 1970s, a shift also occurred in the field of rehabilitation, from institutional care to more independent community-based living for those permanently disabled. Whereas previously, the care of people with major trauma and disabilities such as spinal cord injury, cerebral palsy, and muscular dystrophy had been relegated to institutional settings or to the care of relatives and friends, by the 1970s the pattern began to be reversed. The emergence of independent living programs, adaptive housing, home personal care attendants, and training in independent living skills allowed independent living in a community setting for people with severe disabilities. Advocacy groups such as the National Spinal Cord Injury Association and the Paralyzed Veterans of America added a powerful lobby to the effort, and federal legislation through the Americans with Disability Act fostered the development of rights of the spinal cord injured.

Since the 1970s, trauma research and treatment have increasingly emphasized prevention, community involvement, public education and professional education. The geographic locations and professional standing of trauma centers, hospitals, and public health departments give health professionals a unique opportunity to assume leadership and co-leadership roles in each of these areas in their respective communities. Linking existing systems and sharing resources also enhances the ability to confront violence where it occurs (Tellez and Mackersie 1996). The field of rehabilitation has become less agency-dominated and more focused on the individual client in the past 20 years as disability activists have assumed greater influence. More importantly, a philosophical shift has occurred, stemming from the "acknowledgement that disability is a natural part of the human experience and that people with disabilities have the right to live in their communities, to interact with individuals in the broad mainstream of society, to be employed in meaningful jobs, to be independent, to make choices about daily living, and to participate in decisions about the services they receive." (Giordano and D'Alonzo 1995)

The expanding or new universe of disability resulting from violence and abuse will require a research and practice agenda that forges new partnerships, adopting new styles, taking risks, and employing all the knowledge available in order to effectively deal with a growing segment of this young client population. Among the developments predicted for the rehabilitation field in the next 25 years are increases in community-based rehabilitation services, increases in supported employment programs, greater control of programs by people with disabilities, emergence of culturally sensitive rehabilitation counseling models, and models for developing rehabilitation personnel through non-traditional programs (Giordano and D'Alonzo 1995).

The health disciplines must also more deliberately address the issues of custodial care of a different sort, the widespread and lengthy incarceration of adolescents as a solution to the problem of interpersonal violence. The public health implications of incarceration, a risk factor for further violence, are issues that the field will need to address more fully. As more funds are invested in removing these young people from society, the generating conditions that lead to violence go unchallenged. For the rehabilitation field, this is an issue that has already surfaced as young people with violence-induced disability are serving time, often lacking the medical care required to keep them minimally healthy and mobile in prison facilities. On a different level, the sentencing to death of juveniles and young adults (often for the death of their peers) poses other, larger issues about the state's use of force against children. It also presents a challenge to the health community to begin to include the eradication of such practices in their scope of violence prevention work.

The study and practice of violence prevention requires a principled, ethical stance that the young people who are affected by violence are fully human and have intrinsic human rights, that they are capable of change, are full of potential, and are entitled to excellent care. The study of violence does not differ from the previous efforts to study and raise awareness about other forms of trauma:

> The study of war trauma becomes legitimate only in a context that challenges the sacrifice of young men in war. The study of trauma in sexual and domestic life becomes legitimate when it challenges the subordination of women and children. Advances in the field occur only when they are supported by a political movement powerful to legitimate an alliance between investigators and patients and to counteract the ordinary social processes of silencing and denial. In the absence of strong political movements for human rights, the active process of bearing witness inevitably gives way to the active process of forgetting. Repression, dissociation and denial are phenomena of social as well as individual consciousness (Herman 1997, 9).

CHAPTER 8

Conclusion

In the absence of mid- and long-range policies to reduce youth violence, a limited but promising approach to violence prevention efforts lies in treatment innovations, better systems coordination, and interdisciplinary approaches that encourage the process of behavioral change. Although these recommendations will not solve the underlying causes of violence, and only offer a technical fix, they can help to assure care for the victims of violence and diminish the likelihood of re-injury or death to self and others.

Mid- and long-range policies to prevent violence require that the "hard surfaces of life" be impacted. These surfaces are the economic, political, stratificatory realities that contain all individuals and the biological and physical necessities on which those surfaces rest. The stories of the young people speak to such dimensions and the importance of enacting policies that can reach the "deep-lying turtles"—the difficult and elusive dynamics of personal change in therapeutic or intervention settings—as well as shape the complex, stratified environment which surrounds these settings. As illustrated by the stories of the young study participants, violence prevention policies must also address larger questions about identity, development, race, ethnicity, status, power, death, disability, legitimacy, urbanization, inequality, and immigration. According to young participants, the key spheres of influence that policies to promote non-violent development among children and adolescents should address are health care, education, job training and employment preparation, community and youth development, juvenile and community justice.

POLICY IMPLICATIONS: ADDRESSING BARRIERS TO HEALTH

The study findings show how a group of young people affected by violence was able to reduce violence in their lives. This research also begins to delineate the design of prevention programs for vulnerable populations, as suggested by the High Risk Communication Study, directed by the Public Health Service Office of Disease Prevention and Health Promotion:

> Virtually all of the young people reported that violence—along with drugs, alcohol and sex—is "a way of life," says the report, and many do not expect to live past their seventeenth year. With this fatalistic view, these young people feel little threat from the possible long-term consequences of their current risky behaviors. Therefore, they cannot be reached by communication campaigns alone. Such campaigns must be integrated with efforts to encourage youth/adult interaction, to link programs with health services, to include input from high-risk youth and their families, and to support safe havens and productive activities (NHIS 1994).

To reduce violence on a national scale requires "coordinated, comprehensive violence prevention programs to at least 80 percent of local jurisdictions with populations over 100,000" (NHIS 1994), a goal established in 1994 which remains to be attained. Public policies need to support such programs on a far greater scope than the present. A large-scale, comprehensive and longstanding federal initiative similar to the Head Start program, funded in the 1960s to help families in poverty as part of President Johnson's war on poverty, could begin to address the host of social problems associated with youth violence, such as family turmoil, academic failure, peer and community/neighborhood factors. (See Table 8 for program level public policy recommendations.)

Table 8. Public policy recommendations: program level

- Increase the funding base for programs that help children, adolescents and adults develop negotiation, communication, anger management, problem solving and coping skills that exclude violence as an acceptable form of resolving conflict.
- Develop and support anti-violence programs that emphasize teaching preadolescents and adolescents to build emotional, cognitive and creative abilities, academic, vocational, social and cultural competencies required for a healthy adulthood
- Expand anti-violence programs to emphasize both perpetration as well as victimization prevention
- Enhance cultural diversity and representation in programmatic efforts to reduce and prevent violence by mandating the participation by the subjects and community in the development, implementation and evaluation of these efforts as precondition of funding.

Funding quality violence prevention and intervention programs, however, is a small piece of a broader health promotion policy for young people who have been impacted by violence. Prevention programs should not be the sole focus of health care policies that influence the well-being and development of this sub-sector of young people. Among the health policies that have the most effect on child and adolescent development are those that regulate access to care, and disparities in care received.

A major problem is discrimination against children, youth and their families in the many spheres of health (and public life in general). Policies to eliminate discrimination should identify, confront, and transform the social arrangements and ideologies in which discrimination is rooted and reproduced.

Institutional racism and discrimination are well-established risk factors for violence causation, a range of other health problems, and maldevelopment among adolescents from disadvantaged communities. The stories of the young people in this study underscore the significance of discrimination experienced in multiple, reinforcing forms in various worlds. These forms of discrimination were variously experienced as based on race, ethnicity, gender, nationality, legal status, age, gang and violence involvement, and welfare and medical insurance status, among others.

Our society needs policies to address structural inequalities in the access and distribution of medical care. A World Health Organization (WHO) survey examining the quality, distribution, and cost of care in each country, ranked the United States as inferior to those of most other industrialized nations because it is the most expensive and yet fails to provide adequate care to the poor. The United States leads the world in its average annual medical expenditure yet ranks lower than its industrialized counterparts because, too often, its indisputably world-class medicine is not available to those without money. R. Christopher Murray, WHO's director of global programs, describes the United States as really three Americas, with the bottom 5 or 10 percent, made up of Native Americans living on reservations, the inner city poor, rural blacks, and Appalachia constituting the third America. Murray concludes that health conditions in this bottom third of the United States are as bad as those in sub-Saharan Africa (Mishra 2000). Health care policies promoting an equitable distribution of care are required to redress these tremendous disparities. Public health policymakers, researchers, and activists can use these perspectives along with data on the astronomical costs of gunshot injury, to demonstrate how little is spent in prevention, and how this disparity impedes the healthy development of children and youth from the "third America."

As we look ahead to respond to the health care needs of children growing up over the next twenty-five years, a key to the quality and equity of services will be the extent to which the federal government is accountable for guaranteeing basic services and rights. Private advocacy groups and constituent lobbies and rights groups will play an increasingly important role in safeguarding rights, monitoring such developments, and advocating for just policies. It is clear that, given the inequities in U.S. society, some groups will be far better positioned than others to protect their interests and rights. Health professionals (and their allies who work with children and youth) are challenged to play a more direct and active role in addressing operational, institutional, and the larger structural barriers to health for this disadvantaged youth.

ADDRESSING BARRIERS TO EDUCATION AND PREPARATION FOR EMPLOYMENT

Violence prevention requires the transformation of school culture, involving the commitment of the principal, teachers, staff, parents, and community as well as the alteration of disruptive and violent behavior among students. To achieve such a changed environment requires policies that explicitly foster a caring ethic and focus on strong adult-child relationships. Those were the ties that had kept Charo and other young participants in school.

Material resources are also important. The young people stressed the importance of enacting policies that correct for the shortage of books, the poor physical condition of buildings, the high student-to-teacher ratio, and the paucity of school activities that engage students in many inner-city schools. Schools with doorknobs, clean bathrooms, fixed-up ceilings, and nice gardens are some of the features they would like to see for their children or younger siblings. Other measures cited that could keep many young people in school include having access to the computers they have seen in more affluent public schools and receiving up-to-date schoolbooks in a well-stocked library. Quality after-school programs (sports, arts, and other activities) and interesting community service opportunities are other means to prevent and intervene in the cycle of violence. Developing stronger ties between schools and parents and community mentoring programs were other measures schools could undertake to diminish the anonymity of students in such institutions and increase accountability. Quality, nonpunitive truancy programs with a home visitation component can help prevent children from dropping out of school, or help redirect them to another school when necessary, and steer them away from violence involvement. Statistics for Los Angeles for 1993 indicated that 85 percent of all daytime crimes were committed by truant youths.[10]

Policies based on zero tolerance laws were seen as ineffective and harmful by the study participants, for they lead too easily to discriminatory actions and forfeiture by the schools of their responsibility to provide an education to their most unruly students.[11] Such policies treat all offenses within certain categories with equal severity, with no regard for intent, extenuating circumstances, or previous record, and reflect a "take no prisoners" attitude toward discipline.

During the lifetime of the study participants, the total number of students being excluded from school in the United States nearly doubled from 3.2 million in 1974 and 1997, according to the Department of Education's Office for Civil Rights. Derived from criminal justice policies, the practice of excluding students from schools adversely affects children, families, and communities. The 24 states (Massachusetts and California included) that do not mandate alternative education should pass laws requiring school districts to provide such programs (Advancement Project 2000). High quality alternative education programs provide much-needed services to this growing population of at-risk students. For many young people, alternative programs offer a last chance to receive an education.

The importance of meaningful engagement and employment in redirecting violence trajectories was underscored in the young people's stories, and in meta-analyses of offender recidivism studies. However, there are few programs to help youth with troubled pasts acquire the job skills needed to secure and maintain meaningful employment. The work generally available to such youth typically is employment in service sector or other unskilled occupations, offering inadequate opportunity for advancement. To improve, education programs need to expand to include specialized adult literacy and skills training programs to prepare youth who are currently locked out of the job market or relegated to a narrow range of employment options in which they are the last to be hired and the first to be fired.

DEALING WITH GUNS IN THE ENVIRONMENT

I was very violent, and, you know, the only reason why I feel that I didn't really critically hurt somebody was because the weapons weren't so available to me.

—Charo

Guns are the main weapon involved in homicide cases involving adolescents. Indeed, the marked increase in gun wounds and killings attributed to adolescents under age 18 has received extensive attention in the media and policy circles. The armed juvenile offender became the focal point of much state and federal legislation in the 1990s, with the enactment of special provisions for crimes, gang gun crimes and drive-by shootings, and the changes in criminal court transfer for young transgressors.

Effective policies to keep handguns away from minors must focus on prevention as well as apprehension. The removal of prohibited weapons from young persons who possess or carry them needs to be accompanied by law enforcement goals to reduce the supply of guns to youth and to reduce the general availability of guns in communities. In his study of American youth violence, Zimring distinguishes three types of gun markets with different kinds of supply mechanisms that need to be addressed: 1) the white market of legally regulated retail suppliers, who account for the majority of transfers of new and used weapons; 2) the gray market of hand-to-hand transfers of guns between individuals who are not dealers; and 3) the illegal market, the bulk purchasing of guns and their sale to persons who the seller knows are not legally permitted to own them (Zimrig 1998).

Addressing the gray market, or influencing the type of familial gun transaction that resulted in Carl's mandatory one-year sentence for gun possession as a juvenile, requires a broader focus on prevention and education. This involves addressing the social status and meaning of handguns in adolescent cultures, street subcultures, and in the larger U.S. society, as well as the perceived or real need for self-defense. Campaigns and policies that seek to influence social values should be a priority focus for public information efforts at many levels, and directed to many segments of the U.S. population, that seek to reduce the risk of gun injuries, disabilities, and death. Involving credible young people and community members who have experienced both the lure and the devastation of handguns is crucial in efforts to help deconstruct the current imagery of the gun in society and adolescence.

The young people from Los Angeles—especially the young people from the neighborhood in East Los Angeles, a community that has one of the highest and oldest concentrations of gang activity in the country and one of the highest homicide rates in Los Angeles, suggest the curtailment on manufacturing, especially of those guns used in violent assaults. Others suggested measures such as shutting down manufacturers of cheap handguns used in many urban crimes. Some of the participants suggested that only police, the army, and the National Guard be permitted to carry the type of guns commonly used in interpersonal crimes and other weapons that are clearly not for hunting purposes.

The impact of such policy measures to address the supply factors will vary according to the characteristics of each city, including gun density.

> The distinction between high-availability and low-availability cities should alert us to the probability that efforts to keep firearms from youths are hostage to the general condition of gun availability. As hard as it might be to reduce the black market availability of handguns in low-ownership cities like New York and Boston, it would seem harder still to reduce gun availability in cities like Atlanta, Miami and Houston (Zimrig 1998).

None of the young participants endorsed the policies implemented in communities under the Gun-free Schools Acts of 1989 and 1994, a spin-off of the Drug-Free Schools Act. These two acts granted increasing federal jurisdiction over schools. Such activities as policing schools, the installing of metal detectors, and conducting locker searches may be needed as a first response in some instances, but generally exacerbate feelings of insecurity and fear. The schools attended by the youth in this study and their peers had inherent structural problems that mere policing responses could not address. Better solutions would have included reducing classroom size to diminish anonymity and offering greater opportunities for youth development, as well as strengthening ties between school and community services.

MAKING A CONNECTION BETWEEN HEALTH AND JUSTICE

The stories of the young people's trajectory towards and away from violence hold serious implications for criminal law and juvenile justice policies. Although this study purposefully did not focus on the trajectory towards violence or the development of these young people's injury or violence "career" as a point of departure, the stories suggest that the young people had varying ages at the time of serious violence involvement, different levels of maturity, culpability, vulnerability, and levels of cognitive abilities to fully comprehend moral reasoning. The ability to control impulses in the context of anger and frustration, and to deflect or resist peer pressure even as they engaged in the same acts of violence, varied. As stated by Zimring in his study of U.S. youth violence, there is no sustained analysis of the factors that justify separate treatment of adolescent offenders in the literature to measure against the known facts about serious youth violence (Zimrig 1998, 75).

The research findings on desistance from violence underscore the need for further exploration of diminished responsibility, culpability, and age on current punishment policies, especially when such policies compromise the long-term interests and rehabilitation potential of young offenders. The fact that young victims of violence are subject to relatively quick changes in the pattern of their behavior and their outlook is a positive sign for the legal process. The stories of these youth suggest that retaining the young people in the juvenile justice system, where their youth development needs can be met along with the corrections and rehabilitation, is a better policy choice to encourage and promote change. The stories in this study also argue for the strengthening discretionary powers of juvenile judges, rather than district attorneys, to decide on the outcome of criminal charges. The youths' large potential for change beg a revision of current policies of capital punishment for crimes committed as a juvenile.

We need further research on the social skills and social experiences of adolescents who are involved in violence and those who mature out or change their behavior to help discern what constitutes penal maturity for young offenders who commit crimes of extreme gravity. A common theory of rehabilitation for young people who have been seriously involved in violence can also contribute indirectly to the development of a common law of adolescent culpability and inform a comprehensive policy towards youth violence and adolescent homicide.

The stories of the young people underscore that victimization and perpetration are often intertwined, and that policies to prevent recidivism need to encompass both dimensions of the phenomenon of interpersonal violence. Federal Department of Justice and state victim compensation funding and the spectrum of victim assistance services, should be extended to young victims and their families, regardless of the circum-stances surrounding the event that led to injury. George, Ronnie, Carl, and Mo had tried to receive assistance for victims legislated by the Victims of Crime Compensation Act, but were unsuccessful because of their criminal backgrounds. George's efforts to advocate for a stipend for a mother to bury her son who had been shot in a drive-by were also futile: she was denied because of her 14-year-old son's suspected gang ties. Just victim compensation assistance will ensure a comprehensive policy towards victims that is not based upon a false innocent victim-perpetrator dichotomy.

Increasing Social Capital

Social capital accumulates not only among individuals but also communities. Policies that increase the individual, family and community social capital can provide the secure and supportive social networks needed to endow young people with the resources to resist and terminate involvement in youth interpersonal violence.

Among the policies suggested by the youth that would increase such capital was the provision of "family days" during which parents would be paid or encouraged to be with their children and engage in family activities, and the city could provide food, refreshments, and family activities for children and youth of all ages. Health, education, and home visitation programs can strengthen the connections between youth, families, and community institutions. Encouraging residents of disadvantaged neighborhoods who "made it" to move back into the neighborhood and/or to continue to "give back to their hood" is a way to further widen the networks of social capital. Employer policies (such as municipal, state workers residency requirements, corporate programs based on solidarity and not charity precepts) are other ways in which networks can be strengthened. Encouraging pastors, social workers, clinical and public health staff to leave their offices and do more work on the street can enrich the ties to the community and enhance professional competence to address the community's salient issues. On a different level, social policies formulated within different spheres should focus on enhancing the public and civic features of life, especially in neighborhoods where private property and resources are few. For example, Ronnie would like to see the city of Los Angeles care for its public parks as much as the private golf courses that are so manicured and accessible to so few.

The cities of Boston and Los Angeles differ substantially in the access to social capital that they provide to violence-involved youth. While Boston can be described as having a social welfare orientation, reflected in the provision of municipal street worker programs and support services for violence-involved youth, Los Angeles provides fewer resources for youth in communities and invests more in crime control and incarceration. City-level policies are especially relevant in fostering social capital-building and mediating positively or negatively the effects of larger state and national policies.

Transcending Identity Politics

Policies that promote the cessation of violent conduct require multi-leveled analysis, fields of action, and mobilization efforts that transcend single disciplinary perspectives, localities or particularized organization. Such a broad and deep analysis has often been lacking in the ways responses to violence have historically been addressed by "out" groups. As Rubinstein describes, writing about the 1960s, group revolts or group improvement movements express "the interests and needs of specific identity groups rather than a more general interest in system change" and rarely take into account the larger forces "driving the members of oppressed domestic groups desperately to assert and defend particularized cultural identities," (Rubinstein 1989) whether they are based on ethnicity or race, or other identities.

> Indeed, rebellious groups in the U.S. more often conceive of themselves as nations-within-the-nation, cultural entities struggling for some form of self-determination, than economic entities linked organically to some larger national or international group (Rubinstein 1989, 315).

Rubinstein's description of the U.S. political system as one "essentially anarchic and dominated by the norm of self-help" rings true as a depiction of the 1990s New Federalist policies of government dismantling and the willingness of the local community to take on the responsibility of fixing problems that are, by and large, structural problems. Since the 1960s, class stratification as a whole and within social classes, paradoxically has further undermined "the coherence of domestic identity groups, but it has also served to strengthen the needs of individuals for particularized group identification." The demand for community control is increased in an era in which social integration has come to mean the increasing subordination of all interests to those of concentrated capital (Rubinstein 1989, 317).

The types of macro-level policy recommendations that have surfaced from this research project require the participation of institutions, multiple networks, and spheres of interest across the city and the country, the involvement of many domestic identity groups, and mobilization beyond self-help approaches. Among the macro-level policies suggested are increasing entry-level worker's pay; increasing the minimum wage; and decreasing the number of hours or multiple job-holding among parents, to allow for more family time and supervision. Other measures include improved public transportation and access to be able to reach better jobs and take advantage of all the pro-social development opportunities available in a city or region. Other policies important to pursue are increasing affordable housing as a means of enhancing stability, and increasing social capital; universal health care; and promoting just, community-oriented policing. Other recommendations include influencing the structure of health, education, social service, and justice programs to allow for a one-on-one, client-centered relationship with children and youth; a broader societal policy agenda that values education over incarceration for disadvantaged youth; and a moratorium on further prison construction.

Monitoring compliance with civil rights, children's rights, victims' rights, and disability rights legislation and litigation to confront, eliminate and transform discriminatory policies are some of the other efforts requiring the sustained engagement of many, over time, to achieve such transformation. At a federal level, the Departments of Maternal and Child Health, and the Department of Education should require all state health departments and school districts receiving federal aid to provide more comprehensive civil rights compliance data, including data on disciplinary actions taken by offense, including the race, ethnicity, and disability status of the child, and information on referrals to law enforcement agencies for in-school conduct. More compliance reviews and investigations to ensure that children are not discriminated against in the adoption or application of disciplinary policies are also needed. This requires active discussion and leadership by the President, the Departments of Education, Health, and Justice, as well as the Office for Civil Rights. Strong support for diverse urban communities by these departments and Housing and Urban Development is also needed. Researching and disseminating successful local practices that create integrated communities and enforcement against housing market and lending practices that spread segregation based on ethnicity, race and wealth can help foster peaceful and just communities. (See Table 9, Public policies to promote violence prevention and cessation, by domain.)

Policies Based on Inclusion and Hope

In morally isolating ourselves from this segment of the population, we confer on it the status of being quarantined. Public fear and distrust assume the appearance of a rational response. Gradually these young men and their would-be families become functionally obsolete in society. As a matter of policy, the environments they inhabit are neglected, and predictably, they deteriorate.

Felton Earls

Table 9. Public policies to promote violence prevention and cessation, by domain

Macropolicies
- Public policies need to recognize that societal change may take 20 years
- Give everyone good health care
- Improve government agency record keeping, communication
- Reduce the prominence of crime prevention in the construction of youth policy
- Do not package youth development programs as crime and violence prevention
- Pay parents enough so they don't have to work 2-3 jobs, so they can be home more
- Promote just, prevention oriented policing
- Value education over incarceration
- Take some money from rich and give to the poor, redistribute wealth
- Structure health, education, social service and justice programs to allow for long-term one-on-one relationships with children and youth
- Improve transportation, accessibility
- Increase safe, affordable housing
- Monitor compliance with civil, children's, victims, and disability rights legislation and litigate to confront, eliminate and transform discriminatory policies
- Challenge use of such rhetorical devices as "super predators" and "feral pre-social being", "lost generation" in policy initiatives for they create a fear of the young
- Invest in "hard core" youth who want to change

Schools
- Provide breakfast and lunch programs in schools
- Create safe schools, community where kids are listened to, respected, not feared
- Have lower student/ teacher ratio
- Fix up schools, provide door-knobs, clean bathrooms, updated textbooks, nice computers
- Lower counselor-to-student ratio in schools, so we know we can go to college or a good trade
- Make it so all schools have equal resources, change property tax allocation
- Provide meaningful community service opportunities
- Fund rich after school programs
- Make program accessible to all youth
- Strengthen truancy programs
- Provide school programs for youth who carry weapons based on youth development policies
- Provide supervision intensive service opportunities for high risk youth

Table 9, continued

Guns

- Remove guns from environment
- Shut down manufacturers of cheap handguns
- Only allow police, army and national guards to carry weapons
- Focus on policies that cut off supply mechanisms

Community

- Have doctors, pastors, social workers leave their offices and do more work on the street
- Break the code of silence about child sexual abuse
- Have as many youth programs as alcohol outlets
- Focus on policies that cut off supply mechanisms
- Have community-based programs visit children and youth in their homes
- Encourage people who left the neighborhood and "made it" to give back and/or move back
- Support community based alternatives that promote change and violence cessation in natural settings
- Smaller case loads for social workers
- Sponsor more "family days" when all families can get together in city parks and have fun
- Make public parks more important than golf courses
- Increase job training or micro-enterprise programs
- Give rides to relatives so they can visit inmates
- Allow child-parent programs like girl scouts in prison

Cultural

- Frame policies in ways that challenge an "eye for an eye" as driving punitive, retributive precept
- Put up billboards that increase the peace
- Encourage positive media, positive images in people's minds
- Pay same amount of money attention as sports Most-Valuable players to superstar teachers, youth workers.
- Regulate "violent trash" on television and movies that shows violence in a hyped-up way
- Glorify youth workers not movie stars and celebrities
- Value all kinds of jobs (housewife, janitor, teacher) not only big degrees
- Portray the story of crime and violence reduction, the youth-fullness of violence prevention change agents

continued

Table 9, continued

Justice
• Do not give juveniles the death penalty
• Educate youth, families, and communities about justice system, consequences of violence involvement and their legal rights
• Smaller caseloads for probation workers
• Government policies should remove imagery of aggression as a symbolic function of preventing violence (e.g., "Getting tough on juveniles" "War on crime")
• Stop building prisons
• Enact policies that grant discretionary power to decide on outcome of criminal charges to juvenile judges, not public prosecutor
• Do not try juveniles as adult
• Policies need to recognize that even a kid who kills, "he is not thinking like an adult when he commits these things."
• Avoid punishments that inflict substantial permanent harm on young offenders so that a healthy transition to adulthood is still possible even when harmful mistakes are made.
• Offer alternatives, a place to go when youth come out of jail
• Mandate and incorporate youth victims of violence as target population of victims of crime monies & services

On a macro level, crime prevention should not be the major element in the complex of government policies that influence the development and life chances of young people in the United States. Policies towards violence-involved youth should be aligned with the precepts that guide youth policy in other contexts. There is a danger in combining health, education and youth development programs under a crime and violence prevention rubric; this approach can contribute to a fear of the young, and paves the way for policies that separate and isolate these children from society. This tendency is manifest in the policies of both the Democratic and Republican parties that had remarkable ideological consistency throughout the 1990s. The creation of a bipartisan positive, comprehensive national youth policy that ensures the right of young people and promotes the development of a continuum of needed social, educational, and health services, is sorely needed, as well as the establishment of a federal advisory committee to coordinate youth policy on a national level.

Divisive rhetoric such as "super predators," "feral pre-social beings," and "lost generation" should be challenged and more closely examined for the racial implications and pseudo-speciation in such texts. As the young people in this study stated, they are not "animals" and they are capable of finding their way back into society. Youth advocates from all disciplines need to explicitly de-construct such terms and increase the barriers and social costs of such savage pronouncements. Government pronouncements should remove the imagery of aggression as a symbolic function of preventing violence. "Getting tough on juveniles," "war on crime" and other bellicose imagery are forms of preemptive hostility, even as the policies enacted are ostensibly meant to protect children and safeguard them from harm.

Advocates and policymakers must offer alternate images of youth's potential, social integration, and rehabilitation. Youth workers, health care staff, teachers, social workers, probation officers, judges, community mentors, the clergy, researchers, employers and a multitude of other adults who have seen positive transformation in the lives of children and youth need to rescue these examples as the generative images driving policy and in the portrayals in the media that shape public perception. Like the rich possibilities and examples of personal and social change embedded in the 20 stories and voices of the young participants, these many narratives can overwrite the tired tale and social policy mantra of the "Lost Generation." In the words of Andres, you need to tell these stories because "if they think about giving up, that we are all knuckleheads, they can think of me. I could change."

STUDY SIGNIFICANCE

The question "What contributes to the termination of assaultive behavior among violence impacted youth?" is a complex one that cannot fully be answered in this preliminary study. Although not providing definitive answers to a complex question, this study contributes to the discussion of factors and processes of termination among a subset of youth highly impacted by violence, a population largely unknown to researchers. The study records the experiences of youth who are hospitalized, and referred to a corrective public health based intervention for their risk of homicide victimization or perpetration; the study group includes nine youth who sustained a spinal cord injury, a population that has been used by epidemiological researchers as a proxy for homicide victims in terms of their risk-taking profile. Seven out of the 20 study participants were young women, and their insights shed some light on the poorly understood phenomenon of serious female delinquency and cessation.

No previous studies examined the perceptions of change of violence-involved adolescents in health and hospital settings. Helpers' perceptions of change as well as the strategies for effecting it are often different from those with whom they are working. This study offers a glimpse of how one sample of self-selecting adolescents viewed this change process, provides a rough profile of young people who are contemplating cessation of assaultive conduct, and identifies associated behaviors and the primary and secondary antecedents to cessation of assaultive conduct. The findings offer a general outline of the characteristics of the process of change, the common experiences, factors, personalities and events that placed and sustained the youth on a trajectory towards non-violence, describing the health, social service, and community re-entry characteristics needed to promote the process of change. The study also delineates the components of a trauma intervention framework and the particular characteristics of successful helpers in clinical and other settings.

The programmatic suggestions contained in the study contribute to the refinement of practice, fleshing out, through individual case study and the collective story of the group, the thin causation and cessation theories and evaluation methodologies that generally guide violence prevention program development. The study suggests intermediate outcomes to assist in developing of future evaluation parameters and research instruments, addressing a methodological limitation of the field.

On another level, the study attempts to contribute to the discernment of a broader theory of change for young persons involved in violence and impacted by trauma. This study offers a glimpse as to how a select group of formerly violence-involved youth who are now practitioners and activists achieved this transformation, and helps explore the boundaries and contents of a restorative health approach to violence reduction. Theories of juvenile perpetration and rehabilitation are based on the very narrow experiences of the segment of youth incarcerated. As such, these theories do not capture the broader, unknown patterns of perpetration, the processes of change and rehabilitation occurring in natural and guided contexts as they unfold in communities across the nation. This research project offers a rare longitudinal view of the process of transformation of these young people, many of whom were selected to take part in this study as they struggled to leave behind a life of violence involvement, not having fully stabilized their new behaviors. This project followed the life stories of these young people from a minimum of six to a maximum of nine years, and traces developments that I closely and directly observed; conversations with other providers and youth workers further enriched the study. Such longitudinal research, even in a qualitative research project based on carefully chosen case studies, is unusual because of the instability in the lives of those who are often studied, and the often short-term engagement of the researchers. The perspectives of this study argue for future participatory engagement as a means of sustaining involvement and enhancing the quality of the data collected and bringing fresh perspectives to the field.

Lastly, the analysis serves as a tool for discussion, reflection, and clarification—and a challenge to collective action. It offers a usable text for youth-and researcher-driven policy development in the area of youth violence prevention and youth development. The analysis is intended as a competing metaphor, of voices of change, to the policy discourses on incorrigible, violent youth.

IMPLICATIONS FOR FURTHER RESEARCH

Far more is necessary to further our understanding of the ways in which young people come to be involved in violence, the consequences, and how they extricate themselves from violent situations. Other types of research methods (quantitative research methods such as surveys or triangulation of qualitative and quantitative methods) should be pursued to provide a fuller picture of the process of change among violence-involved youth. Research should not, however, pre-empt taking steps to address the problem. Methodologies such as action research and other participatory methodologies can help breach the divide between investigation and action.

A comparison of the results produced by these various methodologies, targeted investigations, and comparative perspectives will help promote violence reduction in a more comprehensive way. Needed research in this area is summarized in Table 10.

Table 10. Future research directions

- Build upon research on peer assisted violence termination.
- Conduct longitudinal studies among adolescents to understand the scope and particularities of violence exposure.
- Sponsor research on clinician and helper characteristics on termination outcomes.
- Investigate violence cessation among youth and interplay of individual, situational and structural factors.
- Conduct research on "Batman Syndrome" and resiliency among violence-impacted youth.
- Carry out epidemiological studies on how frequently transformation occurs.
- Investigate the situations faced by injured youth, whether these present conflict and what skills and supports are needed to achieve and maintain healthy functioning and to sustain behavior change.

Table 10, continued

• Explore further the structure of change with stages and processes of change of Prochaska and DiClemente.
• Explore the oscillatory processes of change among youth attempting to change.
• Look at the effects of violence prevention and youth development on prevention of secondary disabling conditions among violence induced SCI.
• Conduct more nuanced research on pre-injury characteristics.
• Re-examine the inconclusive findings about the association between experiencing or witnessing violence and the occurrence of subsequent violence.
• Calculate costs and benefits of rich, supervision-intensive health programs for violence impacted youth.
• Expand nascent body of research on community service and violence prevention.
• Explore the moral and ethical reflection on everyday violence.
• Study variations in regional or national patterns of violence causation, reduction and cessation and on violence prevention.
• Expand the use of participatory and action research methodologies.
• Promote child and youth centered research agenda.
• Recognize inherent potential for abuse in violence research, monitor research trends through ethics commissions.

INVESTIGATING CHANGE AND RESILIENCY AMONG VIOLENCE-IMPACTED YOUTH

To accurately understand violence prevention, we need better information about the frequency, characteristics, and dynamics of violence termination. Epidemiology and surveillance can play a primary role in more accurately determining the characteristics of populations that have matured out or successfully changed, and help identify the causes, contributors and factors conducive to change.

Further research is needed to explore aspects of the "Batman Syndrome," in which children and adolescents turn a negative life event into a positive force for development. Systematic studies of resilience in untreated survivors can shed light on the autochthonous methods and the supportive relationships available naturally to them in their own communities.

The processes of transformation recounted by the young people in this study suggest a number of conclusions that are consonant with and amplify the findings of Prochaska and DiClemente. Future research can further illuminate the structures of change and the oscillatory processes of change among violence-involved adolescents youth. The inconclusive findings about the association between experiencing or witnessing violence and the occurrence of subsequent violence merit further scrutiny as well. The relationship between social inclusion, the rehabilitation process, and the prevention of secondary disabling conditions among youth with violence-induced disability is another area that needs further investigation.

Continuing the early research of peer-assisted violence termination is another critical topic to pursue. Given the importance of helper characteristics on termination outcomes, greater research emphasis should be placed on clinician and helper characteristics in termination outcomes. The importance of participation in social action as part of the recovery from trauma and the process of termination from violence suggest the need to expand the nascent body of research on community service and violence prevention to include young people who are impacted by violence and the effects of participation in social action projects on cessation.

Improving Baseline Data

Further research emphasis should be placed on the ascertainment of the dimensions, characteristics, and extent of youth violence. The priority areas of import to violence cessation programs for impacted youth include studies on out-of-school and street youth, despite the difficulty in developing accurate sampling frames for these subpopulations. Over-reliance on self-report studies with youth who are easier to reach through schools, correctional, or other captive settings will not yield a true picture of the subset of youth most at risk for youth interpersonal violence involvement and victimization, and can minimize influence of more extreme social conditions on violence.

There is virtually no research on children and youth with violence-induced disability, and the incidence and pre-injury characteristics are not well known.

A Broader Lens for the Study of Violence Prevention

Greater research on the influence of less proximal causes on violence desistance is needed. Such influences include the situational, community-level, and societal characteristics that can foster the termination of violence and the development of pro-social behavior.

Some of the required thinking on the issue is beyond the realm of social science, but more properly belongs to disciplines that address larger issues of the meaning of life. Ethicists who study the precepts underlying professional practice need to ask why the death penalty for juveniles is not questioned, and is overlooked in youth violence prevention efforts.

Need for Comparative Perspectives

Violence-involved youth from inner cities all over the world face common problems. The shared experiences of the young people from Boston and Los Angeles underscore such similarities. Indeed, violence-involved youth in the United States share several experiences with their counterparts in developing countries, including those in Latin America and the Caribbean. In some important ways, the similarities of the problems faced across these varied countries are as notable as the differences (Hagan and McCarty 1997). The impact of a changing economic context on the street life of the surrounding society, and the globalization of the problem of guns, drugs, and a violent media culture, affect pockets of urban youth on the margins of society in similar ways.

The problems of violence involved youth transcend regional and national frontiers, posing a set of issues that invite greater cooperation in achieving knowledge and understanding. Youth violence research has been largely linked to the national settings in which it is undertaken, and often discussed in the context of various subgroups of race and ethnicity. Few research projects have looked at variations in regional or national problems and their solutions.

> It is not only important to look at the mechanism of injury but also to investigate other variables and information that may contribute or be associated with particular injuries, especially wounds peculiar to violence. In trauma centers, part of this valuable information is available on gurneys and wheelchairs (Tellez and Mackersie 1996).

Need for Child-Centered and Youth-Centered Investigation

We need programs that are culturally specific, age appropriate, and that involve the target population in the decision-making process. We are not going to reduce violence if our time and our dollars are spent talking at teenagers, for example. We are going to have to talk with our teens and then design violence prevention strategies based on our conversation with them. Those at risk for violence and other poverty related social problems are not unreachable, but we will not reach them sitting in our offices.

—Deborah Prothrow-Stith (1987, 42)

This research project suggests that youths' unique concerns are not always identifiable by adults. If we do not include their voices, we risk failing to achieve the full potential for development and policy ideas that emerges from more inclusive processes and diversity of views. We also risk missing out on the richness and innovative perspectives from young people with varying experiences, and the fresh categories and perceptions they bring to the research.

While children and youth, especially minority and economically disadvantaged young people, have been targeted, tracked, monitored, observed, measured, and tested, seldom have they been active participants in investigating their own issues, setting agendas and research questions, establishing boundaries, or negotiating what is written about their lives. This is also true of violence prevention research. One of the study participants describes being part of a participant-observer study of domestic violence:

They were watching sometimes, and I'd be pissed and I'd be like, "What are you doing looking at me?" You know, they'd write things down. They would be writing like this: "This was her reaction to me looking at her, and then when she was feeding her daughter, maybe her daughter opened her mouth this wide. Maybe children of domestic violence don't open it as wide. And her reaction to me looking at her, she swore and these were her exact words, 'you fuckin' whatever.'" It was just a pain just seeing them looking' at me that way.

This study has solicited the voices of young people, their "subjugated knowledge," and interpretations. Yet, much more work needs to be done in this area. Researchers as well as program developers and policy makers need to engage and more actively seek the voices of youth and their interpretations, in order to better understand the ways in which adolescents are actively involved in the construction of their lives and worlds.

A child-centered and youth-centered research agenda for violence prevention is a needed next step for the field. As with other disciplines like anthropology, this approach has the potential to challenge the implicit adult perspectives, methodological strictures, and theoretical assumptions of the various disciplines. A child-centered research agenda "contains all the elements for a radical paradigm shift, similar to the salutary effects resulting from the feminist critique of the discipline. But to date that process has hardly begun." (Scheper-Hughes and Sargent 1992, 15)

Research and Social Change

When researchers work with children and youth in participatory projects or write about young people, they must take particular care to avoid exploitative relationships within the research enterprise itself. The subjects of violence and trauma lend themselves to exploitative dynamics on many levels. Herman describes how survivors of terrible events are often motivated to volunteer as research subjects in the hope that being of assistance to others may give meaning to their experience and preempt harm to others (Herman 1997). This is also true of young survivors.

On another level, researchers need to be wary of indirectly contributing to the moral panic over youth violence, paving the way for the enactment of draconian and retributive measures against children and youth. Referring to the growing international industry of violence, researcher Scheper-Hughes cautions those engaged in such practices:

> ...one must note that even the contemporary social science writings and discourses on urban violence that are so fashionably popular in the universities and urban institutions of Brazil (as they are in South Africa, Europe, and North America) are themselves 'dangerous.' The over-production of research on violence (responding in part to the theoretical opportunism which this area of study provides) unwittingly contributes— though indirectly and mediated through popular media that appropriate and deform social science writings—to the popular sense of "dangerousness." (Scheper-Hughes and Sargent 1998)

Given the inherent potential for abuse in violence and violence prevention research, studies on violence and its termination should be concerned with social change and social policy questions, contributing to the welfare of the young people and communities being studied, offering practical conclusions as well as augmenting theoretical knowledge. This is the dual responsibility of the field whose larger mandate is the transformation of all types of violent relations and the society in which we live.

EPILOGUE

He was 19. He tried to apply here and they denied him. I guess they didn't have all of the psychological services that he needed. They kept shipping him from crazy hospital to crazy hospital. And I found out he killed himself. I felt like I could have helped him. He was calling me, we were chatting. There were times when we were supposed to hook up and we didn't. And I am sorry for that. God, may he rest in peace. He was trying to change. He was trying to make that turnaround. And nobody was fucking helping him. His mom found him in his bathroom somewhere, dead. He could have made that turnaround if he had had more than me. It takes more than one person. I think this place would have been great. It turned me around. It turned Mo around. Why not? That's just fucked up. It makes me mad. Sick to my stomach. This world is fucked up. He just died like that. He didn't have to die from no services or lack of support.

—Carl

This project was possible due to all the young people, whom I cannot name, that took part in this study and gave it life. It is written for George's brothers, Albert's brother, Charo's baby, Ruby's and Lita's boyfriends, the cousins of Mo, Lita, Flaco, Ronnie, and José; and Carl's 19-year-old friend, all mentioned in this study, and for the many other young people in their lives who are no longer alive. It is also dedicated to José, who died before its completion.

Endnotes

1. According to the 1995 National Report on Juvenile Offenders and Victims, the recent increase in acts of aggression that result in homicide among older juveniles can largely be attributed to the increase in firearm homicides. See Snyder and Sickmund (1995), pp. 24–26.
2. In a retrospective study of current victims of violence in Detroit in 1989, Goins et al. (1992, 431-435) found that 44 percent of the patients were re-injured over a five-year period; the retrospective cohort mortality during the same time period was 20 percent; and rates of both unemployment and substance user among the victims was 67 percent.
3. The pattern of discriminatory enforcement has been so pervasive, according to Miller (1992) that the effect has been to criminalize an entire population. Studies of Washington, DC, the nation's capital, revealed that nearly 50 percent of the African American male population between the ages of 18 and 35 at any given moment are either in prison, on probation or on parole, or have a warrant out for their arrest.
4. The estimated number of nonfatal violent assaults based on self-reports of homicide (i.e., those reported in the National Crime Survey) exceeds 100:1. According to Rosenberg and Fenley (1991), this may underestimate the extent of nonfatal assaultive injury in the United States.
5. If Los Angeles had used Chicago's motive definition, its 1980 peak of 351 gang-related homicides would probably have been set closer to 175 (Klein 1995, 15).
6. The objectives of this approach are to create environments (e.g., adult role models of conflict resolution) that encourage and teach health-enhancing behaviors (e.g., conflict resolution skills) and interpersonal attributes (i.e., values that promote nonviolence) and that weaken support for health-compromising behavior and intra

personal attributes (e.g., role models of intimidation and coercion).
See Perry and Jessor (1985).

7. Initiatives focusing on the other levels (such as changes in groups or individuals, relationships, social structures, or social norms) need to demonstrate change and then tie it to larger shifts in population rates of violence. Difficulty in identifying and matching controls, controlling for confounding and competing variables, and garnering the community support and commitment required to carry out such an initiative makes these efforts challenging and expensive to evaluate. It is also difficult to maintain adequate control over the duration of the intervention and the needed follow-up time to determine lasting effects. See Tolan and Guerra (1994), p. 53.

8. The choice to conduct a participatory research model is no longer merely ideological, but is increasingly a legal decision. As stated by Zola (1994), "It is becoming increasingly commonplace to have lay/consumer representation on all sorts of 'expert' committees, and laws have been passed to assure their representation on all levels of the research enterprise." Within the field of disability research, in particular, this is the operant trend.

9. It can also be found in sympathetic violence prevention accounts. In rallying cries of the public health violence prevention movement which seeks to portray the problem of adolescent interpersonal violence as a preventable and understandable problem, challenging the concept of "dangerous" youth, appeals are often made to safeguard Black males as an "endangered species." Strains of Erik Erikson's notion of 'pseudo-speciation', the tendency to classify some individuals or groups as less than fully (or differently) human also underlie such accounts.

10. For example, statistics for Los Angeles for 1993 indicated that 85 percent of all daytime crimes were committed by truant youths (Stephens 1997).

11. The U.S. Department of Education defines a Zero Tolerance Policy as a policy that "mandates predetermined consequences or punishments for specific offenses" (NCES and BJS 1999).

References

Abraham, A., T.L. Cheng, J.L. Wright, I. Addlestone, Z. Huang and L. Greenberg. 2001. Assessing an educational intervention to improve physician violence screening skills. *Pediatrics* 107(5):68e-68.

Adkins R.H., B. Hume and M. Nabor. 1997. Spinal cord injury identified with violence; community reintegration in urban areas. Submitted as an article to *Topics in Spinal Cord Injury*.

Adler, W.M. 1995. *Land of opportunity: one family's quest for the American Dream in the age of crack*. New York: The Atlantic Monthly Press.

Advancement Project. 2000. Opportunities suspended: The devastating consequences of zero tolerance and school discipline policies. Cambridge, MA: The Advancement Project and The Civil Rights Project, Harvard University.

Ambrosio, T. and V. Schiraldi. 1997. From classrooms to cell blocks: a national perspective. Justice Policy Institute, February.

American Academy of Pediatrics (AAP) Committee on Adolescence. 1998. Firearms and adolescents. *Pediatrics*, 98:784-787.

American Academy of Pediatrics (AAP) Task Force on Adolescent Assault Victim Needs. 1996. Assault victim needs: A renew of issues and model protocol. *Pediatrics*, 98(5):991-1001.

Ammerman, R. T. and M.H. Hersen. 1997. *Handbook of prevention and treatment with children and adolescents: Interventions in the real world context*. New York: John Wiley and Sons, Inc.

Amnesty International. 2004a. *Execution of child offenders: Updated facts and figures*. Media briefing, News Service No: 030, 16 February. Available at: http://web.amnesty.org.

————. 2004b. *Stop child executions! Ending the death penalty for child offenders*. Available at: http://web.amnesty.org.

Anderson, C.J. and L.C. Vogel. 2002. Employment outcomes of adults who sustained spinal cord injuries as children or adolescents. *Archives of Physical Medicine and Rehabilitation* 83:791-801.

Aos, S. P. Phipps, R. Barnoski, and R. Lieb. 2001. *The comparative costs and benefits of programs to reduce crime*. Washington, DC: Washington State Institute for Public Policy.

Arendt, H. 1970. *On violence*. New York: Harcourt, Brace and Company.

Austin, J., K.D. Johnson, and M. Gregoriou. 2000. *Juveniles in adult prisons and jails: a national assessment.* Washington, D.C.: George Washington University Institute on Crime, Justice and Corrections and the National Council on Crime and Delinquency.

Babbie, E. 1992. *The practice of social research.* Belmont, CA: Wadsworth Publishing Company.

Bandura, A 1994. *Self-efficacy: the exercise of control.* New York: WH Freeman Publishers.

Barlow, B., M. Niemirska, and R.P. Gandhi. 1982. Ten years' experience with pediatric gunshot wounds. *Journal of Pediatric Surgery.* 17: 927-932.

Bell, C. and E. Jenkins. 1991. Traumatic stress and children. *Journal of Health Care for the Poor and Underserved* 2(1):175-185.

Bell, D. 1960. *The end of ideology.* Glencoe, IL: Free Press.

Bennett, J. 1981. *Oral history and delinquency - the rhetoric of criminology.* Chicago: University of Chicago Press.

Bernard, B.L. 1991. *Fostering resiliency in kids: Protective factors in the family, school and community.* San Francisco, CA: Far West Laboratory for Educational Research and Development.

Boston City Hospital. 1991. *Sentinel injury surveillance system. Special report on teen victims.* Boston, MA: BCH (Boston City Hospital)Gunshot and Stabbing Project Update.

The Boston Globe. Feb. 8, 1997. *Street Smarts.*

Bronfenbrenner, U. 1979. *The ecology of human development.* Cambridge, MA: Harvard University Press.

Brown, J., P. Cohen, J.G. Johnson and E.M. Smailes. 1999. Childhood abuse and neglect: specificity of effects on adolescent and young adult depression and suicidality. *Journal of the American Academy of Child and Adolescent Psychiatry* 38:1490-1496.

Buber, M. 1952. On the suspension of the ethical. In: *The eclipse of God: studies in the relation between religion and philosophy.* pp. 147-156. New York: Harper and Row.

Cales R.H. and D.D.Trunkey. 1985. Preventable trauma deaths. A review of trauma care systems development. *JAMA* 254(8):1059-1063.

California Department of Health Services. 1996. EPIC Proportions: Violent injuries to California youth. Report No. 7. Sacramento, CA: Department of Health Services.

Camino, L. and S. Zeldin. 2002. From periphery to center: pathways for youth civic engagement in day-to-day life of communities. *Applied Developmental Science* 6(4):213-220.

Canada, G. 1995. *Fist stick knife gun: a personal history of violence in America.* Boston, MA: Beacon Press.

Carrillo, E, J. Gonzales, L. Carrillo, P. Chacon, N. Namias, O. Kirton and P Byers. 1998. Spinal cord injuries in adolescents after gunshot wounds: An increasing phenomenon in urban North America. *Injury* 29:503-507.

Centers for Disease Control and Prevention. 1994. *Homicide among 15-19 year old males - United States, 1963-1991.* MMWR 4340:725-727.

Chambliss, W. 1995. Crime control and ethnic minorities: Legitimizing racial oppression by creating moral panics. In Hawkins, D.F., ed., *Ethnicity, race and crime: Perspectives across time and place*. pp. 235-258. New York: State University of New York.

Citizens for Juvenile Justice. 2000. 2000 Fact Book: Trends and issues in juvenile delinquency. Key facts in Massachusetts juvenile justice. Boston, MA: Citizens for Juvenile Justice.

Clifford, J. 1988. *The predicament of culture: Twentieth-century ethnography, literature and art*. Cambridge: Harvard University Press.

Cloward, R.A. and L.E. Ohlin. 1960. *Delinquency and opportunity: A theory of delinquent gangs*. New York: Free Press.

Cohen, A.K. 1955. *Delinquent boys: The culture of the gang*. New York: Free Press.

Cohen, S. and R. Wilson-Brewer. 1991. *Violence prevention for young adolescents: The state of the art of program evaluation*. Carnegie Council on Adolescent Development Working Papers.

Collins, R. 1981. *Sociology since mid-century: Essays in theory cumulation*. New York: Academic Press.

Comer, J.P. 1988. Educating poor minority children. *Scientific American* 2595:42-48.

Conrad, P. and J.W. Schneider. 1980. *Deviance and medicalization: From badness to sickness*. St. Louis: C.V. Mosby.

Corsica, J.Y. 1993. Employment training interventions. In A. P. Goldstein and C. R. Huff, eds., *The Gang Intervention Handbook*. Champaign, IL: Research Press.

Daane, D.M. 2003. Child and adolescent violence. *Orthopedic Nursing* 22(1):23-29.

Dailey, J.T. 1992. Trauma center closures: A national assessment. *Journal of Trauma* 33:539–547.

Davidson, W.S., R. Redner, R.L. Amdur and C.M. Mitchell. 1990. *Alternative treatments for troubled youth: The case for diversion from the justice system*. New York: Plenum.

Dawes, R.M., A.J.C. van de Kragt and J.M. Orbell. 1990. Cooperation for the benefit of us – not me, or my conscience. In J.J. Mansbridge, ed., *Beyond self interest*. Chicago: The University of Chicago Press.

De Vos, E., D.A. Stone, M.A. Goetz and L.L. Dahlberg. 1996. Evaluation of a hospital-based youth violence intervention. In K. E. Powell and D. F. Hawkins, eds., Youth violence prevention: Descriptions and baseline data from 13 evaluation projects. *American Journal of Preventive Medicine* Suppl. to 12:5.

Debellis, M.D. 1997. Posttraumatic stress disorder and acute stress disorder. In R.T. Ammerman and M. Hersen, eds., *Handbook of prevention and treatment with children and adolescents: intervention in the real world context*, pp. 464-465. New York: John Wiley and Sons, Inc.

Denninghoff, K.R., L. Knox, R. Cunningham, and S. Partain. 2002. Emergency medicine: competencies for youth violence prevention and control. *Academy of Emergency Medicine* 9(9):947-56.

DiClemente, C. and J. Norcross. 1992. In search of how people change: Applications to addictive behaviors, September 1992, *American Psychologist*. 47:1102-1114.

Duany, L. and K. Pittman. 1990. *Latino youth at a crossroad. Adolescent pregnancy prevention clearing house report.* Washington, DC: Children's Defense Fund.

DuRant, R. H., C. Cadenhead and R.A. Pendergrast. 1994. Factors associated with the use of violence among black adolescents. *American Journal of Public Health* 84:612-617.

DuRant, R. H. 1996. Intentions to use violence among young adolescents. *Pediatrics* 98:1104-1108.

Durkheim, E. 1947. *The division of labor in society.* Glencoe, IL: Free Press.

Durkin, M.S., L.L. Davidson, L. Kuhn, P. O'Connor and B. Barlow. 1994. Low-income neighborhoods and risk of severe pediatric injury: a small area analysis in northern Manhattan. *American Journal of Public Health* 84:587-592.

Durlak, J. A. 1979. Comparative effectiveness of paraprofessional and professional helpers. *Psychological Bulletin* 86:80-92.

Earls, F. 1991. Not fear, nor quarantine, but science: Preparation for a decade of research to advance knowledge about causes and control of violence in youths. *Journal of Adolescent Health* 12:619-629.

Eccles J.S, A. Wigfield and U. Schiefele. 1998. Motivation to succeed. In N. Eisenberg, *Handbook of child psychology: social, emotional and personality development*, fifth edition, pp. 1017-1095. New York: John Wiley and Sons, Inc.

Elliott, D.S. 1994a. Serious violent offenders: Onset, development, course and termination. The American Society of Criminology 1993 Presidential Address. *Criminology* 32:1-21.

————. 1994b. *Youth violence: An overview.* Boulder, CO: Center for the Study and Prevention of Youth Violence, University of Colorado.

Erikson, E. 1963. *Childhood and society.* New York, NY: Norton,

————. 1968. *Identity: youth and crisis.* New York, NY: Norton.

Eron, L.D., J.H. Gentry and P.Schlegel, eds. 1994. *Reason to hope. A psychosocial perspective on violence and youth.* Washington, DC: The American Psychological Association.

Fagan, J. and A. Browne. 1994. Violence between spouses and intimates: physical aggression between women and men in intimate relationships. In: A.J. Reiss and A.J. Roth, eds., *Understanding and preventing violence: panel on the understanding and control of violent behavior.* Vol. 3 social influences. pp. 114-292.Washington, DC: National Academy Press.

Farrell, A.D. 1996. Richmond youth against violence: A school-based program for urban adolescents. In K. E. Powell and D. F. Hawkins, eds., Youth violence prevention: descriptions and baseline data from 13 evaluation projects. *American Journal of Preventive Medicine,* 12:5-14.

FBI. 1993. *FBI uniform crime reports 1993,* Cited in R.A. Mendel. 1998. Prevention or pork: A hard headed look at youth-oriented anti-crime Programs. Washington, DC.: American Youth Policy Forum.

Fein, J.A., K.R. Ginsburg, M.E. McGrath,. F.S. Shofer, J.C. Flamma and E.M. Datner. 2000. Violence prevention in the emergency department: Clinician attitudes and limitations. *Archives of Pediatrics and Adolescent Medicine* 154:495-498.

Fein, J.A., N. Kassam-Adams, M. Gavin, R. Huang, D. Blanchard, and E.M. Datner. 2002. Persistence of posttraumatic stress in violently injured youth seen in the emergency department, *Archives of Pediatrics and Adolescent Medicine* 156:836-840.

Fields, S.A. and J.R. McNamara. 2003. The prevention of child and adolescent violence. *Aggression and Violent Behavior* 8:(1)61-91.

Fleming, D.W. 2003. More evidence, more action: addressing the social determinants of health. In Guide to community preventive services: interventions in the social environment to improve community health. *American Journal of Preventive Medicine* (Supplement) 24 (3S): 1.

Ford, D.Y. and J.J. Harris. 1996. Perceptions and attitudes of black students toward school: school, achievement, and other variables. *Child Development* 673:1144-1152.

Foucault, M. 1975. *The birth of the clinic: An archeology of medical perception.* New York: Vintage Press.

———. 1980. *Power /knowledge: Selected interviews and other writings.* New York: Pantheon Press.

Freed, H., D.W. Webster, J.J Longwell, J. Carrese and M.H. Wilson. 2001. Factors preventing gun acquisition and carrying among incarcerated adolescent males. *Archives of Pediatric and Adolescent Medicine* 155:335-341.

Friedman, L. 1993. *Crime and punishment in American history.* New York: Basic Books.

Fromm, E. 1973. *The Anatomy of human destructiveness.* New York: Henry Holt and Company.

Gabriel, R.M., M. Haskins, T. Hopson and K.E. Powell. 1996. Building relationships and resilience in the prevention of youth violence. *American Journal of Preventive Medicine* 12(5):48–55.

Galtung, J. 1969. Violence, and peace research. *Journal of Peace Research* 6:167-191.

Garland, D.E. 1993. *Violence: Prevalence, costs and prevention with emphasis on spinal cord injury.* Paper presented at Annual Meeting of the American Spinal Cord Injury Association, Philadelphia, PA.

Garland, D. and G. Wharton. 1994. Spinal cord injury care: Funding for the future. *Orthopedics* 17:675-678.

Gaston Institute. 1992. *Latinos in Boston*. Boston, MA: Gaston Institute for Latino Community Development and Public Policy, University of Massachusetts.

Geertz, C. 1968. Is America by nature a violent society? *New York Times Magazine*, 25. April 21.

———. 1973. Thick description; toward an interpretive theory of culture. In Robert M Emerson, *Contemporary field research*, 1988. Chicago: Waveland Press.

———. 1983. From the native's point of view: On the nature of anthropological understanding. In Geertz, C., *Local knowledge: Further research in interpretive anthropology*. New York: Basis Books, Inc.

Gendreau, P. and Andrews, D. A. 1990. What the meta-analyses of the offender treatment literature tells us about "what works." *Canadian Journal of Criminology* 32:173–184.

Gil, D.G. 1990. "Work, violence, injustice, and war: Have we really overcome Hitler?" Keynote address at the international Congress on Child Abuse and Neglect, Hamburg, West Germany, September 4, 1990. In *Unraveling social policy: theory, analysis, and political action towards social equality*. Rochester,VT: Schenkman Books.

———. Preventing violence in a structurally violent society: Mission impossible. *American Journal of Orthopsychiatry* 66(1):77-84.

Ginsburg, K.R., P.M. Alexander, J. Hunt, M. Sullivan and A. Cnaan. 2002. Enhancing their likelihood for a positive future: the perspective of inner city youth. *Pediatrics* 109(6):1136-1143.

Giordano, G. and B.J. D'Alonzo,. 1995. Challenge and progress in rehabilitation: A renew of the past 25 years and a preview of the future. *American Rehabilitation* Autumn-Winter:14-21.

Goffman, E. 1988. The interaction order. American sociological review. #48. In R.A. Wallace and A. Wolf. 1991. *Contemporary sociological theory: continuing the classical tradition*. Englewood, NJ: Prentice Hall.

Goins, W.A., J. Thompson and C. Simpkins. 1992. Recurrent intentional injury. *Journal of the National Medical Association* 84:431-435.

Goldstein, A.P. 1990. *Delinquents on delinquency*. Chicago, IL: Research Press.

Gornick, M., J.N. Greenberg, P.W. Eggers and A. Dobson. 1985. Twenty years of Medicare and Medicaid: Covered populations use of benefit and program expenditures. *Health Care Financing Review Annual Supplement*:13-59.

Graham, H.D. 1989. Violence, social theory and the historians: The debate over consensus and culture in America. In T.R. Gurr, ed., *Violence in America: Protest, Rebellion and Reform*. Newbury Park, CA: Sage Publications.

Greenspan, A.I. and A. Kellermann. 2002. Physical and psychosocial outcomes 8 months after serious gunshot injury. *The Journal of Trauma: Injury Infection and Critical Care* 53(4):709-716.

Grossman, J.B. and J.E. Rhodes. 2002. The test of time: Predicators and effects of duration in youth mentoring relationships. *American Journal of Community Psychology.* 30 (2): 199-219.

Gurr, T.R. 1970. *Why men rebel*. Princeton, NJ: Princeton University Press.

———. 1989a. Protest and rebellion in the 1960s: The United States in world perspective. In T.R. Gurr, ed., *Violence in America: protest, rebellion and reform.* pp. 49-76. Newbury Park, CA: Sage Publications.

———. 1989b. *Violence in America: The history of crime.* Newbury Park, CA: Sage Publications.

Hagan, J. 1994. *Crime and disrepute.* Thousand Oaks, CA: Pine Forge Press.

Hagan, J. and B. McCarty. 1997. *Mean streets: Youth crime and homelessness.* Cambridge: Cambridge University Press.

Hanson, B., G. Beschner, J.M. Walters and E. Bovelle. 1985. *Life with heroin–voices from the inner city.* Lexington, MA: Lexington Books.

Harstad. C. 1976. Guided group interaction: Positive Peer Culture. *Child Care Quarterly* 5:109-120.

Hart, R.A. 1997. *Children's participation: The theory and practice of community development and environmental care.* London: Earthscan Publications.

Hartz, L. 1955. *The liberal tradition in America.* New York: Harcourt, Brace and Company.

Hawkins, D.F. 1993.. Inequality, culture and interpersonal violence. *Health Affairs* Winter:85-86.

Henggeler, S.W., G.B. Melton and, L.A. Smith. 1992. Family preservation using multisystemic therapy: an effective alternative to incarcerating serious juvenile offenders. *Journal of Consulting and Clinical Psychology* 60:953-961. In D.S. Elliott, series ed. 1998. *Blueprints for Violence Prevention Book Six: Multisystemic Therapy.* Boulder, CO: Center for the Study and Prevention of Violence.

Herman, J. 1997. *Trauma and Recovery.* New York: Basic Books.

Hill, H.M., F.I. Soriano, S.A. Chen, and T.D. LaFromboise. 1994. Sociocultural factors in the etiology and prevention of violence among ethnic minority youth. In L.D. Eron, J.H. Gentry and P. Schlegel, eds., *Reason to hope: A psychosocial perspective on violence and youth.* pp. 59-100. Washington, DC: American Psychological Association.

Hoffman, J.S. 2003. Book reviews: World Report on Violence and Health. *Injury Prevention* 9:93.

Hofstader, R. and M. Wallace, eds. 1970. *American violence: A documentary history.* New York: Alfred Knopf.

Holinger, P.C., D. Offer, J.T. Barter and C.C. Bell. 1994. *Suicide and homicide among adolescents.* New York: Guilford Press.

Hollin, C.R. 1993. Cognitive-behavioral interventions. In A.P. Goldstein and C.R. Huff, eds., *The Gang intervention handbook.* Champaign, IL: Research Press.

Horwitz, R. 1983. *Honor and the American dream.* New Brunswick, NJ: Rutgers University Press.

Hutson, H.R., D. Anglin and M.J. Pratss. 1994. Adolescents and children injured or killed in drive-by shootings in Los Angeles. *New England Journal of Medicine* 330:324-327.

Illich, I. 1976. *Medical nemesis.* New York: Pantheon.

Jackson, A.W. and G.A. Davis. 2000. Turning points 2000: educating adolescents in the 21st century. New York:Teachers College Press.

Jackson, P.I. 1995. Minority group threat, crime and the mobilization of law in France. In D. Hawkins, ed., *Ethnicity, race and crime: Perspectives across time and place.* pp. 341-359. Albany, NY: State University of New York Press.

Juvenile Justice Digest. 1995. Washington Crime News Services, Fairfax, VA. October 5, p. 8-9.

———. 1996a. Washington Crime News Services. Fairfax, VA. April 18. p.7.

———. 1996b. Washington Crime News Services, Fairfax, VA. February 15, pp. 4-5.

———. 1996c. Washington Crime News Services. Fairfax, VA. January 4, p.2.

Kaufman, J. and Zigler, E. 1987. Do abused children become abusive parents? *American Journal of Ortho Psychiatry*, 57:378-83.

Kawachi, I., B.P. Kennedy, K. Lochner and D. Prothrow-Stith. 1997. Social capital, income inequality, and mortality. *American Journal of Public Health* 87:1491-1498.

King, M.L. 1963. *Strength to love.* Philadelphia: Fortress Press.

Kinnear, K.L. 1995. *Violent children: A research handbook.* Santa Barbara, CA: ABC-CLIO.

Klar, Y., J.D. Fisher, J.M. Chinsky and A. Nadler, eds. 1992. *Self change: social psychological and clinical perspectives.* New York: Springer Verlag.

Klein, M.K. 1995. *The American street gang: Its nature, prevalence, and social control.* New York: Oxford University Press.

Krause, J.S., C.L. Vines, T.L. Farley, J. Sniezek and J. Coker. 2001. An exploratory study of pressure ulcers after spinal cord injury: relationship to protective behaviors and risk factors. *Arch Phys Med Rehabil* 82:107-113.

Krug E.G., L.L. Dahlberg, J.A. Mercy, A, Zwi and R. Lozano, eds. 2002. *World report on violence and health.* Geneva: World Health Organization.

Kuhn, T. S. 1970. *The structure of scientific revolutions.* Chicago, IL: The University of Chicago Press.

Leffert, N. 1997. Building assets: A positive approach to adolescent health. *Minnesota Medicine* 80: 27-30.

Levine, F.J. and K.J. Rosich. 1996. *Social causes of violence: Crafting a science agenda.* Washington, DC: American Sociological Association.

Lipsey, M.W. 1988. Juvenile delinquency intervention. *New directions for program evaluation* 37:63–84.

———. 1992. Juvenile delinquency treatment: A meta analytic inquiry into the variability of effects. In T.D. Cook, H. Cooper, D.S. Cordray, H. Hartmann, L.V. Hedges, V. Light, T.A. Louis and F. Mosteller, eds., *Meta-analysis for Explanation: A Casebook.* pp. 83-128. Newbury Park, CA: Russell Sage Foundation.

Lipton, D., R. Martinson and D. Wilks. 1975. *The effectiveness of correctional treatment.* New York: Praeger Press.

Loeber, R. and D.P. Farrington. 1998. Serious and violent juvenile offenders: A report of the Office of Juvenile Justice and Delinquency Prevention (OJJDP).

Lynch, M. and D. Cicchetti. 1998. An ecological-transactional analysis of children and contexts: The longitudinal interplay among child maltreatment, community violence, and children's symptomatology. *Development and Psychopathology* 10:235-257.

Maguire, K. and T.J. Flanagan, eds. 1990. *Sourcebook of criminal justice statistics.*. Washington, DC: Bureau of Justice Statistics.

————. *Sourcebook of criminal justice statistics.* Washington, DC: Bureau of Justice Statistics.

Maguire, K., A.L. Pastore, and T.J. Flanagan. 1992. *Sourcebook of criminal justice statistics.* Washington, DC: Bureau of Justice Statistics.

Mahoney, M.J. 1991. *Human change processes: the scientific foundations of psychotherapy.* Basic Books.

Martinson, R. 1974. What works? Questions and answers about prison reform. *The Public Interest* 35:22–54.

Massachusetts Department of Public Health. 1993. *Gunshot wounds and stabbings among Boston's residents: Special focus on youth and guns, weapon injury surveillance system.* Boston, MA: Massachusetts Department of Public Health.

Massachusetts Taxpayers Foundation. 2003. State spending more on prisons than higher education, *Bulletin*, November 24,. Boston, MA.

Maxfield, M.G. and C.S. Widom. 1996. The cycle of violence: revisited 6 years later. *Archives of Pediatrics and Adolescent Medicine* 150:390-395.

McCord, J. 1995. Ethnicity, acculturation and opportunities: A study of two generations. In D.F. Hawkins, ed., *Ethnicity, race and crime: Perspectives across time and place.* pp. 69-81. Albany: State University of New York Press.

McGill, D.E. S.F. Mihalic and J.K. Grotpeter. 1998. *Blueprints for violence prevention, Book two: Big Brothers, Big Sisters of America.* Boulder, CO: Center for the Study and Prevention of Violence.

MacKenzie, E.J., J.H. Siegel, S. Shapiro, M. Moody and R.T. Smith. 1988. Functional recovery and medical costs of trauma care: An analysis by type and severity of injury. *Journal of Trauma* 28:281-297.

McLaughlin, M. 2000. *Community counts: how youth organizations matter for youth development.* Washington, DC: Public Education Network.

Mead, G.H. 1934. *Mind, self and society.* Chicago, IL: University of Chicago Press.

Mendel, R.A. 2000. *Less hype, more help: Reducing juvenile crime, what works– what doesn't.* Washington, D.C.: American Youth Policy Forum.

Mercy, J.A., M.L. Rosenberg, K.E. Powell, C.V. Broome and W.L. Roper. 1993. Public health policy for preventing violence. *Health Affairs* 12:7-29.

Miller, J.M. 1992. *Search and destroy: The plight of African American males in the criminal justice system.* Alexandria, VA: National Center on Institutions and Alternatives.

Miller, W. and S. Rollnick. 1991. *Motivational interviewing.* New York: Guilford.

Miller, W.B. 1981. American youth gangs: Past and present. In A. Blumberg, ed., *Current perspectives on criminal behavior.* New York: Knopf.

Mishler, E.G. 1984. *The discourse of medicine: Dialectics of medical interviews.* Norwood, NJ: Ablex Publishing Corporation.

————. 1986. *Research interviewing context and narrative.* Cambridge, MA: Harvard University Press.

Mishra, R. 2000. The Boston Globe, June 21.

Mitka, M. 2002. Hospital study offers hope of changing lives prone to violence. *Journal of the American Medical Association* 287:576-577

Monkkonen, E. 1989. Diverging homicide rates: England and the United States, 1850-1875. In T.R. Gurr, ed., *Violence in America: The history of crime.* pp. 80-101. Newbury Park, CA: Sage Publications.

Moore, B. 1966. *The social origins of dictatorship and democracy.* Boston, MA: Beacon.

Morales, A. 1992. A clinical model for the prevention of gang violence and homicide. In R.E.C. Cervantes, ed., *Substance abuse and gang violence.* pp. 105-118. Newbury Park, CA: Sage Publications

Morash, M. 1983. Gangs, groups and delinquency. *British Journal of Criminology* 4:316.

Mortimer, J. and R. Larson, eds. 2002. *The changing adolescent experience: societal trends and the transition to adulthood.* New York: Cambridge University Press.

Mulvey, E.P and J.F. Rosa. 1986. Delinquency cessation and adolescent development: Preliminary data. *American Journal of Orthopsychiatry* 56:212-224.

National Center for Education Statistics (NCES) and Bureau of Justice Statistics (BJS). 1999. *Indicators of School Crime and Safety, 1999,* Appendix A, Table Al. Washington, DC: U.S. Department of Education and U.S. Department of Justice.

National Center for Injury Prevention and Control (NCIPC). 2000. *National injury mortality reports, 1987-1998.* Atlanta, GA: Centers for Disease Control and Prevention.

National Center for Injury Prevention and Control (NCIPC). Unpublished. *National summary of injury mortality data, 1981-1997.* Atlanta, GA: Centers for Disease Control and Prevention.

National Commission on the Causes and Prevention of Violence. 1969. *Final Report,* Washington, DC: United States Government Printing Office, 1969.

National Health Information Survey (NHIS). 1994. *Building a healthy future: Reaching youth at risk, high-risk youth communication study.* Public Health Service Office of Disease Prevention and Health Promotion, *Health Affairs,* Winter 1993, p. 240.

National Research Council (NRC) and Institute of Medicine (IOM). 2002. *Community Programs to Promote Youth Development.* Committee on Community-level Programs for Youth. J. Eccles and J.A. Gootman, eds.,

Board on Children, Youth and Families, Division of Behavioral and Social Sciences and Education.

National Spinal Cord Injury Statistical Center (NSCISC). 1994. *Annual report for the model spinal cord injury care systems.* Birmingham, AL: University of Birmingham.

Nobunaga, A.I., B.K. Go and R.B. Karunas. 1999. Recent demographic and injury trends in people served by the Model Spinal Cord Injury Care Systems. *Archives of Physical Medicine and Rehabilitation* 80(11):1372-1382

N.O.D. and Harris. 2001. 2000 N.O.D./Harris Survey of Americans with disabilities. Washington, DC: National Organization on Disability.

Norcross, J.C. and D.J. Vangarelli. 1989. The resolution solution: Longitudinal examination of New Year's change attempts. *Journal of Substance Abuse.* 1:127-134.

O'Donnell, L., A. Stueve, A. San Doval, R. Duran, R. Atnafou and D. Haber. 1999. Violence prevention and young adolescents' participation in community youth service. *Journal of Adolescent Health* 24(1):28-37.

O'Brien, R.M. 1983. Metropolitan structure and violent crime: Which measure of crime? *American Sociological Review,* 48:434-437.

OAS. 2001. *Plan of action, Quebec Summit of the Americas.* Organization of American States. Available at: www.summit-americas.org.

Office of Health and Vital Statistics. 1989. *Homicide rates: national comparison, Boston vs. other U.S. cities.* Boston, MA: Office of Health and Vital Statistics, Massachusetts Department of Health and Hospitals.

Office of Health and Vital Statistics. 1993. *Health perspectives.* Boston, MA: Office of Health and Vital Statistics, Massachusetts Department of Health and Hospitals.

Oliver, W. 1994. *The violent social world of black men.* Boston: Lexington Books.

Orleans, C.T., L. George, J. Houpt and K. Brodie. 1985. Health promotion in primary care: A survey of US family practitioners. *Preventive Medicine,* 14, 636-647.

Paget, M.A. 1983. Experience and knowledge. *Human Studies* 6(1):67–90.

Pepler, D.J. and R.G. Slaby. 1994. Theoretical and developmental perspectives on youth and violence. In L.D. Eron, J.H. Gentry and P. Schlegel, eds., *Reason to Hope: A psycho-social perspective on violence and youth.* pp 27-58. Washington, DC: American Psychological Association.

Perry, C. and R. Jessor. 1985. The concept of health promotion and the prevention of adolescent drug abuse. *Health Education Quarterly,* 12:169–184.

Pettigrew, T., ed. 1980. *The sociology of race relations: Reflection and reform.* New York: Free Press.

Phelps, L., M.R. McCart, W. Hobart Davies. 2002. The impact of community violence on children and adolescents. *Trauma, Violence and Abuse* 3:194-209.

Pierce, G. and J.A. Fox. 1992. *Recent trends in violent crime: A closer look.* Boston, MA: National Crime Analysis Program, Northeastern University.

Pittman, K, M. Irby and T. Ferber. 2002. *Unfinished business: Further reflections on a decade of promoting youth development.* Takoma Park, MD: The Forum for Youth Investment

Powell, K.E., L.L. Dahlberg, J. Friday, J.A. Mercy, T. Thornton and S. Crawford. 1996. Prevention of youth violence: Rationale and characteristics of 15 evaluation projects. In K.E. Powell and D.F. Hawkins, eds., Youth violence prevention: descriptions and baseline data from 13 evaluation projects. *American Journal of Preventive Medicine* Suppl. 12(5):3-12.

Presidential Commission Reports, National Commission on the Causes and Prevention of Violence 1968-69. 1969. In Mulvihill, D.J. and Tumin, M.H. *Crimes of Violence: Staff Reports to the National Commission on the Causes and Prevention of Violence*, vols. 1, 11-13. Washington, DC: Government Printing Office.

Prince, C.J. 1993. Violence fuels health costs. *Boston Business Journal*, 1(26):3-9.

Prochaska, J.O. and C.C. DiClemente. 1985. Common processes of change for smoking, weight control and psychological distress. In S. Schiffman and T. Willis, eds., *Coping and substance abuse: A conceptual framework.* New York: Academic Press.

———. 1992. In search of the structure of behavior.change. In Y. Klar, J.D. Fisher, J.M. Chinsky and A. Nadler, eds., *Self change: Social psychological and clinical perspectives*, pp. 87-114. New York: Springer Verlag.

Prochaska, J.O., C.C. DiClemente and J.C. Norcross. 1992. In search of how people change: Applications to addictive behaviors. *American Psychologist* 47:1102-1114.

Prothrow-Stith, D. 1987. *The violence prevention curriculum for adolescents.* Newton, MA: Education Development Center, Inc.

———. *Deadly consequences.* New York: Harper Collins.

Prothrow-Stith, D. and H.R. Spivack. 2004. *Murder is no accident: understanding and preventing youth violence in America.* San Francisco:Jossey-Bass.

Putnam, R. 2000. *Bowling alone: the collapse and revival of American community.* New York: Simon and Schuster.

Pynoos, R.S. and S. Eth. 1985. Children traumatized by witnessing acts of personal violence. In S. Eth. and R. Pynoos, eds., *Post-traumatic stress disorder in children.* pp. 17-43. Washington, DC: American Psychiatric Press.

Ragucci M.V., M.M. Gittler, K. Balfanz-Vertiz and A. Hunter. 2001. Societal risk factors associated with spinal cord injury secondary to gunshot wound. *Archives of Physical Medicine and Rehabilitation* 82(12):1720-1723.

Reiss, A.J. and JA Roth, eds. 1993. *Understanding and preventing violence.* Four volumes. Philadelphia: The National Academy of Sciences.

Reissman, F. 1965. The "helper-therapy" principle. *Social Work* 10:27–32.

Rhodes, M., J. Aronson, G. Moerkirk and E. Petrash. 1988. Quality of life after the trauma center. *Journal of Trauma* 28:931-938.

Rice, D. 1993. Shooting in the dark: Estimating the cost of firearm injuries. *Health Affairs* 12:4, Winter 1993.

Rich, J.A. and D.A. Stone. 1994. *The experience of violent injury for young African American men: The meaning of being a "sucker."* Paper presented at the Annual Meeting of the Society of General Internal Medicine, April 1994, Washington, DC.

Ridel, M. and M.A. Zahn. 1982. *The nature and patterns of American homicide: An annotated bibliography.* Washington, DC: National Institute of Justice.

Roberts, H.B. 1987. *The inner world of the black juvenile delinquent: three case studies.* Hillsdale, NJ: Erlbaum.

Rodriguez, G.P. and S.L. Garber. 1994. Prospective study of pressure ulcer risk in spinal cord injury patients. *Paraplegia* 32:150-58.

Roscoe, B. and T. Kelsey. 1986. Dating violence among high school students. *Psychology* 23:53-59.

Rosenberg, M.L. and J.A. Mercy. 1991. Assaultive violence. In M.L. Rosenberg and M.A. Fenley, eds., *Violence in America: A public health approach.* New York: Oxford University Press.

Rosenberg, M.L. and M. Fenley. 1991. *Violence in America: A public health approach.* New York: Oxford University Press.

Rubinstein, R.E. 1989. Rebellion in America: The fire next time? In T.R. Gurr, ed., *Violence in America: protest, rebellion and reform.* pp 307- 328. Newbury Park, CA: Sage Publications.

Rymer, R. 1992. For gang members in South Central L.A. Sometimes a wheelchair is the only way out. *Health* November/December:58-65.

Sampson, R.J. and Lauritsen, J.L. 1994. Violent victimization and offending: individual-, situational-, and community level risk factors. In A.J. Reiss, Jr. and J.A. Roth, eds., *Understanding and preventing violence. Social influences.* Vol. 3, pp. 1-114. Washington, DC: National Academy Press.

Scales, P.C. and N. Leffert. 1999. *Developmental assets: A synthesis of the scientific research on adolescent development.* Minneapolis, MN: Search Institute.

Schacter, S. 1982. Recidivism and self-cure of smoking and obesity. *American Psychologist*, 37:436-444.

Scheper-Hughes, N. 1992. *Death without weeping: The violence of everyday life in Brazil.* Berkeley, CA: The University of California Press.

Scheper-Hughes, N. and C. Sargent, eds. 1998. *Small wars: The cultural politics of childhood.* Berkeley, CA: The University of California Press.

Schwitzgebel, R.L. 1964. *Streetcorner research.* Cambridge, MA: Harvard University Press.

Schwitzgebel, R.L. and D.A. Kolb. 1964. Inducing behavior change in adolescent delinquents. *Behavior Research and Therapy* 1:297–304.

Schwitzgebel, R.L. and D.A. Kolb. 1964. Inducing behavior change in adolescent delinquents. *Journal of Psychology* 67:72-82.

Serin, R. and S. Kennedy. 1999. Treatment readiness and responsivity: Contributing to effective correctional practice." *Correctional Service of Canada* 2:Oct. 1999.

Serra Hoffman, J. 1994. *Youth violence in the Latino communities: Opportunities for training, research and practice*. Paper presented for the Injury Control and Emergency Services Section at the Annual American Public Health Association Meeting, October 1994,Washington: DC.

Shaw, C.R. [1930] 1966. The Jack Roller: a delinquent boy's own story. Chicago: University of Chicago Press.

Shaw, C. and H. McKay. 1942. *Juvenile delinquency and urban areas: A study of rates of delinquents in relation to differential characteristics of local communities in American cities*. Chicago: University of Chicago Press.

Sherman, L.W., D. Gottfredson, D. MacKenzie, J. Eck, P.Reuter, and S. Bushway. 1997. *Preventing crime: what works, what doesn't, what's promising*. Report. Washington, DC: U.S. Department of Justice.

Shoemaker, W.C., C.B. James, L.M. King, E. Hardin and G.J. Ordog. 1993. Urban violence in Los Angeles in the aftermath of the riots: A perspective from health care professionals with implications for social reconstruction. *Journal of the American Medical Association* 270(23):2833–2837.

Sickmund, M. and Y. Wan. 2001. *Census of juveniles in residential placement databook. Detailed offense profile by sex for the United States, 1999.*Washington, DC: Office of Juvenile Justice and Delinquency Prevention.

Sims D.W., B.A. Bivins, F.N. Obeid, H.M. Horst, V.J. Sorensen and J.J. Fath. 1989. Urban trauma: A chronic recurrent disease. *Journal of Trauma* 29:940-947.

Singer, M., T. Anglin, L. Song and L. Lunghofer. 1995. Adolescent's exposure to violence and associated symptoms of psychological trauma. *Journal of the American Medical Association*, 273(6):477-485.

Slack, C.W. 1960. Experimenter-subject psychotherapy: A new method of introducing intensive office treatment for unreachable cases. *Mental Hygiene* 44:238–256.

Smith, A. 1995. "The Jailing of America," The Boston Globe, December 10.

Smith, W., J.O. Simmonds, Z.S. Alam, and R.E. Grant. 2003. Spinal cord injury caused by gunshot wounds: the cost of rehabilitation. *Clinical Orthopaedics and Related Research* 408:145-151.

Snyder, H.N. 1997. *Juvenile arrest rates for weapons law violations, 1981-1997.* Washington, DC: U.S. Department of Justice, Office of Juvenile Justice and Delinquency Prevention.

————. 2000. *Juvenile arrests 1999*. Washington, DC: U.S. Department of Justice, Office of Juvenile Justice and Delinquency Prevention.

Snyder, H.N. and M. Sickmund. 1995. *Juvenile offenders and victims: A national report.* Washington, DC: U.S. Department of Justice, Office of Juvenile Justice and Delinquency Prevention.

————. 1999. *Juvenile offenders and victims: 1999 national report.* Washington, DC: U.S. Department of Justice, Office of Juvenile Justice and Delinquency Prevention.

Sourcebook of Criminal Justice Statistics. 1994. Table 3. U.S. Department of Justice, Office of Justice Programs. Bureau of Justice Statistics.

Steinberg, L. 2001. We know some things: Parent-adolescent relations in retrospect and prospect. *Journal of Research in Adolescence* 11:1-20.

Stephens, RD. 1997. National trends in school violence: statistics and prevention strategies. In A. Goldstein and J.C. Conoley, eds., *School violence intervention: a practical handbook.* pp. 72-90. New York: Guillford Press.

Stevenson, H.C. 1998. Raising safe villages: Cultural-ecological factors that influence the emotional adjustment of adolescents. *Journal of Black Psychology* 34:44-59.

Stone, D. 1997. *Policy paradox: The art of political decision making.* New York: W.W. Norton.

Stover, S.L., J.A. DeLisa and G.G. Whiteneck, eds. 1995. *Spinal cord injury: clinical outcomes from the model systems.* Gaithersburg, MD: Aspen Publishers, Inc.

Strodtbeck, F.L., J.F. Short, Jr., and E. Kolegar. 1962. The analysis of self-descriptions by members of different gangs. *Sociological Quarterly* 24:331-356.

Sullivan, L. 1997. Hip-Hop *Nation*: The underdeveloped social capital of Black urban America. *National Civic Review*. 86(3):235-243.

Suro, R. 1997. More is spent on new prisons than colleges. *Washington Post,* February 24, p. A12.

Tellez, M.L. and R.C. Mackersie. 1996. Violence prevention and trauma surgeons: descriptions and preliminary evaluation. *Journal of Trauma* 40(4):602-606.

Thompson, E.P. 1963. *The making of the English working class.* New York: Vintage.

Thrasher, F.M. 1963. *The gang.* Chicago, IL: University of Chicago Press.

Tilly, C. 1964. *The vendee.* Cambridge, MA: Harvard University Press.

Tilly, C. 1989. Collective violence in a European perspective. In T. R. Gurr, ed., *Violence in America: Protest, rebellion, and reform.* Newbury Park, CA: Sage Publications.

Tilly, C., L. Tilly, and R. Tilly. 1975. *The rebellious century, 1830–1930.* Cambridge, MA: Harvard University Press.

Tolan, P.H. and N.G. Guerra. 1994. *What works in reducing adolescent violence: An empirical review of the field.* Boulder, CO: Center for the Study and Prevention of Violence.

Trunkey, D.D. 1993. The impact of violence on the nation's trauma care. *Health Affairs* 12(4):162–170.

Turk, A. [1969]1993. *Criminality and legal order.* Chicago: Rand McNally.

Tyroch, A.H., J.W., Davis; K.L. Kaups and M. Lorenzo. 1997. Spinal cord injury: A preventable public burden. *Archives of Surgery* 132:778-781.

U.S. Bureau of Justice Statistics. 1995. National crime victimization survey, 1991. In H.N. Snyder and M. Sickmund, eds., *Juvenile offenders and victims: a national report.* Washington, DC: U.S. Department of Justice, Office of Juvenile Justice and Delinquency Prevention.

U.S. Census Bureau. 1995. Massachusetts Department of Correction, quoted in Boston Globe, March 26.

U.S. Department of Health and Human Services. 1985. *Report of the secretary's task force on black and minority health.* Washington, DC: U.S. Department of Health and Human Services.

U.S. Department of Justice. 1992. *Criminal victimization in the United States. 1991.* Washington, DC: U.S. Department of Justice, National Vital Statistics System.

U.S. Department of Justice. 1993. *Comprehensive strategy for serious, violent and chronic juvenile offenders.* U.S. Department of Justice, Office of Juvenile Justice and Delinquency Prevention.

U.S. Department of Justice. 2003. Prevalence of imprisonment in the US population 1974-2001. Washington: U.S. Department of Justice, Office of Justice Programs, Bureau of Justice Statistics.

U.S. Surgeon General. 2002. Youth violence: Report of the U.S. Surgeon General. Washington, DC:. U.S. Public Health Service.

Uriarte, M. 1990. *The Latino information gap in Massachusetts.* Boston, MA: Gaston Institute for Latino Community Development and Public Policy, University of Massachusetts.

Van Maanen, J. 1988. *Tales from the field: On writing ethnography.* Chicago: University of Chicago Press.

Vigil, J.D. 1990. Street socialization, locura behavior and violence among Chicano gang members. In J.F. Kraus, S.B. Sorenson, and P.D. Juarez, eds., *Research conference on violence and homicide in Hispanic communities.* Los Angeles, CA: UCLA Publication Series.

Violence Prevention Coalition. 1993. *Violence in Los Angeles County.* Violence Prevention Coalition of Greater Los Angeles, Los Angeles, CA.

———. 1994. *Facts About violence in emergency medical services in Los Angeles County.* Violence Prevention Coalition of Greater Los Angeles, Los Angeles, CA.

Violence Prevention Project Papers. 1994. *Homicide, Youth and the Latino Community: Leading Causes of Death in Massachusetts in 1989 for Youth 15–24 Years of Age.* Boston, MA: Violence Prevention Project Papers, Department of Health and Hospitals.

Wacquant, L. 1999. *Les prisons de la misère.* Éditions Raison D'Agir.

Wacquant, L. and W.J. Wilson. 1989. The cost of racial and class exclusion in the inner city. *The Annals* 501:8-25.

Wallace, R. 1990. Urban desertification, public health and public order: "planned shrinkage," violent death, substance abuse and AIDS in the Bronx. *Social Science and Medicine* 31(7):801-813.

Wallace, R.A. and A. Wolf. 1991. *Contemporary sociological theory: Continuing the classical tradition.* Englewood, NJ: Prentice Hall.

Waters, R.L. and R.H. Adkins. 1997. Firearm versus motor vehicle related spinal cord injury: preinjury factors, injury characteristics, and initial outcome comparisons among ethnically diverse groups. *Archives of Physical Medicine and Rehabilitation* 78:306-312.

Waters, R.L., J. Cressy and R.H. Adkins. 1996. Spinal cord injuries due to violence. *American Rehabilitation* Autumn:10-15.

Weingarten, S.I. and P.M. Grahm. 1991. Targeting teenagers in a spinal cord injury prevention program. *Paraplegia* 29:65-69.

Wharton, G.W., J.C. Milani and L.S. Dean. 1988. Pressure sore profile: Cost and management. *Paraplegia* 26:122-124..

Whiteneck, G., S.W. Carlifue, K.A. Gerhart, D.P. Lammertse, S. Manley, R.R. Menter and KR Seedroff. 1993. *Aging with spinal cord injury*. New York: Demos Publications.

Widom, C.S. 1989a. Child abuse, neglect and violent criminal behavior. Criminology 27:251-272.

———. 1989b. Does violence beget violence? A critical examination of the literature. *Psychological Bulletin* 106:3-28.

Wiist, W.H., R.H. Jackson and K.W. Jackson. 1996. Peer and community leader education to prevent youth violence. In Youth Violence Prevention: Descriptions and Baseline Data from 13 Evaluation Projects. *American Journal of Preventive Medicine* Suppl. 12(5):56-64.

Williams, C.W. 1991. *Black teenage mothers: Pregnancy and child-rearing from their perspective*. Boston, MA: Lexington Books.

Williams, T. 1989. *The cocaine kids; the inside story of a teenage drug ring*. Reading, MA: Addison-Wesley Publishing Company.

Willis, P.E. 1981. *Learning to labor*. New York: University of Columbia Press.

Wilson, E.B. 1952. *An introduction to scientific research*. New York: McGraw-Hill,.

Winship, C. 2002. *End of a miracle? Crime, faith, and partnership in Boston in the 1990's*. Cambridge: Harvard University.

Yin, R.K. 1989. *Case study research: Design and methods*. Newbury Park, CA: Sage Publications

Youniss, J. 1980. *Parents and peers in social development*. Chicago: the University of Chicago Press.

Zafonte, R.D. and M.P. Djikers. 1999: Medical and functional sequelae of spinal cord injury caused by violence: findings from the model systems. *Topics in Spinal Cord Injury Rehabilitation* 4:36-50.

Zeeb, K. 1991. Bullet wounds and spinal cord injury. *Spinal Network Extra*. Summer:22-29.

Zeldin, S. and H. Spivak. 1993. *Violence prevention and youth development: Implications for medical clinicians*. Washington, DC: Center for Youth Development and Policy Research.

Zimrig, F.E. 1998. *American youth violence*. New York: Oxford University Press.

Zola, I.K. 1972. Medicine as an institution of social control. *Sociological Review* 20(4):487-504.

————. 1982. *Missing pieces: A chronicle of living with a disability.* Philadelphia: Temple University Press.

————. 1994. *Shifting boundaries – Doing social science in the 1990s: A personal odyssey.* Presidential address delivered at the Eastern Sociological Society Annual Meeting, March 19, Baltimore, MD.

Zunz, L.S. and J.M. Rosen. 2003. Psychosocial needs of young persons who are victims of interpersonal violence. *Pediatric Emergency Care* 191:15-19.

Informed Consent Form

I understand that I am being asked to take part in a research project carried out by Joan Serra Hoffman, a doctoral student at the Heller School for Advanced Studies in Social Welfare at Brandeis University, Waltham, Massachusetts. This research project is sponsored by the Center for Social Change, at the Heller School for Advanced Studies in Social Welfare at Brandeis University.

My participation in the project is voluntary, and will be in the form of taped interviews. I understand that I am free to refuse or discontinue the interview or participation at any point, and that all taped information given by me will be destroyed, and that none of the information given by me will be used for any purpose now or in the future.

If I do decide to complete the interviewing process and consent to it being used in a dissertation or other publications, my confidentiality will be upheld in the following way, should I wish to remain anonymous:

1)   No statements will be included or details given which could be connected to me.

2)   My name and physical description will not be used.

3)   My taped interview and any notes relating to me will be heard and seen only by the researcher and her assistants.

4)   Any unforeseen situations that arise which jeopardize my confidentiality in any way will be handled with the same caution by the researcher.

The information you give me will be used to write a thesis and may be included in additional journal articles and/or books. The dissertation will be available at the Heller School upon completion, and available to you. You may obtain information concerning the final document by contacting Professor David Gil at the Heller School at Brandeis University, or Joan Serra Hoffman at the addresses and telephone numbers listed below. If you have any questions or concerns about the report or your involvement in this study, please call me collect at (617) 522-7819.

MY SIGNATURE INDICATES THAT I HAVE READ THE INFORMATION ABOVE AND THAT I HAVE AGREED TO PARTICIPATE IN THIS STUDY:

Signature of Participant   Date

Brandeis University   Brandeis University
Heller School   Heller School
Center for Social Change   Center for Social Change
Attn: Professor David Gil   Attn: Joan Serra Hoffman
415 South Street   415 South Street
Waltham, MA 02254-9110.   Waltham, MA 02254-9110
(617) 736-3800   (617) 522-7819.

Index